AF574460

# Urban Revisions

Current Projects for the Public Realm

# Urban

# Current Projects for

# Revisions
## the Public Realm

Exhibition organized by Elizabeth A. T. Smith
Edited by Russell Ferguson

with essays by
Mike Davis
M. Patricia Fernández-Kelly
Richard Sennett
Elizabeth A. T. Smith
and Gwendolyn Wright

The Museum of Contemporary Art, Los Angeles
The MIT Press, Cambridge, Massachusetts
and London, England

This publication accompanies the exhibition
"Urban Revisions: Current Projects for the Public Realm,"
organized by Elizabeth A. T. Smith at
The Museum of Contemporary Art, Los Angeles.

"Urban Revisions: Current Projects for the Public Realm"
is made possible through the generous support of the
National Endowment for the Humanities, a federal agency;
the Graham Foundation for Advanced Studies in the Fine Arts;
The Principal Financial Group Foundation, Inc.; Jean and Lewis Wolff;
Melva and Martin Bucksbaum; Jim and Patty Cownie Charitable Trust;
Mr. James Gordon; and Mr. G. David Hurd.

Library of Congress Cataloguing-in-Publication Data
Urban revisions: current projects for the public realm / exhibition
organized by Elizabeth A.T. Smith; edited by Russell Ferguson with
essays by Mike Davis... [et al.]
p. cm.
Exhibition schedule, The Museum of Contemporary Art, Los Angeles,
May 15-July 24, 1994 and others.
Includes bibliographical references.
ISBN 0-914357-34-4
1. City Planning–United States–History–20th century–
Exhibitions. 2. City planning–California–Los Angeles–
History–20th century–Exhibitions. 3. Architecture, Modern–20th
century–United States–Exhibitions. 4. Architecture–United
States–Exhibitions. I. Smith, Elizabeth A.T.. 1958-
II. Ferguson, Russell. III. Museum of Contemporary Art
(Los Angeles, Calif.)
NA9108.U73 1994
711'.4'097307479494–dc20

Edited by Russell Ferguson
Assistant Editor: Sherri Schottlaender
Designed by April Greiman Associates
Printed by Queen Beach, Long Beach



Distributed by
The MIT Press
55 Hayward Street
Cambridge, Massachusetts 02142-1399
MIT ISBN 0-262-69173-6

**Exhibition Schedule**

**The Museum of Contemporary Art, Los Angeles**
**May 15 - July 24, 1994**

**Centre Canadien d'Architecture/Canadian Center for Architecture, Montreal**
**October 19 - January 15, 1995**

**University Art Museum, Berkeley**
**March 15 - June 8, 1995**

**Des Moines Art Center**
**November 11, 1995 - February 12, 1996**

CONTENTS

"Urban Revisions : Current Projects for the Public Realm" is the fifth in a series of major exhibitions initiated and co-organized by The Museum of Contemporary Art that address key developments in contemporary architecture and design. These have ranged from groundbreaking thematic exhibitions—"Blueprints for Modern Living: History and Legacy of the Case Study Houses" and "The Independent Group: Postwar Britain and the Aesthetics of Plenty" (the latter co-organized by MOCA and three additional institutions)–to individual retrospectives of the work of the acclaimed architects Arata Isozaki and Louis I. Kahn. Continuing and extending this tradition of ambitious, investigatory programming, "Urban Revisions" is the first exhibition to provide a major focus on planning and urban design. In so doing it relates the field of architecture to a context of larger social, cultural, economic, demographic, technological, and ecological concerns.

"Urban Revisions" takes as its subject the physical and social space of the contemporary city as it is envisioned by some of today's most innovative architects, urban designers, and planners. The projects selected for inclusion position themselves across a wide range of territory, not only in their disparate geographical and contextual identities, but also in terms of the design problems confronted and solutions proposed. Furthermore, these projects give evidence of a broad spectrum of urbanistic ideologies and approaches currently being brought to bear on the revisioning of cities.



The exhibition presents work that posits a variety of critical attitudes toward conventional urban design and planning practices. Its de-emphasis of purely formal approaches in favor of quality of ideas and breadth of vision is noteworthy, as is its evenhanded attention to the merits of a variety of competing and, at times, conflicting ideological positions about the space of the contemporary city that these projects, taken as a group, embody. Each of the projects included manifests a strong desire to question and rethink accepted strategies of urban form-giving. For instance, the desire for a sustainable future and for alternatives to the automobile—a direct response to the insidious effects of a previous generation's policies of urban renewal—have generated a number of imaginative, forward-thinking proposals for creation and reclamation of transportation corridors that also serve various related urbanistic and social functions. The idea of a sweeping master plan as a way to transform and impose order is replaced by planning as a mechanism to underscore existing contexts and histories through an approach of minimal intervention. The now conventional concept of "mixed use," a reaction to the modernist separation of functions, gives way to an urbanism predicated upon a socially expansive definition of heterogeneity—demographic, economic, temporal, and physical. Additionally, growing recognition of the merits of grassroots design and planning efforts as vitalizing and empowering civic forces, particularly within underserved areas, lends increasing credence to the notion of design for and by communities and profoundly alters the role of the professional designer.

The inextricable linkage of physical design and social vision is a compelling characteristic shared by each of the works in "Urban Revisions." At the same time, this boldness of vision has caused controversy and contentiousness to swirl around the majority of these projects. Indeed, in several instances, the solutions presented here have later been severely adapted and reordered away from their original form by developers, civic agencies, and other such bureaucratic and managerial entities because they diverged too sharply from accepted thinking and practice (as well as for reasons of cost, political expediency, etc.). Also significant in allowing them to be evaluated as a testing ground for new ideas is the exhibition's emphasis on "real" rather than on theoretical or self-generated works. While chronicling the processes behind and examining the issues raised by each, this exhibition looks forward to a future of "Urban Revisions" which will make positive, yet provocative, contributions to both the physical and social shaping of the public realm.

*Richard Koshalek, Director*

*Elizabeth A.T. Smith*

REALIZING A PROJECT OF THIS SCALE AND COMPLEXITY requires the collaboration and assistance of a great number of individuals. First, I wish to extend sincere appreciation and thanks to the architects, designers, artists, and community members whose work forms the subject of this exhibition and publication, and whose visions and tenacious commitment to their realization hold promises for significant physical and social enhancement of the public realm.

My fellow contributors to the content and presentation of "Urban Revisions" have played crucial roles in bringing the project to fruition. I am immensely grateful to Michael Rotondi and his capable staff, including Clark Stevens, Brian Reiff, Tracy Loeffler, and Jin Kim, for their design of the installation and for Michael's spirited response to the content and direction of the exhibition from its inception. To April Greiman, Sean Adams, Lorna Turner, and Ron Romero deep thanks are extended for their masterful design of this publication and of the exhibition's graphic elements. Eric Martin provided inspired advice and invaluable technical assistance regarding aspects of the show's presentation. My deep appreciation goes to Jillian Burt for her early role as liaison among members of the design team and for her thoughtful and insightful handling of an enormously complex set of needs. We also extend our utmost thanks to Mike Davis, M. Patricia Fernández-Kelly, Richard Sennett, and Gwendolyn Wright for the incisive, analytical texts they have contributed to this publication and for their forthright and spirited input into the project's scope and direction along with that of the additional project advisors—Richard Koshalek, Phyllis Lambert, and Donlyn Lyndon.

My colleagues at MOCA have provided crucial support and assistance in realizing all aspects of "Urban Revisions." John Bowsher, Exhibition Production Manager, and his extraordinary staff of preparators have undertaken the show's complex and demanding installation requirements with their consistent skill, alacrity, and sensitivity. Russell Ferguson, Editor, has assured that this publication embodies high standards of rigor and comprehensiveness through his long and sympathetic involvement with the intellectual scope of the project. In the book's organization, he has been ably assisted by Sherri Schottlaender, former Assistant Editor, whose conscientiousness, responsiveness to the subject matter, and good humor were invaluable. Chief Registrar Mo Shannon and Associate Registrar Robert Hollister handled the show's difficult and often unusual transportation requirements with patience, diligence, and consummate professionalism. Their flexibility and spirit of accommodation in terms of the project's frequently shifting demands was essential and is deeply appreciated.

To Richard Koshalek, Director, and to Sherri Geldin, former Associate Director (now Director of the Wexner Center for the Arts), I extend heartfelt thanks for their enthusiastic embrace of the concept behind "Urban Revisions." Their supportive attitude and guidance regarding its realization as one of MOCA's major exhibitions reflects their recognition of the value of architecture within contemporary art museum programming and our shared commitment to its importance as an artistic and social practice. To Colette Dartnall, Curatorial Assistant, I am deeply grateful for her deft handling of numerous aspects of the show's organization and for the profound level and quality of support that she consistently contributes with thoroughness, grace, and intelligence. Many other members of MOCA's staff are also deserving of recognition and thanks for their many and varied roles in bringing this effort to fruition. Foremost thanks are owed to Zazu Faure, project assistant, for her involvement in catalogue and exhibition production and for her incisive and thorough handling of often startlingly disparate requests and problems. David Bradshaw, Audio Visual Technician, was extremely helpful in his facilitation of the project's extensive incorporation of video and audio elements. Dawn Setzer, Press Officer, handled the exhibition's press relations with her usual skillful organization and flair. Alma Ruiz, Exhibitions Coordinator, conscientiously oversaw the complex tour logistics and budgetary components. Vas Prabhu, Director of Education, and Caroline Blackburn, Art Talks Coordinator, coordinated a variety of imaginative education programs geared to attract diverse audiences to the exhibition. Erica Clark, Director of Development, Margaret Steele, Associate Director of Development, and June Scott, Grants Manager, skillfully supervised the project's fundraising efforts. Paul Schimmel, Chief Curator, Kathleen Bartels, Director of Administration, and Jack Wiant, Chief Financial Officer, provided important general advice and guidance throughout the organization phase.



Rick Keating, president of MOCA's Architecture and Design Council; John Chase, Margaret Crawford, John Kaliski, and Julie Silliman of the Los Angeles Forum for Architecture and Urban Design; and Richard Rowe of the Society of Architectural Historians, Southern California Chapter, offered not only crucial support in conceiving and implementing public programs related to the exhibition but also demonstrated a collaborative spirit that made our interactions pleasurable as well as productive. Numerous others have contributed in important ways to this project's genesis. The following individuals offered significant advice, input, and/or assistance during the conceptualization of "Urban Revisions": Joan Abrahamson; Janet Abrams; James J. Amis; Paola Antonelli; Laurel Meinig Brewster; Victoria Casasco; Katherine Diamond; Rosalie Genevro; Aiisa Gulko; Dolores Hayden; Paul Randall Jacobson; Yun Kim; Estela Lopez; Ross Miller; William Morrish and Catherine Brown; Deborah Murphy; Kyong Park; Nick Patsaouras; Alan J. Plattus; Michaele Pride-Wells; Mark Robbins; Judith Scheine; Janet Marie Smith; Doug Suisman; Michael Webb; and many others to whom I am also grateful.

Our colleagues at the institutions participating in the tour of "Urban Revisions" demonstrated an enthusiasm for and commitment to the exhibition's subject matter early in the project's organizational stages. I extend deep thanks in particular to Phyllis Lambert, Helen Malkin, and Nicholas Olsberg at the Centre Canadien d'Architecture in Montreal; Jacquelynn Baas, Bonnie Pittman, Larry Rinder, and Nina Zurrier at the University Art Museum, Berkeley; and I. Michael Danoff and Jessica Rowe at the Des Moines Art Center. To institutional lenders including the Fonds Regional d'Art Contemporain du Centre, Orleans, France; Grand Center, Inc., St. Louis; Maguire Thomas Partners of Los Angeles; the Société d'Habitation et de Développement de Montréal; and The Urban Assembly in New York City, our profound gratitude is offered.

Finally, we wish to express utmost appreciation to the sponsors of "Urban Revisions." The National Endowment for the Humanities, a federal agency, provided major support for the exhibition. The project received crucial early funding from the Graham Foundation for Advanced Studies in the Fine Arts. Additional support was provided by The Principal Financial Group Foundation, Inc., Jean and Lewis Wolff, Melva and Martin Bucksbaum, Jim and Patty Cownie Charitable Trust, Mr. James Gordon, and Mr. G. David Hurd. MOCA's Architecture and Design Council contributed substantially to the exhibition's opening symposium.

To all of the above and to others who furthered the realization of "Urban Revisions: Current Projects for the Public Realm" in myriad ways, we extend heartfelt appreciation and thanks.

2

"Help!" by Herblock. From The Herblock Gallery (Simon & Schuster, 1968).
©1966 Herblock, *The Washington Post.*

# Urban Revisions: Current Projects for the Public Realm

*Elizabeth A. T. Smith*

In 1951 the Bunker Hill area of Los Angeles was an enclave of tenement apartments and boarding houses, moderately priced hotels, and American Renaissance-style homes built in the late 1890s and largely converted to small-scale commercial uses. That same year the area was deemed blighted by the city's newly formed Redevelopment Agency, paving the way for the Bunker Hill redevelopment plan of 1959.[1] Today this district embodies the heart of Los Angeles's corporate and cultural aspirations—the site of high-rise office towers set amid immaculately landscaped and art-filled plazas, luxury apartments, hotels, and facilities for the presentation of music and art. The decades-old vision of its planners has now been brought largely to fruition, yet the district sits in uneasy juxtaposition with many of the surrounding areas that are startlingly dissimilar in function, population, and physical appearance.

During the later 1980s and into the 1990s, a number of significant directions have emerged in the fields of city planning and urban design that diverge sharply from patterns of previous thinking about the evolution of cities. This publication and the exhibition it accompanies seek to identify and analyze these directions by focusing on a group of forward-looking projects that commingle the social and the aesthetic as the basis for new planning and design strategies. These offer serious alternatives to both conventional market-driven practices and to purely theoretical tendencies. Although their ideological and aesthetic approaches differ widely, their common underlying threads include a generally critical stance toward work done, characteristically, by large architectural offices under the direction of commercial and corporate interests, as well as a strong commitment to heterogeneity. In the most provocative instances, the now familiar and often heavily consumerist emphasis of "mixed use" has given way to an interest in physical, social, cultural, and economic interaction among often widely divergent demographies, identities, and histories in a given place.

Commitment to the ideal of a truly heterogeneous urban condition has grown out of widespread recognition of the failure of urban renewal—the clearance and redevelopment of urban areas deemed blighted by local, state, and federal agencies, particularly during the postwar American building boom of the 1950s. First compellingly articulated by writers Jane Jacobs and Lewis Mumford in the early 1960s, a vast body of subsequent critical literature on urban renewal documents and analyzes its impact on the decline of many American center cities as viable living and working environments.[2] In some of the most striking scenarios, as in downtown Los Angeles, the wreaking of

1. Bunker Hill's transformation is chronicled through a vivid pictorial narrative in Arnold Hylen, Bunker Hill: A Los Angeles Landmark (Los Angeles: Dawson's Book Shop, 1976).

2. Two pivotal books published in 1961 are Lewis Mumford, The City in History: Its Origins, Its Transformations and Its Prospects (New York: Harcourt Brace Jovanovich), and Jane Jacobs, The Death and Life of Great American Cities (New York: Vintage Books). Later critical writings range from Martin Anderson, The Federal Bulldozer: A Critical Analysis of Urban Renewal 1949-62 (Cambridge, Mass.: The MIT Press, 1964), and Robert Goodman, After The Planners (New York: Simon & Schuster, 1973) to Trevor Boddy, "Underground and Overhead: Building the Analoguous City," in Michael Sorkin, ed., Variations on a Theme Park: The New American City and The End of Public Space (New York: Hill and Wang, 1992).

North side of First Street, between Grand and Olive, looking northwest across the intersection of Olive Street. Photograph by Arnold Hylen, originally published in Bunker Hill: A Los Angeles Landmark (1976), courtesy of Dawson's Book Shop, Los Angeles.

irrevocable changes to an urban fabric for its complete reorganization, gentrification, and structural subservience to the automobile casts deep social, cultural, and economic disjunctions into high relief.

From our vantage point in the 1990s, the crisis of the American city and of the cultural and social fabric has permeated a wide spectrum of public consciousness. Reformist leanings have penetrated the design professions as a response to the societal and architectural developments of the past decade. Eschewing the making of massive, deep-seated alterations, today's efforts reflect an urge toward relatively gentle and responsive interventions into an existing physical and social fabric. They depart, however, from both the sociological basis of the "as found" aesthetic of Alison and Peter Smithson's and Team X's critique of Modernist planning launched in the 1950s, and the primarily formal emphasis of the "collage city" articulated by Colin Rowe and Fred Koetter in the 1970s, while at the same time having roots in these and other related tendencies in post-World War II urban theory and practice.[3]

3. For a discussion of the Smithsons' early challenges to modernist planning, see David Robbins, ed., The Independent Group: Postwar Britain and the Aesthetics of Plenty (Cambridge, Mass., and London: The MIT Press, 1990). In Collage City (Cambridge, Mass., and London: The MIT Press, 1978), Colin Rowe and Fred Koetter argued against the assumptions of large-scale redevelopment and "total planning" in favor of a design approach of fragmentation, collision, and bricolage.



Since the 1960s, historic preservation and other grassroots community efforts opposing new development, as well as contextualism and mixed use as architectural and planning devices, have sought to overturn the effects of urban renewal and prohibit its future application. These tendencies have led to a variety of ameliorative and restorative urban interventions, the most renowned type being the "festival marketplace" of consumer and tourist-oriented adaptive reuse, such as Boston's Fanueil Hall Marketplace, New York's South Street Seaport, and Baltimore's Inner Harbor. At the same time, recent decades have witnessed an abundance of analysis and criticism of the merits of the festival marketplace phenomenon and of the overall effects of gentrification on predominantly industrial or working class districts. These debates have expanded to encompass many aspects of accepted wisdom about desirability in cities—among them the role of public versus private automobile transportation, of structured versus undifferentiated open space, and of the cultural landscape as defined by marginalized groups. Vehemently rejecting the model of the festival marketplace and other related efforts as solutions to the complexities of today's urban condition, the work of some of the most creative practitioners in the planning and design fields seeks to recognize and embrace a diversity of realities and hierarchies in the contemporary urban context. No single method, approach, or ideology should dominate as a paradigm for today's design and planning strategies. Instead, lessons can be learned from considering a wide variety of ideas and solutions brought to bear on the particulars of specific sites and problems in terms of both the degree of innovation and the appropriateness that they manifest. The best of recent urban design and planning projects adopt a critical stance, yet operate in terms of a clear commitment to public life and the public realm that is transformative while at the same time responsive to and sustaining of the positive elements of present conditions and social realities.

Within the framework described above, the exhibition "Urban Revisions: Current Projects for the Public Realm" focuses on some of the most significant tendencies in contemporary urbanism. The goal of this essay is to provide a more expansive discussion of the various thematic directions around which the exhibition is organized. These include the creation and reclamation of transportation corridors as urban fabrics, the genesis of new neighborhoods in existing urban and exurban contexts, the "minimizing" of the idea and function of the master plan, and the phenomenon of design for and by communities and constituencies other than professional designers and urbanists. The exhibition's scope is limited mostly to the United States and to projects begun during the last seven years, although in two instances, work being done outside the U.S. with special relevance to the exhibition's themes is included. While the exhibition focuses on a limited number of examples, treated in some depth, rather than on a comprehensive survey of developments in each of the categories named above or of the field in general, it does not seek to define a movement or to endorse one formal or ideological position. On the contrary, it privileges the notion of fresh and responsive visions of the urban realm free from otherwise constraining polemics.

> **A contemporary philosopher of urban architecture is faced, then, at the end of the 20th century, not so much with the absolute dialectic of ancient and modern posed by the avant- and rear gardes of the last eighty years, as with the more subtle and difficult task of calculating the limits of intervention according to the resistance of the city to change.**
> **- Anthony Vidler[4]**

4. Anthony Vidler, "Oneirism," in The Architectural Uncanny: Essays in the Modern Unhomely (Cambridge, Mass.: The MIT Press, 1992), pp. 199-200.



TRANSPORTATION CORRIDORS AS URBAN FABRICS: CREATION AND RECLAMATION

Among the most significant and far-reaching current design and planning initiatives are efforts to reconfigure transportation patterns within and around cities. Beginning in the 1930s, and particularly in the period since World War II, the American urban landscape has been transformed by endless miles of highway corridors, freeways, and expressways to serve the developing automobile culture. Often as an outgrowth of postwar urban renewal programs, highway and freeway systems were introduced directly into the heart of cities such as Boston, New Haven, San Francisco, and Los Angeles to facilitate commuting from the burgeoning suburbs. Proceeding from a vision rooted early in the century in the work of European futurists and modernists, the primacy of high-speed automobile access within and around cities became institutionalized in massive mid-century American public works projects. The best known examples include Robert Moses's masterminding of the extensive expressway and parkway systems in the New York metropolitan area, and the installation of the freeway network and parallel dismantling of the light rail lines in Los Angeles.[5] Conceiving such projects as elements of modernization and improvement of the business climate and crucial for the economic health of cities, their instigators characteristically overlooked the presence of poorer communities standing in the path of a desired roadway. Deeming many such areas blighted, urban planners and policy makers operated on the principle of replacement and displacement of those not vocal or organized enough to react against orders of clearance imposed upon their neighborhoods.

5. Moses's works are extensively documented in Robert A. Caro, The Power Broker: Robert Moses and The Fall of New York (New York: Vintage Books, 1975).

The past twenty-five years have witnessed a dramatic shift in conventional thinking about the impact of the automobile on urban environments. Fueled by the growth of the historic preservation movement and the rise in political empowerment of grassroots community-oriented initiatives since the sixties, a number of incipient urban roadway projects such as New York City's Westway have been questioned, redirected, or halted altogether.[6] Moreover, with the entry of urban planners and public policy makers educated in the sixties and seventies into the ranks of local and regional bureaucracies, an increasing emphasis on the preservation and articulation of existing urban fabrics and on responsiveness to popular constituencies has come to the fore. Alongside and intertwined with these tendencies has been the growth of postmodern theory and

6. Carter Wiseman, "Case Study in Changing Urban Priorities," Architectural Record A4, no.2 (February 1986): 81-83, succinctly traces the genesis, evolution, and subsequent discrediting of the concept behind New York City's Westway from 1969 to 1985.

Johnson Fain and Pereira Associates.
Chatsworth Metrolink Station with library building in background. Drawing by Norman Konady.

practice in planning and design, marked by a respect for context—historical and vernacular, an interest in elements of symbol and scale, and an orientation to the pedestrian on the model of the traditional European city.

While postmodernism and contextualism have influenced, in varying degrees, much of today's urban planning and design, they have particular significance in the context of a discussion about transportation corridors as generators of urban form. Several major American cities have recently developed or are currently introducing public transportation systems intended to eliminate or lessen complete dependence on the automobile and to enhance the urban fabric by providing a service geared to the pedestrian. In some instances, as in Baltimore, this framework adapts itself neatly to the structure of a fairly fine-grained context already containing the basis of a successful pedestrian orientation: medium to high density historical housing stock in proximity to commercial and recreational facilities and workplaces. In other locations, such as Miami or Los Angeles, the existing structure of the city, with the exception of a few neighborhoods, largely inhibits its successful adaptation to a completely viable pedestrian orientation.



In Los Angeles, however, where the rapid transit system currently under construction is at present the nation's largest public works project, attempts to rethink the integration of transit with land use patterns are underway. Under the aegis of the city's Metropolitan Transit Authority, a variety of studies have been commissioned from local architects for ways to direct the growth of areas surrounding future stations. Owing much to the "transit-oriented development" concept promulgated by Peter Calthorpe in the late 1980s, these studies range from conventional, even banal, schemes of multi-tiered mixed-use construction (retail, commercial, residential) with adjacent open space, to more innovative attempts to consider a broad variety of needs, demographics, and architectural/spatial configurations appropriate to the demands of transit but also to the realities of the sites, which are both urban and suburban.[7] At the Vermont/Santa Monica station in Hollywood, for example, Koning Eizenberg Architecture developed a proposal to cast the station as a "context modifier," maintaining the small scale of the existing residential blocks and establishing a neighborhood identity by clustering small market stalls and a larger mercado around the station. Housing options envisioned range from a single-room occupancy hotel to a larger residential building, both four stories over retail and commercial space at street level. In a suburban context, Johnson Fain and Pereira Associates conceived a master plan for a Metrolink station in the town of Chatsworth. Here, with the community discouraging the incorporation of housing, the master plan seeks instead to establish the station as a hub of civic and commercial services, including a replica of the historic Chatsworth Station and a child care center. Additionally, the plan underscores the site's proximity to a magnificent natural landscape by its incorporation of pedestrian and bicycle paths also serving the station. Its urge to create links among larger systems of transportation, landscape, and recreation reflects the thinking behind a related Greenway Plan for Metropolitan Los Angeles developed by Johnson Fain and Pereira Associates. This project's macrocosmic approach to revitalizing 400 miles of abandoned rail and infrastructure rights-of-way as well as river and flood control channels is currently being incorporated into the city of Los Angeles's revision of its general plan.

7. The plethora of transportation-related land use studies recently initiated by Los Angeles's MTA are discussed in James R. Gilson and F. Michael Francis, "Planning for Joint Development in Los Angeles," Urban Land (June 1993): 30-32, and Judith Scheine, "Los Angeles Builds on Transportation," Architecture 83, no.8 (August 1993): 93-99.

Balmori Associates, Inc.,
Farmington Canal Greenway, New Haven.

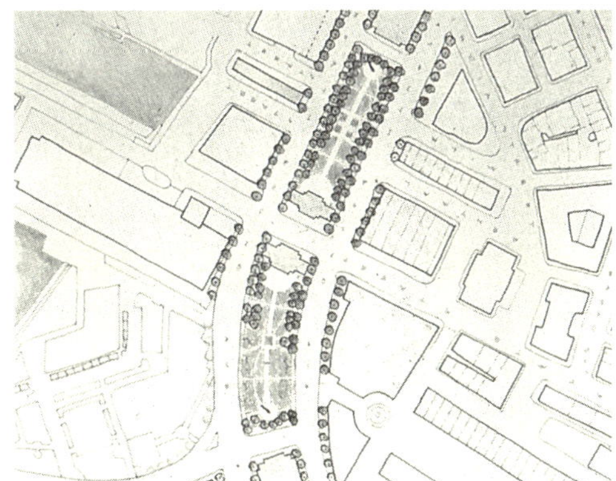

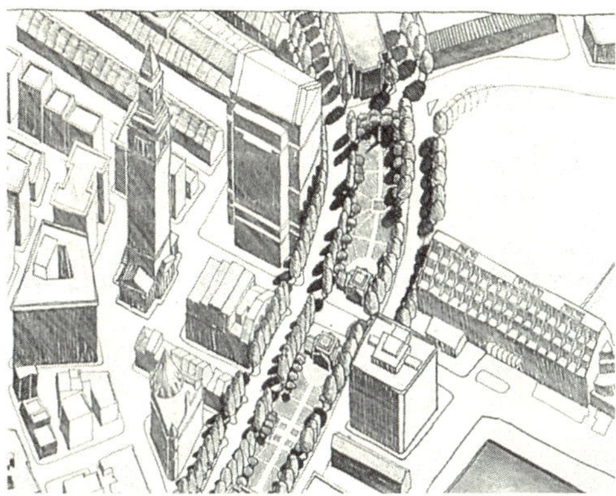

Chan Krieger & Associates,
Planning Study for Central Artery, Boston.

8. This effort is not without significant controversy. According to the architect, among the concerns raised by those opposing the project is alarm at the prospect of increased criminal activity due to improved mobility of those in underserved areas of the city.

Occupied residence in Overtown, Miami; the black owner refused to yield to the freeway. Photograph by Everett Fly.

9. Fly's study of historic black enclaves of Miami-Dade County and preparation of a conceptual revitalization plan for the Overtown district was sponsored by The Black Archives, History and Research Foundation of South Florida, Inc. as part of "Dialogue '81: A Conference on Neighborhood Revitalization."

Several transit-related urban design projects planned for East Coast cities distinguish themselves by the depth of their larger social vision as a determinant of their proposed reconfiguration of the urban landscape. The Farmington Canal Greenway project for New Haven, Connecticut, spearheaded by landscape architect and urban designer Diana Balmori, seeks to introduce a light rail system and greenway along the path of an abandoned canal and rail line, once an important regional transport system that connected New Haven to the center of the state and up to the Massachusetts border. The vision of Balmori and her collaborators is to remake the site, which passes through districts that are widely disparate although in close proximity, into a viable linear connector that offers both a means of access via light rail and an enhanced pedestrian orientation. The project's goal of establishing positive linkage between physically, socially, and economically segregated areas of the city, the rifts between which were exacerbated by a previous generation's disastrous attempts at urban renewal, provides not just a means of physical movement, but also improved access to possible sources of employment in the city and around the region through increased mobility for many of its inhabitants.[8] It also represents a tangible way in which to reintegrate Union Station with the rest of the city.



Likewise, Boston's Central Artery Corridor project seeks to ameliorate an urban fabric rent asunder by the thrust of a busy expressway through the heart of a formerly vital, lower-middle-class residential and commercial district. While the project, as currently being executed, involves massive infrastructural reconfiguration of the roadways going in and out of the city and other complex engineering problems stemming from the substitution of a tunnel for the existing elevated expressway, its urban design component concerns the restoration of an urban fabric in the linear space of the former highway. A study done by Alex Krieger, planning consultant to the project, proposed an intricate mixture of open space and built or programmed areas in the corridor. His plan represents an alternative to related ideas that have been put forth for its development either as completely built infill or as predominantly undifferentiated open space. While the final design ultimately adopted by Boston's Planning Department dedicates 75 percent of the corridor as open space, Krieger's ideas about the desirability of a more complex articulation of the site's historical resonance and past and present functions represents an important evolution of the debate about the role of open space in the public realm.

A variety of other significant ideas have arisen in recent years countering the eradicative tendencies of transportation corridors imposed on urban neighborhoods and proposing instead a regenerative effect. Among these is a study done in 1980 by architect Everett Fly for the Overtown district of Miami, undertaken in the wake of intensive civil unrest in the area.[9] Fly proposed altering the path of a future elevated public transit line so as to avoid the razing of sites significant to the history and identity of Overtown's African-American community. In addition to his emphasis on unearthing and preserving a little-known history, Fly articulated a set of broader social and economic directives for reshaping the future of this marginalized community that, since the time of Fly's study, has itself been transformed both by physical changes and by waves of immigration.

## NEW NEIGHBORHOODS IN URBAN AND EXURBAN CONTEXTS

The drastic imposition of automobile-oriented transportation corridors in and around urban centers was inextricably linked to postwar suburban residential development and the resulting exodus of the middle classes from the city center. As early as 1958, William H. Whyte voiced alarm at the phenomenon of urban sprawl which threatened to disfigure the American landscape. Pointing to the "vast, smog-filled deserts that are neither city, suburb, or country," he noted that "in the great expansion of the metropolitan areas the subdivisions of one city are beginning to meet up with the subdivisions of another."[10] Indeed, one of the most substantially transformative planning elements to have emerged in the modern period is the creation of completely new neighborhoods and residential districts in both urban and exurban contexts. Antecedents range from Ebenezer Howard's turn-of-the century Garden Cities, residential neighborhoods conceived as antidotes to the squalor of life in the heart of the industrial city, to Le Corbusier's vision of modern housing blocks set within gardens, as in his schemes for the Plan Voisin and City of Three Million Inhabitants, to Frank Lloyd Wright's utopian studies for Broadacre City, which privileged private space and automobile transportation among zones of differentiated usage. Wright's vision was partially realized following World War II as vast suburban tracts such as Levittown, New York, and the sprawling developments in California's San Fernando Valley sprouted across the United States. Made possible by the widespread use of the automobile and by the availability of easy financing for new home purchases geared especially to a new generation of veterans entering the housing market, these dramatically altered the American exurban landscape, way of life, and relationship to cities.

10. William H. Whyte, "Urban Sprawl," Fortune (January 1958): 102.

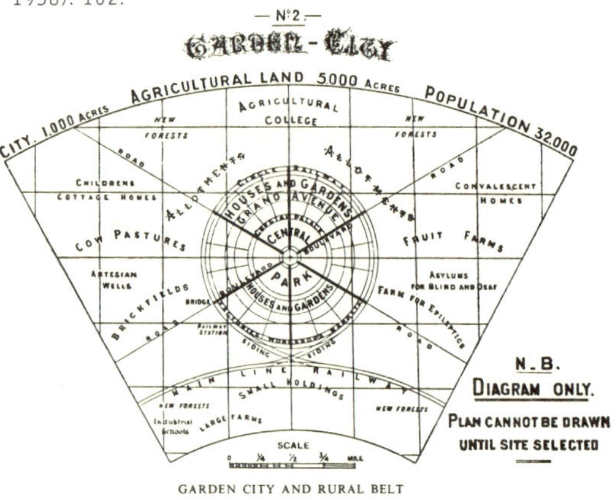


Ebenezer Howard, diagram for a garden city and its territory (1898). Originally published in Garden Cities of To-Morrow.



In Europe, a plethora of predominantly residential new communities also arose to replace and modernize those destroyed during World War II. New Towns—essentially self-sufficient communities built in previously undeveloped areas—flowered in postwar Britain, conceived on the Garden City model in a reformist vein to offer the middle and working classes a series of salutary, village-like living environments at some remove from the urban center. Milton Keynes, built in 1969-70 with a population of approximately 85,000, stands at the pinnacle of the postwar British New Town movement, in which ideals of social experimentation and adaptation to evolving patterns of contemporary living—such as the near-universal automobile ownership of its inhabitants—represented the foremost concerns of its planners.[11] At the same time, the provision of social housing was accomplished by the erection of large highrise multi-family housing complexes based on the examples of Le Corbusier's postwar Unités d'habitations. In the United States, as well, modern highrise public housing became accepted and realized on a widespread scale in the decades following World War II. Some of the best-known examples of these massive structures set in the midst of large open spaces in generally outlying or underserved urban areas include New York's Co-op City, Chicago's Cabrini Green, and St. Louis's Pruitt-Igoe, the 1972 demolition of which stands now as a famous symbol of the failure of the Corbusian model of mass public housing.

11. Jeff Bishop, Milton Keynes: The Best of Both Worlds?: Public and Professional Views of a New City (Bristol, England: School for Advanced Urban Studies, 1986), provides a thorough analysis of the physical planning and social structure of Milton Keynes from an urban sociological point of view.

Demolition of Pruitt-Igoe housing development, St. Louis. Missouri Historical Society, photograph by Richard Moore.

As the middle and working classes increasingly abandoned life in the central cities, suburban development continued to flourish in the United States. Although diametrically opposed in their demographic and physical makeups, both types—urban highrise public housing and suburban single-family tracts—became predicated on multiple segregations, by class, by race, and by activity. Meanwhile, a progressive breakdown of confidence in

12. The ideological and environmental basis behind the genesis of Arcosanti is described in Paolo Soleri, Arcosanti: An Urban Laboratory? (Scottsdale, Ariz.: The Cosanti Press, n.d.).

13. From among the numerous publications documenting and providing an analysis of Seaside, the most substantive include Alex Krieger and William Lennertz, eds., Andres Duany and Elizabeth Plater-Zyberk: Towns and Town-Making Principles (New York: Rizzoli, 1991), and Janet Abrams, "The Form of The (American) City: Two Projects by Andres Duany and Elizabeth Plater-Zyberk," Lotus International 50 (1986): 7-29.

the societal and cultural values that spawned this system of planning and land use began to emerge in the 1960s, giving rise to such concrete manifestations as the utopian community of Arcosanti in the Arizona desert, established in 1970 as an ecologically and socially regenerative alternative to the physical form and normative social framework of conventional land use patterns and sprawling suburban development.[12]

At the opposite spectrum from Arcosanti in terms of planning principles and aesthetics, yet similarly committed to a fundamental healing of the American suburban condition are the relatively recent phenomena of neo-traditionalism and the "new urbanism." The former is epitomized in the resort community of Seaside, Florida, the master plan for which was drawn up in 1979-80 by architects Andres Duany and Elizabeth Plater-Zyberk.[13] It stands as the most renowned contemporary example realized to date of attitudes about scale, structure, and hierarchy of building types drawn from turn-of-the-century concepts of Civic Art and Beaux-Arts principles of classical composition, as well as from the anti-modern theories of the architect and polemicist Leon Krier, first articulated by him in the 1970s. Glorified in the popular press, Seaside has been both lauded and vilified in architectural circles. Its notoriety succeeded in launching the careers of Duany and Plater-Zyberk as the foremost American practitioners of neo-traditional planning. They have since designed the building codes and plans of over forty new residential communities and subdivisions, in addition to numerous design and planning projects for existing contexts.

Andres Duany and Elizabeth Plater-Zyberk. Seaside, Florida. Aerial view from the Gulf.

Playa Vista, Los Angeles. Typical residential district.

While the work of Duany and Plater-Zyberk represents an extreme in the spectrum of commitment to traditional and vernacular typologies as determinants of urban form, a number of other contemporary practitioners have developed related, yet less polemical and often more expansive, approaches. Interest in the traditional European city and/or in the vernacular American townscape as a paradigm for restoration of the urban fabric has been a key component in the thinking of architects whose work ranges broadly in stylistic and philosophical tenor. These include Charles Moore, Denise Scott Brown and Robert Venturi, Rodolfo Machado and Jorge Silvetti, and Fred Koetter and Susie Kim, as well as others more properly described as neo-traditionalists or "new urbanists" such as Peter Calthorpe, Elizabeth Moule and Stefanos Polyzoides, Steven K. Peterson and Barbara Littenberg, and Daniel Solomon, among others.

A major current project that incorporates these concerns yet applies them in the context of the late twentieth-century American metropolis is Playa Vista, a 900-acre mixed use district, the first phase of which is now underway in Los Angeles. Planned by a team of architects consisting of Duany and Plater-Zyberk, Moule and Polyzoides, Ricardo Legorreta, Laurie Olin, and Buzz Yudell, Playa Vista seeks to introduce a new standard of density into Los Angeles's urban framework. By emphasizing pedestrian orientation and firmly delimiting the height and massing of buildings and the hierarchy of street and spatial types, Playa Vista's planning takes its cues from neo-traditional principles. However, the project's scale, orientation to a complex regional infrastructure, and incorporation of measures responsive to community demands (including affordable housing, recycling of waste water, restoration of neighboring wetlands, and traffic mitigation measures) go far beyond the historicist and vernacular impulses of that movement's urge to recreate community on the model of a turn-of-the-century American town.[14]

14. The concept of "new urbanism" refers to a shared body of work and ideas about scale, mixed use, and pedestrian orientation in urban contexts being developed by such practitioners as Peter Calthorpe, Andres Duany and Elizabeth Plater-Zyberk, Elizabeth Moule and Stefanos Polyzoides, and others. The first Congress for the New Urbanism took place on October 8-11, 1993, in Alexandria, Virginia, attempting to codify a movement that its organizers envision as "patterned after the CIAM, which once completely changed the prevalent model of urbanism," as quoted in Arnold Berke, "Seeing a Broader Vision for a Better American City," Historic Preservation News (December 1993-January 1994): 18. See also Peter Katz, The New Urbanism (New York: McGraw-Hill, 1994).

Faubourg Québec, Montreal. Existing site.

Another major instance of commitment to providing new residential communities within the cities as an antidote to suburban sprawl is the currently developing Faubourg Québec project in Montreal. Focused on a neighborhood adjacent to the historic old city and port of Montreal, this project aims significantly to increase the availability of desirable and affordable housing stock in close proximity to existing commercial and recreational facilities and workplaces. A desire to create a vital new community in direct opposition to the tabula rasa approach characteristic of the urban renewal of the recent past led to a lengthy process of envisioning the possibilities for the district in relationship to its genius loci and the larger urban morphology. Furthermore, instead of a single vision shaping its outcome, the planning process of Faubourg Québec involved the participation as consultants of numerous architects with wide-ranging ideas about the genesis of urban form, including Daniel Solomon, Herman Hertzberger, and Peter Rose.

The project's most significant precursor in Montreal is the middle and working-class neighborhood of Milton Parc. Threatened with extinction during an urban renewal project of the 1960s that was halted by the galvanizing of a grassroots effort to preserve and upgrade the neighborhood while keeping its existing residents and avoiding gentrification, Milton Parc is one of the most remarkable examples to date of a community taking control of and directing its own transformation.[15] Its residents are now cooperative owners not only of their own rehabilitated housing, but also of the adjacent spaces for commercial facilities providing neighborhood-oriented services. As a populist phenomenon, a model of community, and an urban fabric, Milton Parc has left a substantial legacy for the planners and developers of Faubourg Québec.

A vastly different history characterizes the genesis of New York's Battery Park City. This 92-acre new district of commercial, residential, and open space created on a formerly undeveloped site adjacent to the water's edge has been hailed as a triumph of innovative planning and urban design, particularly for the quality and extensiveness of its public spaces. Critics of the project, however, point to a checkered political history regarding the progressive dwindling, then complete disappearance, of the number of low-income housing units intended for inclusion in Battery Park City from its inception in 1966.[16] As a market-rate and luxury residential and commercial environment, Battery Park City stands as a prime example of gentrification and urban enhancement. With notable successes in contributing to the city a series of imaginatively configured, artist-designed open spaces, the requisite economic and social bases of its residential and commercial components continue to raise questions about the responsibility of the public sector in the shaping of both the urban context and the public realm.

Given the difficulty of overcoming predominant suburban development and land use patterns, a relatively small degree of innovation has characterized the creation of new neighborhoods in American exurban contexts. The community of Laguna West in Sacramento, California, planned by Peter Calthorpe, is being closely watched as the first built middle-income residential community to espouse a new set of land-use principles. These include a hierarchical layout of residences radiating from the focal point of a community center/transit plaza, and the incorporation of day care and recreational facilities as well as the integral presence of a major employer directly adjacent to the neighborhood. Although numerous conventional elements characterize

15. The history of Milton Parc is documented in Phyllis Lambert, "Land Tenure and Concepts of Architecture and The City: Milton-Park in Montreal," in Gilbert A. Stelter and Alan F.J. Artibise, eds., Power and Place: Canadian Urban Development in The North American Context (Vancouver: University of British Columbia Press, 1986), pp. 133-50, and in Claire Helman, The Milton Park Affair: Canada's Largest Citizen-Developer Confrontation (Montreal: Véhicule Press, 1987).

16. An incisive critique of Battery Park City is found in Rosalyn Deutsche, "Uneven Development: Public Art in New York City," October 47 (Winter 1988): 3-52, a view that contrasts sharply with such assessments as Carter Wiseman's "The Next Great Place: The Triumph of Battery Park City," New York (June 16, 1986): 34-41.

Milton Parc Street Festival. Banner welcomes all to the festival while others attend from their balcony. Montreal, July 27-27, 1970. Photograph: Bill Robson, Montreal Star. National Archives of Canada.

Ricardo Bofill, Spaces of Abraxas, Marne-la-Vallée, France. Photograph by Tony Schuman.

the plan of Laguna West, the effort is an experiment in the reconfiguration of a suburban community to mitigate the effects of complete dependence on the automobile for access to employment and services, as well as the lack of community spirit and sense of placelessness often associated with suburban sprawl.

While suburban Laguna West differs in scale from a dense community such as Playa Vista, both are preeminent examples of the tendency toward the application of traditional planning principles as a corrective measure within late twentieth-century urban and suburban contexts. In Europe, the extension of the New Town phenomenon has continued to mark the evolution of new neighborhoods and communities adjacent to cities. A relatively recent flurry of such developments occurred in France in the 1970s and 1980s, many containing massive public housing projects designed by Ricardo Bofill's Taller de Arquitectura. The best known of these is the Spaces of Abraxas, completed in 1983 in Marne-la-Vallée, a New Town east of Paris. This project, like other Bofill works such as Antigone in Montpelier, France, is conceived as a massive stage set, in order to endow the life of its residents with a sense of theatricality and grandeur. An insensitive and even brutal solution to the problem of providing viable and sustaining living environments for lower-income citizens, the monumental Spaces of Abraxas caricatures the lives and aspirations of its inhabitants, despite the apparent historical resonance of its architecture.[17] A vastly different solution to the provision of mass housing outside the city, albeit at a smaller scale, is being generated by architects Marc Angélil and Sarah Graham in the town of Esslingen, near Zurich, Switzerland. Unlike a New Town, this project creates a center for an existing village, offering a relatively dense configuration of new services, offices, and residential fabric oriented around a railroad station. With the station as its dominant civic building, the town center's environmental mandate is further integrated into its planning and design via a complex system of solar energy application for the interconnected heating and cooling of its buildings. Rejecting historicism and conventional formal contextualism, this project instead emphasizes technology as the determinant of its framework and form, seeking to define new standards of ecological design as a foremost imperative.

17. Tony Schuman, "Utopia Spurned: Ricardo Bofill and The French Ideal City Tradition," in Diane Ghirardo, ed., Out of Site: A Social Criticism of Architecture (Seattle: Bay Press, 1991), pp. 220-49, cogently evaluates the civic value of Bofill's large-scale work, positing that, "His formal symbols . . . offer us refuge in an idealized past, dressing up the status quo with dazzling images that promote a false consciousness." (p. 220).

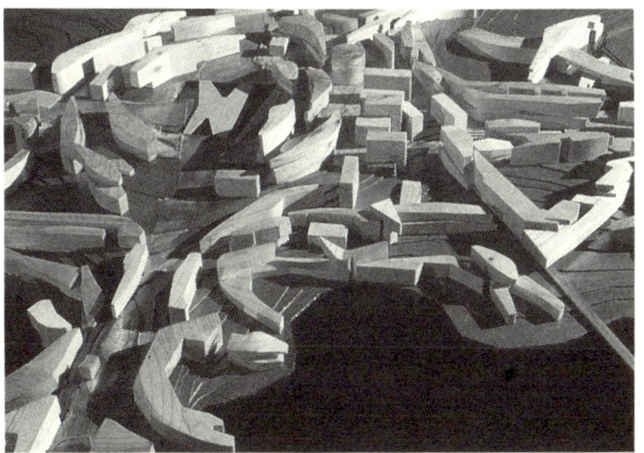

Michael Sorkin. Plan for military base conversion. Model.

An investigatory project by architect and writer Michael Sorkin takes the environmental mandate characteristic of much current thinking about the planning of new communities to an extreme. The one purely hypothetical project to be included in "Urban Revisions," Sorkin's design for a city on land formerly used as a testing ground by the U.S. military near Yuma, Arizona, envisions a socially, economically, and ecologically utopian presence on an otherwise derelict site. Informed by a deeply optimistic commitment to the spirit of invention rather than to pragmatic constraints, the design of this community constitutes an analogue of the uncertainties and potentials of real life and a model for the genesis of form rather than form itself.

## RETHINKING THE MASTER PLAN

The most innovative instances of recent planning and design approaches to both transportation corridors and new neighborhoods evince a profound rethinking of the idea and function of the master plan. Its definition as a strategy to envision and delimit the physical usage of a place over time is being thoughtfully reconsidered and recast in a number of projects addressing themselves to a broad array of urban spaces and focal points. With goals ranging from overall conceptualization to actual configuration and design of buildings and spaces, these vastly different projects strive to reconsider

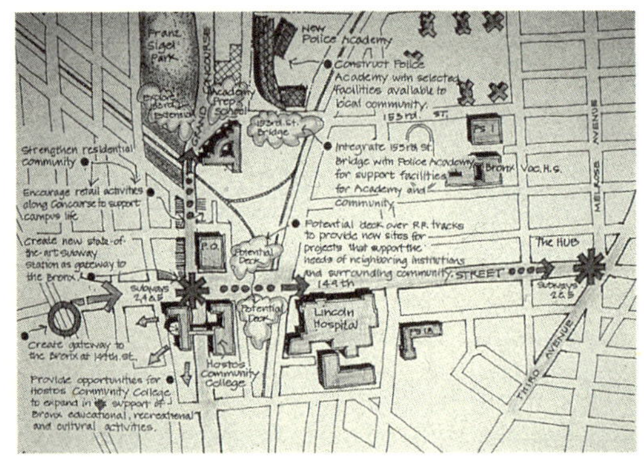


Bronx Center. Plan.

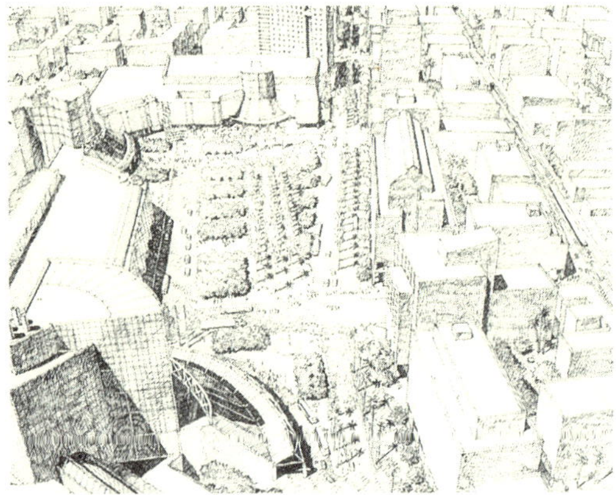

Downtown Strategic Plan, Los Angeles. Convention Headquarters Hotel and Hotel District. The project will catalyze appropriate levels of cooperation among existing and future hotels in the interest of providing appropriate hotel, retail, and transportation services for convention-goers.



conventional approaches. They do so for a myriad of reasons, among them the desire to realistically confront and respond to the social and economic conditions of cities and their populations as well as the urge to ameliorate the physical workings and aesthetic presence of the urban realm. Three types of projects are chosen here for analysis—those that deal with an entire city or a substantial portion thereof; those that treat a district dedicated to arts, culture, and recreational uses; and those that seek to transform a small unit of space—a city block—into a socially beneficial, aesthetically pleasing, and productive site while still maintaining its character as predominantly open space.

Typically, master plans for cities or large parcels of land within or near them are developed under the aegis of government bureaucracies and/or private interests seeking to maximize the economic health and future investment potential of the area under consideration. While similar concerns inform the projects to be discussed here, their designers and participants have brought to bear numerous questions about the role of community members in the planning process, the desirability of gentrification as an urban phenomenon, and the value of minimal rather than deep-seated or radical physical intervention, among other issues. The resulting works succeed in putting forth challenging concepts about both the physical character of public space and the workings of the public realm.

## THE CITY

The Bronx Center project, currently underway in New York City, epitomizes the notion of urban reclamation given life by a master planning process. Yet it was the development of a master plan itself against which the consortium of interests now known as Bronx Center came into being, with the goal of halting the process and application of a plan that had been prepared without community knowledge and participation. The current effort involves a concerted process of physical, social, and economic analysis of the South Bronx with the direct participation of those who live and work in the area. Its outcome is a series of recommendations for initiatives that address residents' primary concerns about housing, jobs, services, and safety, as well as about maintaining a voice and a presence in the community. These recommendations range from the preservation and upgrading, rather than demolition and replacement, of existing housing stock to the creation of a magnet high school for law enforcement adjacent to the soon-to-be-built new Police Academy building, for which a design competition had been won prior to the involvement of the Bronx Center group.

Like the Bronx Center effort, Los Angeles's recently completed Downtown Strategic Plan represents an attempt to lay a foundation for the future on existing physical, social, and economic conditions rather than on a sweepingly transformative vision. While it has a strong community component, it differs from Bronx Center in that the character and composition of the downtown Los Angeles community reflects primarily government and business interests, with residential communities, social service agencies and the populations they serve, and the arts and culture all assuming tangential roles. From a vision of the intersecting futures of these disparate constituencies as well as from careful consideration of their particularized needs and circumstances, the plan has taken shape as a set of physical recommendations, but also as a document of advocacy for the area's traditionally underserved populations and uses.[18] The goal of the planning team, led by Elizabeth Moule and Stefanos Polyzoides, has been to augment the evolving pedestrian and transit orientation of downtown, thus allowing for greater connection among its often distinctly physically and socially separated districts, and to propose several "catalytic projects" as infill for sites in particular need of regeneration.

18. Important social and economic questions about the Downtown Strategic Plan emerge in Aaron Betsky, "All Roads Lead Downtown: The Emerald City Plans its Future," LA Weekly (November 12-18, 1993): 17-19.

Agrest & Gandelsonas, Architects. Vision Plan for Des Moines. Computer-generated drawing.

Recognizing the complexity of the current urban collage, the plan seeks to sustain and enhance it without resorting to either sweeping urban renewal or to its counterpoint, strict historic preservation leading to gentrification.

The Vision Plan for Des Moines, conceived by architects Diana Agrest and Mario Gandelsonas, finds its starting point not in social but in formal innovation. Based on a close study of the physical structure of the city and its morphology, the plan evolves directly from an understanding of the urban fabric particular to Des Moines, and, in the architects' view, to the American city in general. With its intensive focus on the city's physical framework as the generator of potential for a wide spectrum of future economic opportunities as well as new residential areas, recreational sites, etc., the plan seeks to suggest rather than to mandate and to inspire a vision rather than a strict hierarchical ordering. In opposition to the workings of many such efforts, the Des Moines Vision Plan proceeded not from a pragmatic consideration or realistic imaging of the city and its spaces, but rather from the architects' characteristic and highly abstract renditions of formal and spatial configurations and points of connection. These were then employed to stimulate discussion with members of an extensive civic advisory group about the needs, workings, and image of the city.



THE DISTRICT—ARTS, CULTURE, AND RECREATION

STUDIO WORKS.
Conceptual master plan for Grand Center, St. Louis. Model.

Several current and recent projects for urban and exurban districts oriented primarily to arts, culture, and recreation offer a variety of innovative and investigatory tactics for the reclamation of public space. A proposed master plan for Grand Center, an eight-block historic theater district in central St. Louis, took form as a series of seven distinct, yet overlapping strategies for the revisioning and reconfiguration of the area's urban fabric. Developed at a conceptual level by the office of Studio Works in collaboration with an interdisciplinary team of architects, designers, and artists, the master plan for Grand Center took its cues from the site's history and identity as a theater district and grew out of earlier proposals for lighting devised by architect Robert Mangurian of Studio Works with artist James Turrell. Their relatively simple and even ephemeral series of proposed interventions sought to effect profound changes in both the "onstage" (streetscape) and "backstage" (functional spaces such as rear parking lots and alleys) areas of the district, returning it to a position of importance and vitality in the cultural and economic life of the city.

A plan developed for the open space surrounding the North Carolina Museum of Art in Raleigh also rethinks the idea of massive physical transformation in favor of a more directed, responsive approach to the essential conditions of the site at hand. "Imperfect Utopia: A Park for the New World," the title of the master plan devised by the team of architects Henry Smith-Miller and Laurie Hawkinson, landscape architect Nicholas Quennell, and artist Barbara Kruger, recognizes and even calls attention to aspects of the suburban open site surrounding the museum that might otherwise be overlooked or downplayed, i.e., its proximity to a residential area, a prison, and a busy highway. The actualization of the plan's first phase, also being designed by the team, positions an interactive series of installation and filmic elements adjacent to the museum building as a transitional outdoor space signalling a zone of active cultural engagement, rejecting the notion of placing a conventional (passive) sculpture garden in the landscape. Other zones of the park will be dedicated to a range of uses and will include replanting the original growth that at one time graced the site; historical markers and signage will also make evident other aspects of the area's past and its unique physical, social, and cultural identity.

Rashid + Couture / ASYMPTOTE. "Steel Cloud": West Coast Gateway, Los Angeles. Scale model.

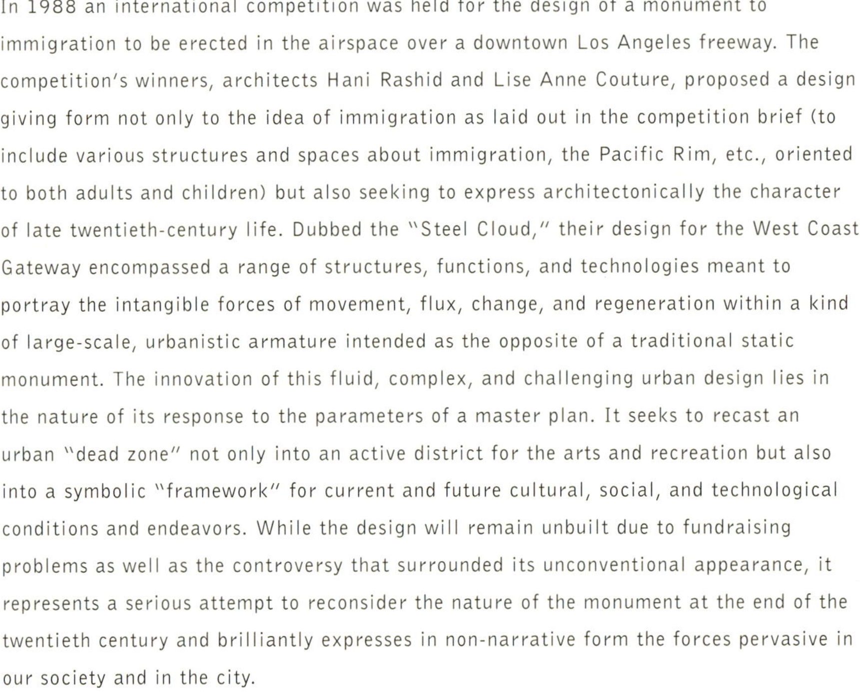

In 1988 an international competition was held for the design of a monument to immigration to be erected in the airspace over a downtown Los Angeles freeway. The competition's winners, architects Hani Rashid and Lise Anne Couture, proposed a design giving form not only to the idea of immigration as laid out in the competition brief (to include various structures and spaces about immigration, the Pacific Rim, etc., oriented to both adults and children) but also seeking to express architectonically the character of late twentieth-century life. Dubbed the "Steel Cloud," their design for the West Coast Gateway encompassed a range of structures, functions, and technologies meant to portray the intangible forces of movement, flux, change, and regeneration within a kind of large-scale, urbanistic armature intended as the opposite of a traditional static monument. The innovation of this fluid, complex, and challenging urban design lies in the nature of its response to the parameters of a master plan. It seeks to recast an urban "dead zone" not only into an active district for the arts and recreation but also into a symbolic "framework" for current and future cultural, social, and technological conditions and endeavors. While the design will remain unbuilt due to fundraising problems as well as the controversy that surrounded its unconventional appearance, it represents a serious attempt to reconsider the nature of the monument at the end of the twentieth century and brilliantly expresses in non-narrative form the forces pervasive in our society and in the city.



## THE BLOCK—REENVISIONING OPEN SPACE

Baratloo-Balch, Architects. Master Plan for Bathgate Avenue Community Park. Bronx, New York.

Two current projects stand out from among the many efforts being undertaken in American cities to reclaim open space for productive and congenial neighborhood-oriented usages. At the level of the city block, otherwise derelict and underused open spaces are being reconfigured for purposes specific to the needs of their surrounding communities instead of being dedicated to generalized, non-specific recreational activity. The Uhuru Garden project in the Watts section of Los Angeles is perhaps the foremost current example of experimentation in the area of purposeful structuring of open space. Designed by landscape architect Achva Benzinberg Stein, Uhuru Garden will replace an empty block with productive agriculture, facilities for instruction in its production, irrigation, etc., and for its distribution and sale. Usage will be limited to those who wish to participate in, maintain, or take instruction in any aspect of work associated with the site, including residents of the adjacent public housing project, students at the nearby public school, and members of a local drug rehabilitation project engaged in the production and sale of goods as therapeutic and job-training activity. Its design incorporates native California vegetation, examples of indigenous irrigation techniques, and other physical elements that will reinforce its role as a focal point in the community it will serve.

In New York City's South Bronx, the Bathgate Avenue Community Park is another example of open space being reclaimed for use by a wide cross section of individuals who live, work, and study nearby. Currently considered dangerous because of criminal activity, and thus off-limits to all but an intrepid few, the park is being redesigned by architects Mojdeh Baratloo and Clifton Balch to better serve the needs of its neighborhood. As in the Uhuru Garden project, a highly structured plan zoned according to specific activity and usage replaces the principle of undifferentiated open space. While the site is small, it offers a varying topography that accomodates such unrelated functions as gardening, ballplaying, supervised playgrounds for small children, etc.

These are being strictly delimited by the designers and positioned for maximum safety and visibility throughout the park. Its situation within the neighborhood itself is being subtly yet firmly reinforced by an "urban zone" of street trees and perimeter fencing around its periphery, acting as a buffer from the street without rigidly or harshly effecting physical separation.

## COMMUNITY SPACES AND PROCESSES

Crenshaw Neighborhood Plan Workshops, Los Angeles.

A significant degree of community input and involvement has informed the genesis and development of the projects discussed above. Instead of applying unilateral bureaucratic decisions and extravagant and/or unmediated architectural visions, these projects attempt seriously to answer to the needs and desires of those with a stake in their future. This phenomenon represents a substantial shift away from previous generations' imposition of urban plans and designs onto a city or district with little or no interaction with the inhabitants and users of a given site. It has now become commonplace for public and private interests to seek community involvement and support from the outset of a project, in part because of the numerous instances where community groups have succeeded in derailing or causing major changes to projects after the fact. By the same token, architects and urban planners have, of necessity, become increasingly cognizant of and responsive to such articulated needs and desires in their vision of the shaping of the public realm. Indeed, the interaction between the design professional and the untrained, yet committed, layperson is a crucial component of the successful outcome of today's work in urban planning and design. As stated by veteran urban planner Denise Scott Brown,

> **Urban design requires thoughtful, knowledgeable and able designers, who can intervene in the urban processes in a supportive and understanding way and who will know when, in their given role, it is appropriate to design, and when it is more creative not to.**[19]

The Bronx Center project, discussed above, stands as perhaps the foremost example of community-based planning to date in terms of the role being played in the decision-making process by those who live and work in the area. It represents the pinnacle of a movement that first manifested itself in the anti-establishment climate of the 1960s toward the involvement of grassroots community groups and residents of the inner cities in local planning and design efforts. Numerous related projects, although on a smaller scale than Bronx Center, are presently underway around the country. In Los Angeles, following the civil disturbances of spring 1992, several significant neighborhood-based planning efforts came into being as a way for residents of underserved areas to gain a greater stake in the sustainment and improvement of their immediate districts. The process of evaluation, interaction, and recommendation undertaken by laypersons who chose to become involved in these efforts alongside trained professionals has resulted in improved knowledge of the public process and the social fabric that, if implemented, will profoundly impact the future of these areas. If progress in the physical and social realms is to be achieved, the public and private sectors and the design community will need to give increasing recognition to the importance of these efforts and continue the interactive processes whereby alliances are formed, understanding is gained, and truly public places are made.

19. Denise Scott Brown, "The Public Realm: The Public Sector and The Public Interest in Urban Design," in Andreas C. Papadakis, ed., Denise Scott Brown: Urban Concepts (London: Academy Editions, and New York: St. Martin's Press, 1990), p. 29.

# Migration, Race, and Ethnicity in the Design of the American City

*M. Patricia Fernández-Kelly*

And they said to one another, let us build us a city and a tower, whose top may reach unto heaven; and let us make us a name, lest we be scattered abroad upon the face of the whole earth. - Genesis: 11:4



## INTRODUCTION

Two contrasting themes run through the history of urbanization. In one, the city stands as a symbol of modernization, cultural progress, and industrial vitality. In the second, the city represents almost the opposite: moral decay, squalor, and danger. For more than a century Americans have entertained versions of this dual account. In recent years, however, negative perceptions about the city appear to have galvanized into a distinct metaphor of the other; large cities, in particular, tend to be equated with crime, unbridled immigration, racial discord, and slack morality. Is this image of the American metropolis truly new? How did the city become synonymous with difference?

The answer to those questions is found in the social and economic forces that have shaped urban landscapes in the United States to a larger extent than the creative efforts of architects and planners. American cities bear the imprint of industrial capitalism, as do cities throughout the world. Exceptional in the international context, however, is the extent to which race, migration, and ethnicity have designed and redesigned the American city. Suburbs, barrios, immigrant enclaves, and ghettos are all manifestations of segregative and resegregative pressures stemming from the intersection of large economic trends and distinctive social dynamics. Below, I focus on processes that accelerated during the second half of the twentieth century but that began much earlier, forging the jagged patterns of residential concentration and deconcentration that give American cities their unique profile.

## URBANIZATION, TECHNOLOGY, AND CAPITALIST DEVELOPMENT

Slightly more than a hundred years ago, a brief but momentous period of technological innovation fomented the emergence of cities as we know them today. Between 1877 and 1889, steel frame buildings, electric power lines, the light bulb, elevators, electric trolleys, the internal combustion automobile engine, subways, and telephones were introduced. These inventions, together with the mechanization of agriculture, the rise of corporations, developments in banking and finance, and new mass-production methods—including the manufactory and the conveyor belt—spurred the growth of metropolitan areas. As in other countries, the modern American metropolis emerged as the visible center of economic and political control under industrial capitalism.[1]

1. For a classic account of the intersection between technological development, urban evolution, and class formation, see Eric Wolf, Europe and the People Without History (Berkeley: University of California Press, 1982).

The emerging city acted as a centripetal force. Investment patterns and the growth of markets prompted competition for central locations and the clustering of commercial activities in business districts near the confluence of transportation lines. Rising labor demands were met by a steady flow of European immigrants, who provided the grist for a burgeoning economy. In cities like New York, Boston, and Chicago, industrial success coincided with the intensification of class antagonisms, militancy, and the eventual consolidation of workers' organizations. After the ruthless elimination of its most radical strands, trade unionism flourished as part of a social compact that translated into lavish profits for investors but also rising standards of living for workers.[2]

2. Larry J. Griffin, Michael E. Wallace, and Beth A. Rubin, "Capitalist Resistance to the Organization of Labor before the New Deal: Why? How? Success?" in American Sociological Review 51 (April 1986): 147-67.

Starting in the 1880s, multistoried buildings transformed urban skylines in the United States, and by 1929, when the construction of Manhattan's Rockefeller Center began, the skyscraper had become a widespread symbol of modernity. Throughout that period and well into the 1950s, the interdependence between industrialists and workers grew, partly due to technological constraints that hampered capital mobility. Although foreign ventures expanded and transnational corporations materialized by the early 1900s, most American investment was domestic, and domestic too were its benefits.



Improved personal and household incomes led to an intensified use of automobiles and trucks during the 1920s and that, in turn, to accelerated urban deconcentration which slowed dramatically only during the Great Depression. The strengthening of the American state and the implementation of New Deal reforms also affected urbanization processes. During the 1930s, numerous public works programs stimulated the creation of peripheral water reservoirs, electric power and telephone lines, and paved roads that laid the foundation upon which many suburbs grew following World War II.[3] Finally, this period witnessed an increased black migration from the rural South that enlarged the pool of labor in metropolitan areas.[4] Stiff racial demarcations confined the new arrivals to segregated neighborhoods, many of which had been occupied at an earlier stage by impoverished European immigrants.

3. W. Parker Frisbie and John D. Kasarda, "Spatial Processes," in Neil J. Smelser, ed., Handbook of Sociology (Newbury Park: Sage Publications, 1988), p. 630.

4. Karl E. Taeuber and Alma F. Taeuber, Negroes in Cities: Residential Segregation and Neighborhood Change (Chicago: Aldine, 1965).

By the 1950s a well-developed suburban infrastructure enhanced by government-subsidized home mortgages, zoning regulations, and federal highway programs resulted in the greatest period of suburbanization in American history. The city now radiated centrifugal forces. Racial desegregation and the Civil Rights movement, combined with persistent black migration, quickened the departure of whites from urban centers. Outward movement from the cities continued apace during the 1960s as metropolitan belts modernized, attracting retail and consumer service establishments. While outer rings received comparatively affluent populations, poverty swelled in the urban core. Unable to compete with brand new shopping malls in the suburbs, and lacking a strong consumption base, businesses floundered in the inner city. At the same time, a period of unparalleled economic prosperity allowed for government initiatives to promote urban renewal, the expansion of public assistance programs, and subsidized housing projects. By the 1970s most of the United States was fully urbanized.

Yet urbanization was only part of a larger story about to undergo an unforeseen twist. By the late 1960s a major tendency towards economic internationalization was apparent, made possible largely by the application of computer technology to productive activities.[5] Facing foreign competition—mainly from Japan and other industrializing countries in Asia—as well as rising wages and government regulations in the United States, companies searched for new ways to realize profits. Diminishing costs in air

5. June Nash and M. Patricia Fernández-Kelly, eds., Women, Men and the International Division of Labor (Albany: State University of New York Press, 1983); Alejandro Portes and John Walton, Labor, Class and the International System (New York: Academic Press, 1981); Michael Storper, "Technology and Spatial Production Relations: Disequilibrium, Interindustry Relationships, and Industrial Development," in Manuel Castells, ed., High Technology, Space, and Society (Beverly Hills, Calif.: Sage, 1985), pp. 265-83.

transportation and improvements in the transmission and storage of information enabled them to retain headquarters in the United States while at the same time relocating labor-intensive operations to less developed countries. This new arrangement provided investors with unprecedented flexibility but also altered the balance of power between capital and labor.

6. Barry Bluestone and Bennett Harrison, The Deindustrialization of America: Plant Closings, Community Abandonment, and the Dismantling of Basic Industry (New York: Basic Books, 1982).

Advanced technology rapidly accelerated capital mobility across international borders. Employers' dependence on American workers was greatly diminished as was the social compact that had created the world's most prosperous working class in the preceding decades. The search for lower production costs and hospitable conditions for investment resulted in a virtual epidemic of plant closings and worker displacement during the 1970s and early 1980s. According to some estimates between 32 and 38 million jobs were lost during the 1970s as the direct result of private disinvestment in American business.[6] Union membership plummeted from 33 percent of the labor force in the 1960s to less than 15 percent in the late 1980s.



As the economic base shifted from manufacturing to services and information processing, cities like Detroit, Pittsburgh, New York, and Baltimore experienced fiscal turmoil and, in some cases, near-bankruptcy. Urban centers deteriorated amidst the rubble of defunct factories. Declines in real earnings, dislocation, and rising unemployment among native-born Americans coincided with the arrival of new waves of immigrants, this time primarily from Asia, Latin America, and the Caribbean.

7. Saskia Sassen, The Global City: New York, London, Tokyo (Princeton: Princeton University Press, 1991).

Paradoxically, the vacuums created by capital flight created new opportunities for investment in many cities. Professionals linked to lucrative sectors of the economy—international banking and finance, communications, producer services, and software design, among others—converged on otherwise decaying metropolitan centers, stimulating gentrification and invigorating the demand for goods and services often provided by immigrants. This new type of urban conglomerate, the global city, emerged from the ruins of the old industrial city as a strategic location for the centralization of coordinating functions vis-à-vis the international economy.[7] Global cities like New York and Los Angeles are the modern counterparts of the ancient Babel: polyglot assortments where poverty and unparalleled affluence coexist side by side.

## URBAN DESIGN AND THE POLITICS OF RACE AND ETHNICITY

8. Alejandro Portes and Rubén G. Rumbaut, Immigrant America: A Portrait (Berkeley: University of California Press, 1990), p. 99.

Two great sagas—international migration and racial polarization—have left their indelible marks on American cities. Praises to the forbearance and determination of an immigrant ancestry are deeply ingrained in American lore. At the same time, immigrants have almost always been seen as social contaminants, the purveyors of disease, ignorance, and dubious morality.[8] Few and far between have been the instances when foreigners have not been received with suspicion and hostility by those who had claimed this land at an earlier date. A consistent pattern in U.S. metropolitan areas has been the departure of older, mostly white, populations after every arrival of immigrant and racial minorities.

Although many immigrants have spontaneously arrived in this country driven by hopes for a better life, active recruitment played a major role in the beginning. As a budding economic power, the United States experienced rising labor demands in the nineteenth century but its emerging opportunities were not well known abroad. Employers, therefore, had to mobilize to attract labor. Business delegates were sent to Mexico,

Ireland, southern Italy, and the Austro-Hungarian empire to enlighten potential workers about the favorable terms available from the eastern canal companies and the western railroads. At the turn of the century, central and eastern Europeans were actively enlisted for work in the Midwest following the development of capital-intensive industries in that region—first steel and then auto manufacturing. Several decades before, labor recruitment by the Hudson and other canal companies moved contingents of Irish and Italian workers towards the routes followed by canal construction. In the West, Chinese workers moved inland after mass recruitment by the railway companies. The Union Pacific and the Central Pacific also recruited Mexicans. About the same time, Finnish workers made their appearance in northern Wisconsin, Minnesota, and the Michigan Peninsula, hired by the copper mines and timber companies.[9]

9. Ibid., p. 13.

Geographical proximity to their points of origin influenced the settlement patterns of early immigrants. That explains why the majority of European immigrants gathered along the mid- and north-Atlantic Seaboard, Asians clustered in California and other Pacific states, and Mexican immigration concentrated in the Southwest. The importance of geographical propinquity was most vividly manifested by immigrant communities established right by the waterfront, in port cities of both coasts. The "Little Italys" nestled along the harbor in Boston, New York, Philadelphia, and Baltimore, or San Francisco's "Chinatown," remain as evidence of immigrant flows that, having reached U.S. shores, would venture no farther.[10] Clusters of foreigners of varying nationalities dotted urban landscapes throughout the latter part of the nineteenth century.

10. Ibid., p. 29.



By the early 1900s, the United States was receiving unprecedented numbers of immigrants per year; foreigners represented up to 21 percent of the American labor force and close to half of the urban population. In contrast to picturesque appraisals written many years later, reports of the time evince a persistent alarm over living conditions in immigrant settlements. As "slum" and "foreign colony" became interchangeable terms, a perception grew that immigrants, especially those from southern and eastern Europe, had "hereditary peculiarities" that threatened the fabric of American institutions. Even at that early stage, government agencies invested personnel and resources to investigate the social pathologies contained in immigrant neighborhoods. A major report issued in 1894 by the Department of Labor compared Baltimore, Chicago, New York, and Philadelphia, and defined slum as "an area of dirty back streets, especially when inhabited by a squalid and criminal population."[11] The rawness of its phrasing notwithstanding, that description eerily evokes contemporary accounts of the inner city.

11. Carroll D. Wright, The Slums of Baltimore, Chicago, New York, and Philadelphia. Seventh Special Report of the Commissioner of Labor (Washington, D.C.: Department of Labor, 1894), p. 3.

An illustration of the conditions and changes endured by the immigrant slum is found in Upton, a West Baltimore area that grew in the late eighteenth century as a result of European migration. Irish, German, Polish, and Bohemian waves first, and then Eastern European Jews, coexisted in Upton with manumitted slaves in a manner akin to that which characterized the slums of other developing cities. Many residents were unskilled manual workers and domestic servants employed in expanding commercial districts and wealthy homes.[12] Following a national pattern, this working class neighborhood emerged in relative proximity to more affluent residential areas.

12. Sherry H. Olson, Baltimore: The Building of an American City (Baltimore: Johns Hopkins University Press, 1980), p. 121.

The early nineteenth century witnessed increases in the rates of homicide and pauperism in Upton. Observers noted a rise of disease, filth, and crowded living conditions. Epidemics of smallpox, diphtheria, and measles were common by 1821 when a noted physician characterized a section in Upton as "A nest of houses tenanted by negroes and divided by an alley [where] disease and death have year after year luxuriously rioted among the miserable and abandoned victims who have there nestled together."[13] By the 1860s, local government sought to make provision for the protection of "unfortunate helpless maniacs" who were appearing on the streets of West Baltimore. There was a great increase of idle and wandering poor, chiefly women with children and without husbands, and old men destitute, helpless, and without work. Historical accounts also mention multitudes of arrivals, especially Irish, "worn-out negroes," and infant beggars.[14]

In West Baltimore as in other urban areas, European immigrants followed a well-known trajectory: they lived poorly and worked tirelessly; they saved, hoping to move to better places. They viewed the slum and the sordid tenements as temporary calamities to be endured in the search for a good life. For the majority, economic advancement meant relocating to other, more prosperous, neighborhoods. Social reconfigurations were mirrored by spatial rearrangements. However, moving to better neighborhoods was out of reach for African Americans, who were shunned as a result of strict racial demarcations. As immigrants moved to more attractive locations, permanent enclosure, on the basis of color and race, became Upton's trademark. West Baltimore epitomizes a common phenomenon: the transformation of immigrant slums into black ghettos.[15]

The gradual integration of immigrants and their children into American society paralleled the expansion of metropolitan areas and, as delineated in the previous section, the tendency towards suburbanization. As upwardly mobile populations searched for more attractive residential areas, a new class of real estate brokers and developers grew. Larger demographic and economic changes further contributed to the dispersion of older populations. In particular, the industrial expansion in the North created an increased demand for labor which, at the time of World War I, began to be filled by black immigrants from the rural South, where cotton agriculture was declining. The impact of black northward migration was profound. In 1910, almost 90 percent of blacks were living in the South, but sixty years later, little more than half remained there. Streams of southern blacks to the North and West reached epic proportions from 1940 to 1970, with almost 1.5 million blacks leaving in each of these three decades.[16] Moreover, this migration was almost wholly to the cities, making blacks an increasingly urbanized population.

African Americans arrived in cities like Chicago, New York, Boston, and Philadelphia with expectations of upward mobility identical to those of older European immigrants and under conditions which early students of ethnicity regarded as optimum for assimilation.[17] For that reason, they posed a threat to white workers in the North, and the violence and intimidation that had characterized southern race relations became a national phenomenon. Competition for work and housing, and growing impatience among blacks, translated into an increase in the frequency and severity of black/white hostilities.[18]

At the same time, despite the barriers of discrimination, many blacks rose to middle class status and, like other Americans, they sought to move to more attractive residential areas. Ironically, this opened opportunities for real estate speculators willing to profit from the rising aspirations of blacks and the prejudice of whites. Profits to be made in buying homes from white owners at below market prices and reselling them to

13. Dr. G. S. Townsend as quoted in W. Thomas Griffith, Annals of Baltimore (Baltimore: W. Woody, 1833), p. 288. See also Thomas Scharf, The Chronicles of Baltimore (Baltimore: Turnbull Brothers, 1874).

14. Olson, The Building of an American City, pp. 53-54.

15. For an excellent account of this subject see Thomas Lee Philpott, The Slum and the Ghetto: Neighborhood Deterioration and Middle-Class Reform, Chicago, 1880-1930 (New York: Oxford University Press, 1978).

16. Martin N. Marger, Race and Ethnic Relations: American and Global Perspectives (Belmont, Calif.: Wadsworth, 1994).

17. See, for example, Ernest W. Burgess, "The Growth of the City: An Introduction to a Research Project," in Robert Park, Ernest Burgess, and Roderick D. McKenzie, eds., The City (Chicago: University of Chicago Press, 1925), pp. 47-62. Those early expectations for the assimilation of African Americans did not materialize. What has been most striking about urban black ghettos is their persistence over time. Although other ethnic groups have clustered in barrios and slums, their eventual integration into desegregated neighborhoods has been much higher. See Douglas S. Massey and Nancy A. Denton, "Trends in the Residential Segregation of Blacks, Hispanics, and Asians: 1970-1980," American Sociological Review 52: 802-25.

18. See, for example, William M. Tuttle, Jr., Race Riot: Chicago in the Red Summer of 1919 (New York: Atheneum, 1970).

blacks for exorbitant sums ignited the practice of blockbusting.[19] Real estate agents began placing middle-class black families in previously all-white neighborhoods, triggering panic about potential losses in property values. In the process, all-white areas were quickly transformed into all-black areas and, often, into extensions of older ghettos. Blacks invariably paid more for the housing than the former residents, enabling realtors to boost their commissions. Such practices yielded substantial fortunes in every major American city.

19. A chilling account of these practices, as manifested in Boston, is provided in Hillel Levine and Lawrence Harmon, The Death of an American Jewish Community: A Tragedy of Good Intentions (New York: The Free Press, 1992). See also Philpott, The Slum and the Ghetto, and Olson, The Building of an American City.

20. Joe R. Feagin and Clairece Booher Feagin, Discrimination American Style: Institutional Racism and Sexism (Englewood Cliffs, N.J.: Prentice-Hall, 1978).

Although significant, blockbusting was only one of several factors maintaining residential segregation. Government policies, for example, created much of the framework necessary to perpetuate it. Since the 1930s, the federal government encouraged home ownership among middle- and working-class people through the establishment of the Federal Housing Administration (FHA) and other housing-related agencies. Their purpose was to provide low-cost financing by providing government-backed mortgage insurance. From the outset, the FHA discouraged integration by refusing to guarantee loans for homes that were not in racially homogeneous areas.[20] Although this policy was altered in 1962—when non-discriminatory pledges were required from loan applicants—it laid the basis for persistent residential segregation.



Banks and other lending institutions contributed to the same system by redlining, that is, designating certain areas within which real estate loans would not be made. Zoning regulations were established specifying the types of housing that could be built in particular neighborhoods; these were designed to exclude low-income, mainly black, units. Restrictive covenants and other similar agreements were also used to bar blacks and other minorities from white residential areas. Until the Civil Rights Act of 1968 prohibited discrimination in housing, such covenants were widely applied and were even supported by law until 1948.[21]

21. A counterpart of these developments consisted of the recalcitrant tendency to locate publicly-subsidized housing projects in impoverished, mostly African-American, neighborhoods. The infamous projects contributed to further concentrate poverty in the inner city. For an eloquent illustration of this process in Chicago's Governor Henry Horner Homes—"The Hornets"—see Alex Kotlowitz, There Are No Children Here: The Story of Two Boys Growing up in the Other America (New York: Doubleday, 1992).

22. See William J. Wilson, The Truly Disadvantaged: The Inner City, the Underclass, and Public Policy (Chicago: University of Chicago Press, 1987), pp. 95-104.

The result of these formal and informal policies was the consolidation of a dual housing market in the United States: one predominantly white and the other mostly black. Driven by forces that were largely economic (like the search for financial gain) but also social (like racial prejudice), the real estate industry, banks and lending institutions, and government agencies played a role in the maintenance of a system which has had far-reaching consequences. For example, redlining in black neighborhoods had a major negative repercussion on public school financing, which has historically depended on taxation based on property values. The exodus of affluent populations and the concentration of impoverished groups in central cities created serious financial problems for local governments which were doubly exacerbated, in recent years, by the loss of manufacturing jobs.[22] Deteriorated and boarded-up housing units, high vacancy rates, and a paucity of business activity in black neighborhoods are among the visible manifestations of institutional arrangements that have persisted for most of the twentieth century.

23. Ibid., pp. 60-62.

Finally, and perhaps most insidiously, residential segregation has resulted in the truncation of social ties upon which processes of successful incorporation into the larger society depend. A substantial number of African-American children continue to grow up in urban environments as highly segregated as those that existed more than thirty years ago, before the beginning of the Civil Rights Movement. Largely for that reason, their experience differs markedly from that of youngsters living in more affluent neighborhoods.[23] Thus, the most disturbing effect of residential segregation may have been the shrinkage of experience created by insularity, confinement, and the dearth of resources of superior quality available to new generations.[24] Although other immigrant groups have endured harsh treatment in their journey towards assimilation, African Americans stand alone as an illustration of stubborn exclusion even in the face of recent governmental efforts to promote incorporation.

Immigration and racial polarization—the two great American dramas—have left a durable imprint upon cities in the United States. The chronicle of immigration contains complex sub-processes such as the dynamics of attraction/repulsion evident in the coexistence of immigrant recruitment and stigmatization that paralleled the formation of urban slums at the turn of the century. The same is true about racial divisions: legislative attempts to promote inclusion have continuously clashed with a collective will to maintain rigid demarcations. In both cases race and ethnicity have reflected larger processes of class domination and subordination. The assimilation of older immigrant groups entailed their ascent up social and occupational ladders but also their actual movement away from the slum. The perpetuation of poverty among African Americans has been mirrored by the hardening contours of the urban ghetto.[25]

24. M. Patricia Fernández-Kelly, "Social and Cultural Capital in the Urban Ghetto: Implications for Economic Sociology," in Alejandro Portes, ed., The Economic Sociology of Immigration: Essays in Networks, Ethnicity, and Entrepreneurship (New York: Russell Sage Foundation Press, 1994).

25. See Douglas Massey, American Apartheid: Segregation and the Making of the Underclass (Cambridge, Mass.: Harvard University Press, 1993); also, "Black Migration, Segregation, and the Spatial Concentration of Poverty" (working paper, 1993, Population Research Center, The University of Chicago).



## DIVIDED FATES: IMMIGRANTS AND RACIAL MINORITIES IN THE NEW AMERICAN METROPOLIS

Starting in the mid-1960s a major shift towards economic globalization was made possible by revolutionary changes in technology. The invention and refinement of the semiconductor, as well as the design of affordable computers of manageable size and increased capacity for the storage and transmission of information, recast the options of consumers and producers, workers and employers.[26] The dazzling array of high-tech innovation also had a visible impact upon cities in the United States and abroad. A major effect of computer technology has been the creation of international communication and production networks that have greatly diminished the constraints imposed by geographical distance and linked urban spaces in ways never seen before.[27]

Although technological development does not occur independently of economic, cultural, and political processes, high-tech innovations have been of such magnitude as to mark the beginning of a new stage in capitalist development. The application of advanced technology to production propelled a shift from manufacturing to services and information-based industries. Automation and the abandonment of traditional factories resulted in reductions in the number of unionized jobs and the migration of people from older manufacturing cities. At the same time, high-tech and white-collar service sectors grew rapidly. Vast increases in communications capacity stimulated a corporate strategy of interregional and international production regardless of the social and economic consequences for local areas. Government contributed to this process by providing support for capital growth in the form of defense spending and reduced social expenditures throughout the 1970s and, especially, during the 1980s.[28]

High-technology industries have promoted new spatial patterns of production. In the United States, old industrial centers, ports, and depots have been replaced by pools of technical and scientific workers, centers of defense spending, sources of innovative venture capital, and strategic nodes in a communication network. In the same vein, changing technology has altered the locational behavior of industry and encouraged the growth of new regions. Older sites constituted by an assortment of physical places have

26. See Leni Siegel, "Delicate Bonds: The Semiconductor Industry," (Mountain View, Calif.: Pacific Studies Center, 1984). See also Joel Shurkin, Engines of the Mind: A History of the Computer (New York: W. W. Norton, 1984).

27. See T. K. Bradshaw and M. Freeman, "The Future of the Electronics Industry in California Communities" (Institute of Governmental Studies, University of California: 1984). See also A. Glassmeier, A. R. Markusen, and P. Hall, "Defining High Technology Industries" (Working Paper No. 407) (Berkeley: University of California, Institute of Urban and Regional Development, 1983); and M. Castells, "Towards the Informational City, High Technology, Economic Change and Spatial Structure: Some Exploratory Hypotheses," Working Paper No. 430 (Berkeley: University of California, Institute of Urban and Regional Development, 1985).

28. See Manuel Castells, "High Technology, Economic Restructuring, and the Urban-Regional Process in the United States," in Manuel Castells, ed., High Technology, Space, and Society (Beverly Hills, Calif.: Sage Publications, 1985).

been infiltrated, and in some cases replaced, by intangible spaces formed by flows of information.[29] This, in turn, is constituting a new hierarchy of functions and power accessible in varying degrees to social groups differentiated by class, race, ethnicity, and gender.

29. The notion of new intangible spaces created by communication flows is more than a metaphor. One of the major developments in 1993 was the emergence of the information highway connecting individuals and institutions vying for access to the most advanced scientific, financial, and technical data.

The electronics industry, which has been part and parcel of these processes, embodies some of the critical changes undergone by the broader economy over the last three decades. The export of jobs to less developed countries, low rates of unionization, and the combination of automation in the United States with labor-intensive operations abroad, are all features of electronics manufacture. In Manhattan, an early clustering of large, vertically integrated corporations gave way during the late 1970s and early 1980s to a multiplicity of small companies in its periphery, including neighboring counties in New Jersey. Restructuring encompassed shifts in the spatial distribution of firms of various types and a movement towards specialized activities which in many cases resemble a new form of artisanal production. Many of the new entrepreneurs in the New York metropolitan area are individuals previously associated with larger, vertically integrated firms which pioneered development in the electronics industry. Those new entrepreneurs are especially skilled in areas such as design and tend to subcontract to a variety of firms while at the same time "putting-out" part of the production process to smaller, often unregulated—or informal—establishments and home workers. Thus, the lowest echelon of the industry is characterized by the presence of industrial home workers, many of whom are women.[30]

30. M. Patricia Fernández-Kelly, "Labor Force Recomposition and Industrial Restructuring in Electronics: Implications for Free Trade," Hofstra Labor Law Journal 10, no. 2 (Spring 1993): 644.



In Southern California, where the largest number of electronics firms was contained during the 1980s, variations of the same critical features are apparent. There, electronics firms have resorted to a series of strategies to retain a competitive edge, including an explicit avoidance of unionized work forces, a move away from vertically integrated operations, reductions in plant size, and a shift toward subcontracting. High-tech firms have favored locations in sprawling suburban conglomerates and fostered the employment of immigrants and refugees, while at the same time providing few opportunities for native-born minorities, especially African Americans.

A distinct effect of the rise of global or informational cities in the United States has been the growth in the demand for professional workers with high levels of education and endowed with symbolic skills. About one-third of the jobs created by the new economy require specialized knowledge.[31] Engineers, lawyers, communications experts, computer designers, software developers, and related consultants of all kinds have tended to converge in large cities characterized by their integral location within the new world economy—New York, Los Angeles, Boston, Chicago—and, to a lesser extent, in smaller cities like Baltimore and Atlanta. Many of those specialists have entered the economy as members of two-earner households, thus representing highly lucrative prospects for real estate markets and related sectors of production and consumption.

31. Robert Reich, The Work of Nations: Preparing Ourselves for 21st-Century Capitalism (New York: Alfred A. Knopf, 1991).

The concentration of professionals in pivotal metropolitan areas has had a dual effect. First, it has spurred processes of gentrification encompassing the renovation of declining neighborhoods, with the consequent rise in property values, and the displacement of older and/or low-income populations. At the same time, local governments trying to attract high-technology industries, as well as tourism, have provided tax incentives to developers engaged in urban revitalization projects. Old industrial areas in Baltimore, Pittsburgh, and even Detroit have been transformed into showcase displays of customized entertainment and associated services. Revitalizing efforts have, in most cases, bifurcated the urban space into a glittering stratum, traversed by affluent citizens and tourists, and a less conspicuous layer of rotting infrastructure inhabited by impoverished populations.

Second, the new technocratic class has invigorated the demand for a variety of labor-intensive activities ranging from domestic service to restaurants and customized furniture and apparel. This has created interstices for the employment of recent waves of immigrants, primarily from Asia, Latin America, and the Caribbean, many of whom are undocumented.[32] New panethnic formations constituted by the combination of immigrant businesses and workers sharing a common language but stratified in terms of social class, race, and national origin have emerged in places like Los Angeles, Washington, and, especially, New York.

32. For excellent descriptions of this process see Saskia Sassen, The Mobility of Capital and Labor (Cambridge: Cambridge University Press, 1988), and The Global City: New York, London, Tokyo (Princeton: Princeton University Press, 1992).



Jackson Heights, in the borough of Queens, is an apt illustration of this phenomenon. Noticeable in that area, along Roosevelt Avenue, is a vibrant cluster of mostly Colombian and some Dominican businesses thriving in what was once a predominantly Irish neighborhood. With few exceptions, commercial establishments bear fresh-paint traces of their recent establishment. Several miniature malls house Korean and Colombian businesses, most of which hire Mexicans as low-skilled workers. In the lateral streets, industrial home work—mainly in garment manufacture—flourishes in a multitude of modest apartments and lofts. Also attesting to the vitality of a burgeoning unregulated economy, myriad street merchants sell cheap goods and food alongside formal restaurants offering delicacies from Ecuador, Mexico, and the Dominican Republic. The external perception is that Jackson Heights is a Hispanic residential area, but from within, high levels of heterogeneity in terms of race, nationality, and class are noticeable. Paradoxically, the age of advanced technology has not expunged older forms of labor supply; it has merely transformed them.

The concentration of immigrants in particular locations within or in the proximity of global cities depends on the characteristics of labor demand but also on the existence of transnational social networks formed by individuals who comfortably cross borders from specific points in areas of origin to specific points in areas of destination. At least for the time being, many of those immigrants appear less interested in assimilating to the larger society than in acquiring the means to maintain their status and visibility in their sending communities. The advantages of low-cost transportation that have enabled investors to relocate manufacturing operations to the less developed world have also facilitated the emergence of a new type of immigrant who sees cities in the United States as attractive places for employment but not necessarily as permanent residences. Transnational labor markets appear to be one of the less obvious, albeit profoundly significant, consequences of globalization.[33]

33. See Sassen, "Immigration and Local Labor Markets," in Alexander Portes, ed., The Economic Sociology of Immigration: Essays in Networks, Ethnicity, and Entrepreneurship (New York: Russell Sage Foundation Press, 1994).

A relatively short ride away from Roosevelt Avenue, in Washington Heights, a flourishing cluster of Dominican businesses merges almost imperceptibly with Harlem, the most notorious black area in New York. From an external vantage point, the two neighborhoods consolidate into a single black ghetto. From within, heterogeneity is again readily apparent. In contrast with the vitality of Washington Heights, Harlem bears all the traces of despair associated with the presence of an urban underclass—abandoned houses, unemployed men dealing drugs on street corners, violence, high numbers of female-headed households dependent on public assistance, and numerous births out-of-

34. Similar questions may be asked about Haitians clustered on the fringes of Liberty City, one of two ghettos in Miami, and about Mexicans and Central Americans in South Central Los Angeles. See Alejandro Portes, "Children of Immigrants: Segmented Assimilation and its Determinants," ibid.

wedlock to adolescents. Dominicans share residential spaces and schools with these most vulnerable populations. Outside their homes, Dominican children mingle with and mimic the fashions, style, and mode of speech of impoverished African Americans. This raises questions about the extent to which assimilation, among these new immigrants, will mean becoming black Americans, with the consequent extension of stigma, isolation, and dismemberment from the larger society.[34] The options of new immigrants in the restructured economy may well divide depending on spatial locations and the concomitant access to differential social networks and economic resources.

Narratives focusing on the new informational or global city have focused on the awe-inspiring transformations brought about by computers. Nevertheless, there is another side to the same story: the application of advanced technology is part and parcel of processes that have stiffened social polarization and altered the prospects of both immigrants and native-born Americans. That bifurcation is being echoed every day in the reconstitution of urban spaces. The same city inhabited by the purveyors of symbolic skills is populated by less prominent but more numerous groups, some of whom are providing muscle for the new economy and others who languish without purpose or function in the occupational ladder.



## CONCLUSIONS

Since its inception, as part of the historical developments that brought about the Industrial Revolution in the nineteenth century, the modern city has endured a split identity: at the same time a place of progress and cultural innovation and a field where the nightmares of modernization are played out without respite. In the collective mind, the city has always been constructed as a place of difference. What has changed is the extent to which long-lived social and economic processes threaten to create a permanent division between those who are part of a revitalized capitalist enterprise and those who are now, for all practical purposes, evicted from the system of production.

Beyond its shimmering patina of computers, automated teller machines, video games, and information superhighways, the global city surges as the visible expression of new forms of incorporation of professionals and immigrants and the exclusion of native-born racial and ethnic minorities. Therein lies the paradox of continued immigration nourishing the ranks of the post-industrial working class, in coexistence with the agony that suffocates the urban ghetto. There too reside the forces that, in the most fundamental way, design the American city.

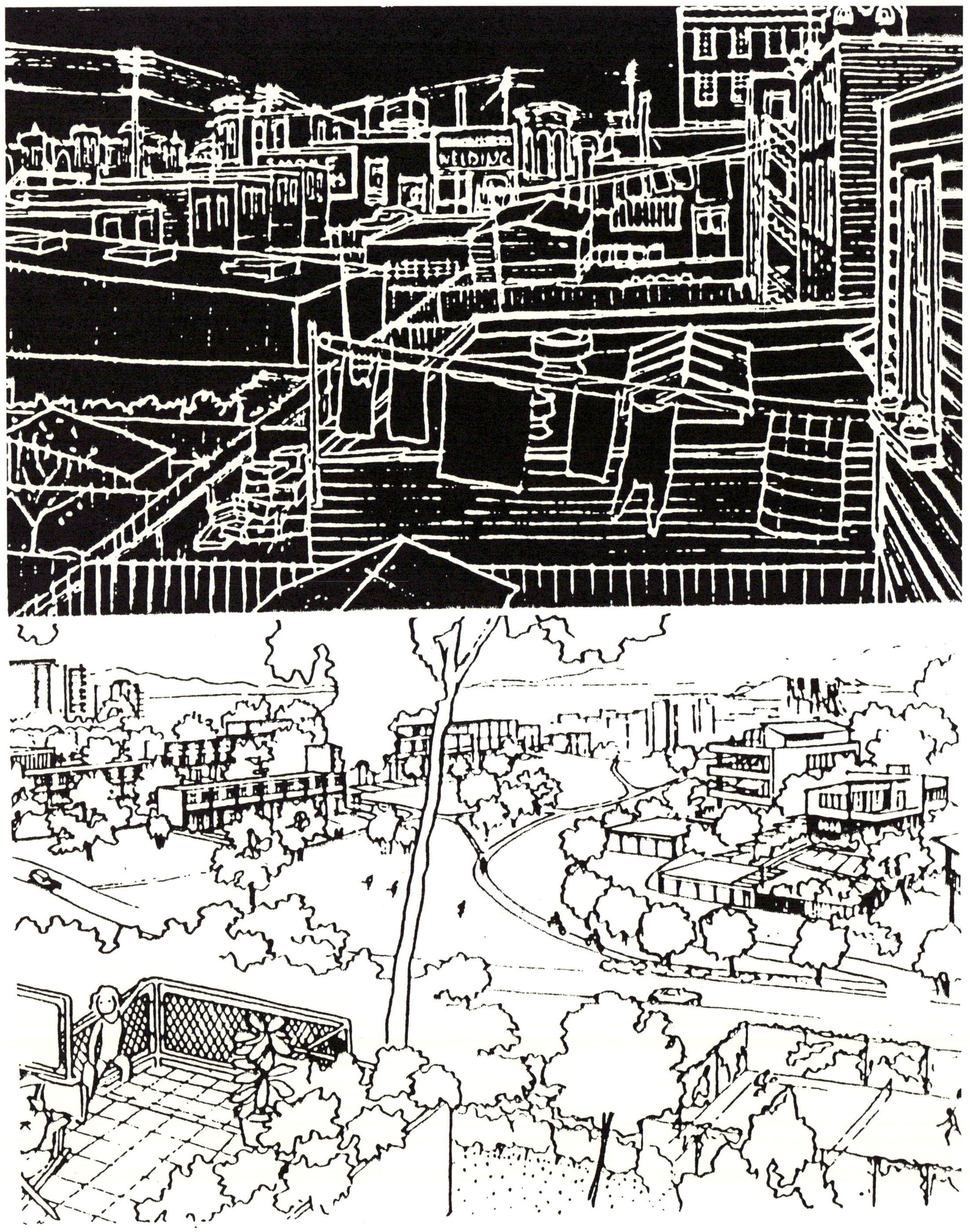

"Living environment as it was it was in 1940 and 'as it should be.'" From a 1940 Telesis exhibition at the San Francisco Museum of Modern Art.

# Inventions and Interventions: American Urban Design in the Twentieth Century

*Gwendolyn Wright*



Some fifty years ago, during the years between the two world wars, European theories of modernism arrived in the United States. The rules of modern architecture, a language of ideas and formal patterns, were modified here—indeed, it sometimes seemed there were no rules at all. American architects often envisioned their buildings not as isolated objects, but as part of cohesive communities within existing cities and towns. They employed a vernacular diction that drew more from local history and ordinary speech than from abstract rhetoric. Most rejected the idea of universally beautiful forms or solutions, seeking instead to adapt each design to its particular context—social, historical, architectural, and environmental.[1]

1. See, in particular, Richard Pommer and Christian Otto, Weissenhof 1927 and the Modern Movement in Architecture (Chicago: University of Chicago Press, 1991), which traces early European notions of a purely formal definition of modern art, preceding the more polemical and didactic concept of the International Style, as used by Philip Johnson in 1932.

There are resounding echoes of this earlier time in today's debates about ecologically and socially appropriate urban design. Architects again look to contingencies and even irregularities, rather than utopian standards, for inspiration. They play with technology and evoke local historical references, renouncing the rigors of the modern movement in favor of its experimental spirit. Indeed, the "Urban Revisions" of the 1980s and 1990s represent the instauration of a modernism that coalesced two generations ago, only to be obscured by the uncompromised, grandiose conformity of postwar urban renewal and suburban sprawl. Contemporary forms are quite different from those of the interwar years, to be sure, yet some of the most interesting proposals are motivated by similar concerns and even expressed in comparable language.

This is not to say that contemporary design is historically derivative; indeed, few architects practicing today are even aware of the parallels. Nor is there an unassailable, "authentic" modernist legacy to be found in this previous generation. History provides no such easy assurances. It is neither a justification for present actions, nor a nostalgic impediment to creativity. Instead there is an ongoing process, using a series of different filters, that lets us view the past and our own circumstances from new perspectives.

For example, many commentators, then and now, have contended that American modernism emerged in a cultural vacuum and developed without formal principles or political imperatives, oblivious to the "true" meaning of the modern movement. It is now possible to put forward a more fluid and inclusive configuration of that moment and of modernism as a design philosophy. Debates and contradictions can be seen as the core of this intellectual enterprise, rather than as conflicts to be overcome; ambiguity and diversity seem intriguing. History thus offers an opportunity to reframe social and formal problems that continue to preoccupy us, appraising strengths and weaknesses, disentangling intentions and influences, charting what has come of various aspirations.

What then were the principal characteristics of this early modernist epoch in the United States, especially among architects interested in urban design? To take on this question, one must first shift away from the usual focus on isolated masters. Architecture involves a much larger community, including both the mainstream of the profession and the avant-garde. They have necessary commonalities as well as divergences. Many traditional designers observed and learned from the best examples of modern American and European architecture, even if they remained aloof from the modern movement and its stylistic crusade. Like their more establishment counterparts, avant-garde architects openly considered some rather quotidian matters—ordinary social practices, budgetary constraints, even hustling for work—as well as high cultural ideals.

Active collaboration—the opposite of the myth of individual genius—defined much of the best American work of this period. Such teamwork had characterized the civic centers and campus plans of the City Beautiful era at the turn of the century. It continued into the 1920s when individuals and firms joined forces to produce large commercial, institutional, and residential building groups, ranging from Rockefeller Center to Cleveland's Terminal Tower and the Los Angeles Civic Center, from Radburn to Coral Gables and Westwood.[2] Governmental agencies played a major role during the next two decades, hiring teams and subsuming individual names into collective enterprises like the Public Works Administration (PWA), Tennessee Valley Authority (TVA), Civilian Conservation Corps (CCC), and Farm Security Administration (FSA). Landscape architect Garrett Eckbo contended that the best ideas of the era could only be developed in a "completely collaborative group."[3]

The intellectual context developed new dimensions, too, as advocacy and study groups coalesced, sometimes around a school or a journal, most often around the cause of local environmental problems. Architects wrote for T-Square and Twice a Year, for Fortune and the New Republic, as well as the established professional magazines. They became members of the Regional Plan Association in New York, the Architectural Research Group in Philadelphia, or Telesis in San Francisco. Museums helped organize special committees, resulting in exhibitions designed to situate problems and proposals for their own cities within a national and transnational vision of modern progress.[4] The matrix of such associations remained loosely structured and highly decentralized. Yet the intensity and frequency of collaboration produced new forms of architectural "discourse"—in a Rortyian rather than Foucaultian sense of the term, based upon ongoing wide-ranging conversations.[5]

Programmatically, too, communities represented the formal and ideological focus of many design projects, as architects tried to capture the forces that drew people together. They did this first under the commercial auspices of the 1920s, creating a multitude of settings for public gatherings and entertainment that embodied the vitality of urban life. Designers carefully analyzed how to entice various crowds: the cosmopolitan elite at nightclubs, bedazzled audiences at cinemas, cheering fans at baseball stadiums, eager consumers at neighborhood shopping centers. Public space radiated a pulsating modern vivacity.

Terminal Tower, Cleveland.

2. On the midwestern complexes see Edward W. Wolner, "The City-Within-a-City and Skyscraper Patronage in the 1920's," Journal of Architectural Education 42 (Winter 1989): 10-23. For a transnational consideration of the era, including New York, see Jean Clair, ed., The 1920s: Age of the Metropolis (Montreal: Montreal Museum of Fine Arts, 1991).

3. Garrett Eckbo, "Site Planning," The Architectural Forum 76 (May 1942): 267.

4. Among these exhibitions are The Museum of Modern Art's "Modern Architecture" show of 1932; that museum's numerous other exhibitions—including "Architecture in Government Housing" (1938), "Regional Building in America" (1941), "Wartime Housing" (1942), and "Look at Your Neighborhood" (1944); the Dallas Museum of Art's "Architecture of the Southwest" (1940); and the San Francisco Museum of Art's "Domestic Architecture of the San Francisco Bay Area" (1949).

5. On this sort of "discourse" see David Hollinger, "Historians and the Discourse of Intellectuals," in John Higham and Paul Conkin, eds., New Directions in American Intellectual History (Baltimore: Johns Hopkins University Press, 1979), reprinted in Hollinger, In the American Province: Studies in the History and Historiography of Ideas (Bloomington: University of Indiana Press, 1985); and Thomas Bender, "Recent Trends in the Historiography of Intellectuals in the United States," unpublished paper.

By the 1930s architects focused on less commercialized kinds of public buildings: governmental institutions, neighborhood community centers, and especially schools. Each type was conceived as a multipurpose facility, with general-purpose meeting rooms as well as specialized services, operating twenty-four hours a day. Under the economic and social duress of the Depression, public space sought to provide a "democratic" setting, reinforcing the bonds of public participation while providing equal access to a variety of services and pleasures. Later, during World War II, this ideal infused American rhetoric about designs for postwar cities and suburbs—designs that claimed to embody the values of freedom and well-being for which the war was being fought.[6]

The factors that might encourage or at least represent civic participation focused largely on site planning and placement. A central location embodied the building's centrifugal force over local residents. Ample playgrounds, green spaces, and transparent walls of glass emphasized a continuous flow of activity between the interior, the surrounding landscape, and the streets beyond. Simple diagrams documented the supposed process of inclusion.



Attention turned as well to the people who constitute a community. Allusions to national and regional identity elicited nostalgic symbolism, but the primary and more interesting scale was that of the residential enclave. Although many architects continued to produce refined private dwellings in modern or historical styles, the impact of the Depression reoriented the profession toward the larger scale of "housing" in groups. Whether for workers in the city or the middle class in the suburbs, such housing emphasized a collective identity. Describing a 1933 exhibition on housing sponsored by New York's AIA, Lewis Mumford proclaimed, "the community rather than the individual dwelling is taken as the unit of design."[7]

View and site plan of the Crow Island Elementary School, Winnetka, Illinois (1940), by Eliel and Eero Saarinen with Perkins, Wheeler, and Will.

Replication of dwelling units supposedly represented the cohesive quality of the social group. Yet Americans were never fully comfortable with the idea of uniformity, disliking its associations with visual monotony and social homogeneity. Intentional variety in massing, roof lines, or detailing seemed to counteract the threat of tedium and conformity. Soon after he began work on Broadacre City, Frank Lloyd Wright alluded to comparable dangers for the architect when he declared, "Standardization is a mere, but indispensable tool"; embraced without reserve, it risked becoming "a prison house for the creative soul and mind."[8]

A major consideration in housing design, as with public settings, involved the open space around dwellings. Not simply a residue or a viewpoint for architecture, nor a calibrated source of light and air, these spaces were purposefully designed for a variety of activities. Site plans articulated specific areas for children's play, adult recreation, socializing, or pleasant vistas. Ideally all these elements coalesced to make a pleasant environment for residents and neighbors alike. As one official publication described Arthur Brown, Jr.'s Holly Courts in San Francisco (1940), "the buildings avoid austerity by their informality, their close relation to the play spaces, and their warm friendly color and texture."[9]

Holly Courts, San Francisco.

Implicitly the model for most American housing projects of this era remained that of the village, in which individual autonomy and collective identity seemed to balance harmoniously. Indigenous historical precedents for community design were often invoked, extending from eighteenth-century New England towns to the planned suburbs of the 1920s. But the most important model for residential design was undoubtedly Clarence

6. On this concept see, for example, "The United States in a Changing World Builds for Defense," Pencil Points 22 (February 1941): 115-22; Dorothy Rosenman, "Housing Speeds Production," The Architectural Record 91 (April 1942): 42-46; Roland Wank, "Planned Communities: A Speculative Survey of Their Future," The Architectural Record 93 (February 1943): 44-48; and "New Buildings for 194x," The Architectural Forum 78 (May 1943): 69-152.

7. Lewis Mumford, "The Planned Community," The Architectural Forum 58 (April 1933): 253.

8. Frank Lloyd Wright, "In the Cause of Architecture: What 'Styles' Mean to the Architect," The Architectural Record 63 (February 1928): 145.

9. "Holly Courts," Special Bulletin of the San Francisco Housing Association 1 (1940): 2.

Arthur Perry's concept of the "neighborhood unit": a specific social organism and planning unit serving 750-1,000 families.[10] Facilities for these families included decent housing, abundant park space, and, above all, the representational and sociological force of the "social center" as a nucleus. In principle, the concept would extend to higher densities of population with an appropriate scale and complexity for each constituency: a neighborhood elementary school, a district high school, and a centralized cultural center serving an entire city.

10. Perry's neighborhood unit was developed in the 1910s under the auspices of the Russell Sage Foundation, then taken up by the Regional Plan Association as well as the architects of Forest Hills Gardens and Radburn. By the 1930s it had become familiar in Europe and a mainstay of all American discussion about residential design. See, in particular, Perry's Housing for the Machine Age (New York: Russell Sage Foundation, 1939).

If urbanism was certainly a central tenet of modern architecture on both sides of the Atlantic, it took on various meanings in each locale. American efforts most closely paralleled those of Ernest May in Frankfurt and Henri Sellier in Paris, where decentralization meant affordable land, a regional network, and picturesque possibilities in site planning. Here the private sector as well as local, state, and federal governments undertook large-scale housing, both for profit and with limited dividends as reform efforts. Yet the greatest difference was that American architects did not seek to reinvent the city; rather they sought to make it more equitable, orderly, and attractive in all its parts—from the bustling downtowns to the frayed edges.

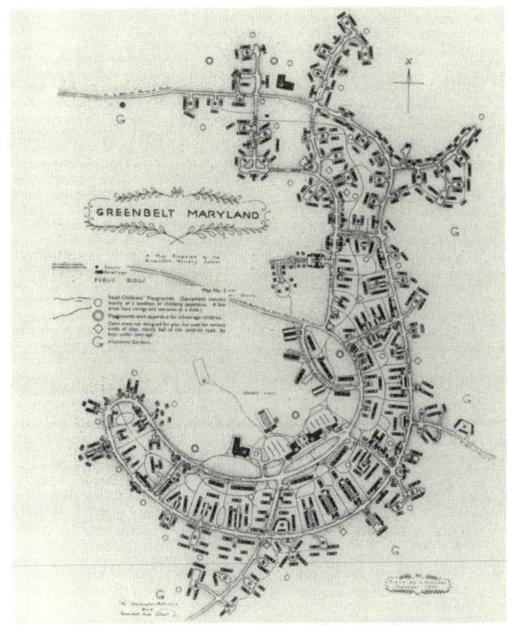


General plan of Greenbelt, Maryland, a Resettlement Administration town of 1935-37, highlighting recreational facilities for various ages in relation to housing.

In the United States, when architects spoke of an urban scale during these years, they usually meant a fragment, carefully inserted into the surrounding context: a distinctive skyscraper complex or residential neighborhood in the 1920s, a cultural center or housing project in the 1930s or 1940s. Those architects who designed whole entities usually restricted themselves to small communities: the FSA towns for migrant workers in California and the Southwest, the TVA town of Norris, or the several Greenbelt towns for white-collar suburban families. Unlike Le Corbusier or Ludwig Hilberseimer, even visionaries like Frank Lloyd Wright or Richard Neutra, both of whom explored large, truly metropolitan dimensions of design, based them on the emerging physical structure and varied social patterns of existing cities and suburbs.

Architectural historians have often disparaged American modernism for its parochialism and lack of rigor, charging that this country's architects failed to grasp the true social and formal meaning of the modern movement.[11] This template assumes a single, universal orthodoxy, obscuring the variety of national, regional, and individual interpretations that in fact existed—not only in the United States, but in eastern Europe, the USSR, the colonial world, and in western Europe, too. These alternatives should not be seen as deviations, but as vital evidence of modernism's real complexity. For it is only by accepting such disparities and differences that a cultural movement can thrive, and not simply dominate.

11. One characteristic example will suffice. "But the mass of American architecture continued in its old derivative courses," wrote J. M. Richards in 1940, "and even when isolated buildings of modern design began to appear they were regarded by most people simply as a new fashion—the latest from Europe" (An Introduction to Modern Architecture [1940; reprint ed., Harmondsworth: Penguin, 1970], p. 94).

12. See Jean-Louis Cohen and Hubert Damisch, eds., Américanisme et modernité (Paris: EHESS and Flammarion, 1993).

While modern architecture was not universal, it was transnational, with ideas and images moving quickly across great distances, yet always filtered through the particularities of local tastes and conditions. This applies not only to Americans' growing interest in the European modern movement, but to the equally strong allure of américanisme in Europe.[12] Beginning about the time of World War I, the United States seemed to embody the conditions of modernity in its supposed freedom from historical traditions and its extraordinary technological accomplishments: towering skyscrapers, landscaped parkways, the pulsating lights of Times Square, the mass production of cars and other commodities.

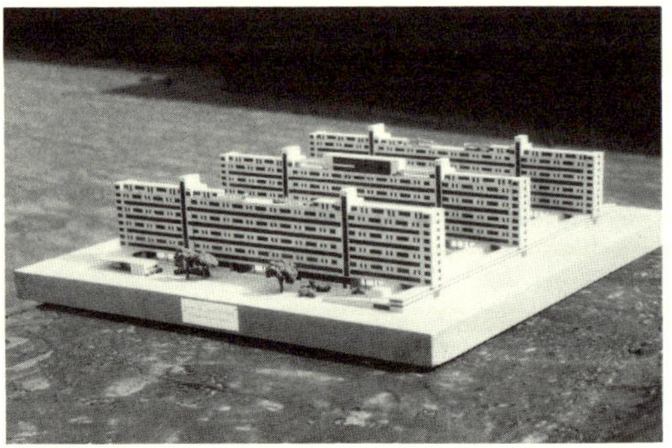

Original model of the Carl Mackley Houses in Philadelphia, by Oscar Stonorov and Albert Kastner, prepared for the 1932 "Modern Architecture" exhibition at The Museum of Modern Art. Stonorov Collection, American Heritage Center, University of Wyoming.

Mackley Houses, Philadelphia, completed in 1935.

This was reality, propelled by the visionary dreams of engineers and advertising designers as well as architects, yet always a physical and experiential actuality as opposed to an unfeasible individual fantasy. Such a perspective accepted the rather awkward and fragmented quality of modern urban life in the United States, the rapid pace of change in culture and fashion, the heterogeneous nature of public taste. It also recognized the limits of and resistance to these forces of modernity.

By the 1930s many commentators characterized American modernism as an effort to "humanize" the austerity of the European modern movement, especially as it had been represented in Philip Johnson and Henry-Russell Hitchcock's canonical "Modern Architecture" exhibition and catalogue of 1932.[13] Thirteen years later, in 1945, The Museum of Modern Art in New York produced a sequel and antidote, "Built in USA." Elizabeth Mock, the curator, described a design philosophy for architecture that sought to be "'humanly satisfactory' in the broadest sense."[14] She asked whether architecture shouldn't "tell a story," and noted the figurative quality of recent buildings, which downplayed pure abstraction in favor of vernacular forms and familiar elements.[15]



Here too, of course, the phenomenon was not unique or restricted to Americans. This sensibility affected European émigrés, most notably Walter Gropius and Richard Neutra, and it found parallels in the more organic, textured work of Le Corbusier or Alvar Aalto in the 1930s.[16] But "humanism" took on special significance in this country, where the political scientist Howard Woolston contended that a "humane" process of socialization had to emphasize individuality and idiosyncracy.[17]

Such goals encouraged a spirit of flexible compromise, rather than authoritative exactitude. Design and construction often involved a give-and-take process in which the architect had to take account of diverse constituencies. Oscar Stonorov's Carl Mackley Houses in Philadelphia, built in 1933 under the auspices of the PWA, exemplifies this evolution. The severe slabs of the original scheme represented an international manifesto on design, geared principally to the audience who admired the model at The Museum of Modern Art in 1932. Later modifications addressed another audience, that of the future residents, members of the Full Fashioned Hosiery Workers Union. Stonorov now broke up the relentless straight lines typical of German social housing, set in uniform rows called Zeilenbau. Instead he used irregular massing and gave precedence to landscape over built form. A clubhouse and swimming pool, augmented by underground garages, responded to American standards of pleasure and convenience.[18]

The familiar precepts of the modern movement were thus encoded in a system that downplayed spatial discipline and abstract metaphor. American architecture highlighted comfort, variety, and legibility. The shift in emphasis extended to many of the basic tropes of modernism.

For example, while Americans assumed that new technology would help define their urban visions, it remained a useful toolbox of materials and techniques rather than a visual metaphor of scientific rationality. Technological images were not abstract references to the machine's potential, but tangible statements about modern corporate strength and American engineering skills. This imagery reverberates in the majestic skyscrapers of the 1920s, symbols of the market's power. It propelled the abundance of

13. The official name was "Modern Architecture—An International Exhibition." See Terry Riley, The International Style: Exhibition 15 and The Museum of Modern Art (New York: Rizzoli, 1992).

14. Elizabeth Mock, ed., Built in USA: Since 1932 (New York: The Museum of Modern Art, 1945), p. 23.

15. Ibid.

16. See in particular William Jordy, "The Aftermath of the Bauhaus in America," in Donald Fleming and Bernard Bailyn, eds., The Intellectual Migration: Europe and America, 1930-1960 (Cambridge, Mass.: Belknap Press of Harvard University Press, 1969), pp. 485-543.

17. Howard Brown Woolston, Metropolis: A Study of Urban Communities (New York and London: D. Appleton-Century Company, Inc., 1938), pp. 92-115.

18. Stonorov worked in association with Alfred Kastner as his draftsman/designer and (since neither of these two were registered) with an established Philadelphia architect, W. Pope Barney. See Richard Pommer, "The Architecture of Urban Housing in the United States during the Early 1930s," Journal of the Society of Architectural Historians 37 (December 1983): 235-42; Eric J. Sandeen, "The Design of Public Housing in the New Deal: Oskar Stonorov and the Carl Mackley Houses," American Quarterly 37 (Winter 1987): 645-67; and Gail D. Radford, "Modern Community Housing: New Responses to the Shelter Problem in the 1920s and 1930s" (Ph.D. dissertation, Columbia University, 1989).

ingenious prefabricated housing experiments in the 1930s and 1940s. The poet Archibald MacLeish, who anonymously wrote a book on the housing problem for Fortune magazine, euphorically declared that such schemes would allow American dwellings to "be replaced at five-year intervals or at ten-year intervals as automobiles are now replaced."[19]

19. The Editors of Fortune [written by Archibald MacLeish], Housing America (New York: Harcourt, Brace and Company, 1932), p. 155.

Urban infrastructure has always played a pivotal role in the American celebration of modern technology. Highways embodied an entirely positive public dimension, facilitating access to the countryside and to other urban areas; they promised to unify every region and to liberate every individual. Raymond Hood in New York and William Christian Mullgardt in San Francisco drew up visions of colossal skyscraper bridges during the 1920s, stressing the metropolitan quality of urban extensions.

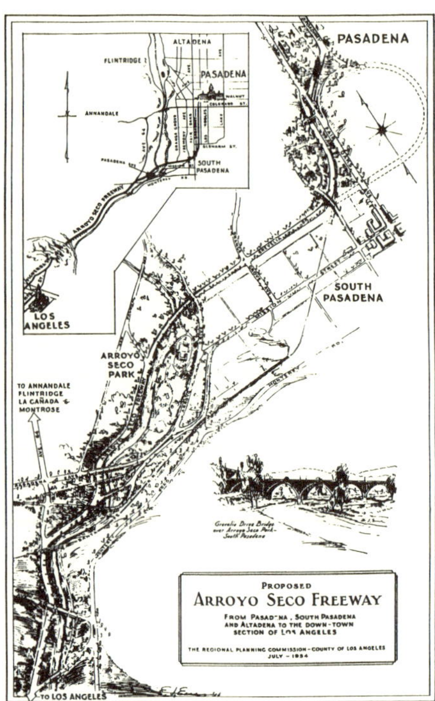


Proposed Arroyo Seco Freeway from Pasadena to downtown Los Angeles, 1934 (Los Angeles County Regional Planning Commission, Master Plan of Highways, 1941).



Every American city began to rethink its urban pattern in terms of automotive traffic, setting aside space for parking, widening major thoroughfares, cutting through new streets and parkways, hoping to systematize and expand the continual movement. Los Angeles made particular strides in its efforts to reconceptualize urban design and experience around new definitions of the intraurban highway. Beginning in the early 1930s, the State Division of Highways and the local city planning commission joined forces to design a new system of "super" highways: continuous, high-speed corridors traversing and unifying the city's sprawl. Richard J. Neutra praised the result as "crisscross communicating in all directions," such as he had envisioned in his earlier utopian proposal, "Rush City Reformed."[20]

20. Richard J. Neutra, "Homes and Housing," in George W. Robbins and L. Deming Tilton, eds., Los Angeles: A Preface to a Master Plan (Los Angeles: Pacific Southwest Academy, 1941), p. 191. Neutra began work on his remarkable "Rush City Reformed" in Berlin in the early 1920s; it continued to evolve in New York, Chicago, and Los Angeles throughout the 1930s. Drawings were first published in Wie baut Amerika? in 1926. Looking back in the 1950s, the architect insisted that the proposal did "not base itself on an abstract and theoretically rigid scheme," but rather on "a belief in the wholesome flexibility of city planning" (Willy Boesiger, ed., Richard Neutra 1923-1950: Buildings and Projects (New York: Praeger, 1964), p. 195, cited in Thomas S. Hines, Richard Neutra and the Search for Modern Architecture (New York: Oxford University Press, 1982), p. 61).

A similar fascination propels contemporary projects such as the Conceptual Master Plan for Grand Center in St. Louis, the Vision Plan for Des Moines, and the Central Artery Corridor in Boston. Street grids and traffic arteries have again become the basis for design intervention, highlighting the human contact that takes place alongside animated urban thoroughfares. Today's architects usually adopt a more ironic stance, cognizant of the destructive impact of automotive and other technologies. Yet they are responding in kind when they too focus on the conditions of everyday life.

Simultaneously, in these and other projects, the natural environment again figures prominently in American conceptions of modernism. In the 1930s nature represented a locus for recreation and other active, even commercialized, forms of public entertainment. Such an emphasis characterized much of the policy as well as the projects of the New Deal. Extensive undertakings in rural areas—shelter belts, dams, highways, electrification, and artificial lakes—modernized the landscape and radically changed the lives of Depression-era Americans, connecting them to distant neighbors and new leisure activities. Every town and metropolis added parks, playgrounds, and public beaches, both within the city and along its periphery.

Focus on the particularity of various ecologies produced vivid architectural modifications: solar heating panels in the Liberty Square housing project in Miami, louvers in the H. H. Berg Homes in the Virgin Islands, concrete balconies with brick parapets at Lakeview Terrace in Cleveland. Formerly useless terrains and oppressive climates now became the very basis of design. "The modern architect enjoys the challenge of these climactic difficulties . . . and rugged land," explained Elizabeth Mock.[21] Using as a cover illustration Burnham Hoyt's Red Rocks Amphitheater, carved into a majestic mountainside near Denver, the Magazine of Art christened the phenomenon "Geo-Architecture."[22]

21. Mock, Built in USA, pp. 21, 23.

22. "Geo-Architecture: America's Contribution to the Architecture of the Future," Magazine of Art 37 (October 1944): 16-21.

Aerial view of Harlem River Houses, New York, 1937. Architects: Archibald Manning Brown, Chief; Horace Ginsbern, Charles F. Fuller, John Louis Wilson, Frank J. Forster, Will Rice Amon, and Richard W. Buckley, Associates. From The Architectural Forum 68, no. 5 (May 1938).

In 1936 Frank Lloyd Wright's celebrated Fallingwater, straddling a waterfall in rural Pennsylvania, epitomized the new sensibility at its most lyrical and personal. At the same time, site planning was becoming the basis for many public housing designs, especially if the site was difficult and hilly, as at Chatham Village in Pittsburgh or at Channel Heights outside Los Angeles. Of course, such terrains had the value of being inexpensive, but they also modulated the regularity of building facades and tied buildings to their surroundings in an informal, seemingly organic manner.

Once again architects are using landscape design to make nature more accessible, without disrupting its actual complexity. The architectural team responsible for Playa Vista in southern California emphasized the sensitivity of the wetlands site, turning a problem into an asset. Their design protects the fragile ecology, winning the support of environmentalists and the enthusiasm of potential buyers.

This same spirit of modified cooperation extends to the surrounding built environment. Cities as far apart as Montreal and Los Angeles seek to accentuate the architectural and social character of their downtowns, rather than promoting radical transformation. Architects carefully study the morphology of street patterns, the distinctive styles of building, the delicate mix of existing uses and housing needs. The resulting plans avoid grand gestures in favor of an incremental approach that tries to reinforce what is already in place.



By and large new housing of the 1930s also deferred to its context, replicating the prevailing pattern of streets, orientation, and scale, even as it organized units and blocks into more commodious groups. Row houses generally followed the street wall, often modulating it with regular setbacks and generous openings onto landscaped courtyards; even buildings turned at an angle usually echoed that line at the punctuation of their corners.[23] The best of the PWA site plans, such as New York's Harlem River Houses and San Francisco's Holly Courts, built upon and even strengthened the plan of their environs. Commodious public spaces at junctures with major streets served as linkages, providing significant connections to the surrounding neighborhoods.

In all of these senses, American architects responded to the physical and social actualities of cities and urban life, seeking to improve what was there. Such visions were "more preventive than remedial. . . subject to a number of limitations."[24] Most intercessions accepted both the pattern and the diversity of American life, rather than trying to reformulate them into a single mold. Le Corbusier's urban visions were seldom emulated until after World War II, for they seemed conspicuously ideal types, demanding a complete transformation, rather than feasible interventions in the existing fabric and life of a city.

Here, too, exceptions prove the validity of a basic, yet never absolute, trend. The most notable and exacting applications of Le Corbusier's Radiant City scheme were those of William Lescaze, sometimes called the "Le Corbusier of America."[25] His PWA housing, known as Ten Eyck (later called the Williamsburg Houses) in Brooklyn (1935-38), rationalized the layout as a sequence of uniform geometric shapes. Interlocked along a vast superblock, the buildings stood purposefully aloof from the surrounding streets and houses; nature became a sea of blank greenery, a backdrop to the regularity of the built forms. But this remained the sole instance of Lescaze's several similar housing proposals to reach fruition. Comparing Williamsburg unfavorably with the Harlem River Houses, Talbot Hamlin charged that the pleasures of Lescaze's systematic order could appeal "only [to] the esoteric few and not the people."[26]

23. Joseph Hudnut insisted that "the walls of buildings should follow the lines of streets. I would restore the street as the basic element in my pattern. The street . . . is a theatre for a habit of life invented near the beginnings of social growth, and perhaps we should think at least twice before we decide that zigzags in a park are truly more appropriate to a habit of life thus embedded in history," in "The Art of Housing," The Architectural Record 93 (January 1943): 60-61.

24. Albert Mayer and Julian Whittlesey, "Horse Sense Planning I," The Architectural Forum 79 (November 1943): 62.

25. Lorraine Welling Lanmon, William Lescaze, Architect (Philadelphia: Art Alliance Press, and London: Associated University Presses, 1987), p. 93.

26. Talbot Hamlin, "New York Housing: Harlem River Homes and Williamsburg Houses," Pencil Points 19 (May 1938): 286-87.

Aerial view of Williamsburg Houses, Brooklyn, New York, 1937. Architects: Richmond H. Shreve; Matthew W. Del Gaudio, Gurney and Clavan, Arthur C. Holden, Holmgren, Volz and Gardstein, John W. Ingle, Jr., William Lescaze, Paul Trapani, and Harry Leslie Walker. From The Architectural Forum 67, no. 6 (December 1937). Site plan by Lescaze.



Adaptive restraint defined the majority of American housing projects built during this era. Despite the use of modern systems of construction, structures remained low-rise—at most four stories high, except in New York City. Though the European avant-garde acclaimed the spartan beauty of the Existenzminimum (a functional minimal standard for human dwelling), American architects considered it far too severe and institutional. They acknowledged the desire for informal massing and ornamented facades, preferably with historicist references, characteristic of popular taste. Even the smallest project featured copper roofs, ceramic tiles, sculptural friezes, wide corner windows, and handsome brickwork. Designers often incorporated motifs drawn from historic dwellings in the area: Georgian doorways in Boston, wrought iron railings in New Orleans, stucco and arcades in the Southwest. The heterogeneity of mass culture and local habits was thus assimilated into a modern aesthetic.[27]

American modernism during these years entailed more than contextual sensibilities and collaborative compromise. It also involved an explicit stance against any absolute order. Most architects rejected the idea that universally beautiful forms could provide appropriate solutions in every circumstance or setting. In overall terms, the American goals and methods exemplify what Barbara Herrnstein Smith, in Contingencies of Value, has recently called "the local figuring/working out, as well as we, heterogeneously, can, of what seems to work better rather than worse."[28]

The collaborative architecture-landscape project called "Imperfect Utopia: A Park for the New World," at the North Carolina Museum of Art epitomizes a new self-consciousness in this regard. The design team purposefully chose to accept the constraints of the museum's rather unkempt suburban surroundings. This entailed a return to certain natural conditions, and a willingness to let the space change with time and use. The park is based upon a sequence of phases, each one a combination of permanent and temporary structures, reforestation and common agricultural crops. The goals are provocatively simple, at once theoretical and practical: "To anticipate change and invite alteration. . . . To have no end in sight."[29]

The earlier aversion to orthodoxy was less an avant-garde transgression against rules than a concerted rejection of any standardized solution. The U.S. Public Housing Authority issued specific warnings against "architectural fantasies," calling instead for designs that "begin with a frank recognition of the economic and social problems. . . . [The architect] must really become a 'functionalist' in the full sense of the word."[30] Organizing an exhibition on such housing in 1936, The Museum of Modern Art sought to "interrupt abstract arguments," replacing them with "concrete examples of new construction which may be of vast significance in the future, not only of our architecture, but of our entire environment."[31] Given the broad range of such sentiments, what we might call a "pragmatic" attitude in architecture and urban design—so readily associated with American culture, so often dismissed as uncritical compromise of European ideals—merits closer attention.

This is not to say that architects studied pragmatists like William James or John Dewey, or even that they self-consciously tried to work out their own theory of design. But they did employ both a language and a method of resolving problems that echoed those of pragmatism. Writing in The Architectural Forum in 1943, Albert Mayer and Julian Whittlesey called it "Horse Sense Planning."[32] More eloquently, Garrett Eckbo insisted, "Good site planning is largely a matter of real common sense, aided by a completely open mind, a lack of esthetic prejudice and an uninhibited sense of form."[33]

27. In any case, the PWA was in business to provide jobs during its early years, so its Housing Division imposed few restrictions on cost or design before 1934.

28. Barbara Herrnstein Smith, Contingencies of Value: Alternative Perspectives for Critical Theory (Cambridge, Mass.: Harvard University Press, 1988), p. 179.

29. Laurie Hawkinson, Barbara Kruger, Nicholas Quennell, Henry Smith-Miller, "The Theory" in Imperfect Utopia (Raleigh: North Carolina Museum of Art, 1989).

30. National Housing Agency and Federal Public Housing Authority, Public Housing Design: A Review of Experience in Low-Rent Housing (Washington: Governmental Printing Office, 1946), p. 3.

31. The Museum of Modern Art Committee on Architecture and Industrial Art, "Architecture in Government Housing," bound typescript, 1936, unpag.

32. Mayer and Whittlesey, "Horse Sense Planning," The Architectural Forum (November 1943): 59-74; (December 1943): 77-82; (January 1944): 69-74.

33. Eckbo, "Site Planning," p. 265.

34. Giles Gunn, Thinking Across the American Grain: Ideology, Intellect, and the New Pragmatism (Chicago: University of Chicago Press, 1992), pp. 12-15.

35. William James, "The Teaching of Philosophy in Our Colleges," Nation 23 (1876): 178, quoted in ibid. p. 36.

36. Joseph Hudnut, "The Art in Housing," The Architectural Record 93 (January 1943): 59.

Giles Gunn speaks of the site of pragmatism as a ludic or liminal space, a border or transitional zone between two other conceptions of space.[34] To one side is the shared, familiar environment of everyday events and experiences; to the other, a place of solitude and completely independent thought. A pragmatist does not simply replicate existing reality, nor withdraw into a hermetic domain. In between the two extremes, the individual artist or thinker tries to look at the familiar environment in a different way, envisaging new possibilities. William James called pragmatism no more than "the habit of always seeking an alternative, of not taking the usual for granted, of making conventionalities fluid again, of imagining foreign states of mind."[35] One finds a similar outlook, together with the technique of continual adaptation, in much American urban design, especially during the interwar era.

Yuba City, California, 1940. Farm Security Administration town, with multifamily housing and trailers for migrant workers. Chief architect: Vernon DeMars.

I am not suggesting a philosophical movement or a coherent theoretical foundation, but a definite set of attitudes—even principles—about the process of architecture, its goals, and ultimately the forms that resulted. Yet one must ask: How clear, strong, and consistent did those principles prove to be? How much were they merely rationalizations of an easy simplification? Did the principles turn into a tedious formula in the hands of less thoughtful designers and bureaucrats? How often did the focus on the commonplace turn into a celebration of the banal, whether in national parks or in urban neighborhoods?

We cannot take even this gentle theorizing too literally, no more so than the European appeals to functionalism and universal benefits. Common sense alone, without the counterforce of imagination, cannot produce good design. The problems fall into two categories. At a formal level, the aesthetic of restraint was seldom inspiring. Much of the housing is rather tedious, barracks-like in its austerity or sentimental in its historicism, despite the sensuous relief of the excellent site planning. Only a few public buildings command a truly monumental presence.

37. "Farm Security Administration," The Architectural Forum 74 (January 1941): 3. The photographers included Dorothea Lange, Russell Lee, and Arthur Rothstein. These photographs, focusing on family life and the simple, clean quality of the living arrangements, represented an attempt to counter stiff opposition to the FSA camps from California agribusiness. By 1942, when Mexican laborers were imported because of shortages during the war, the FSA had ninety-five camps with housing for seventy-five thousand people. See Arthur Rothstein, "FSA Migratory Labor Camp," in Carl Fleischhauer and Beverly W. Brannan, eds., Documenting America, 1935-1943 (Berkeley: University of California Press, in association with Library of Congress, 1988), pp. 188-205.

Second, even when architects embraced difference and ambiguity, they did so without challenging the dominant order. Social diversity was acknowledged, in contrast to a normalized focus on "modern man." Joseph Hudnut declared emphatically, "No four-family apartment is suitable for every family: Irish or Polish, Yankee or Middle West, Catholic or Puritan, tradesman or industrial worker."[36] Yet only one governmental agency took the matter seriously enough to explore the particular needs and cultural habits of their clients. Despite severe budgetary restrictions and a fast-track schedule, architects with the FSA built temporary and permanent communities for farm laborers: primarily displaced midwestern farm families and later, after 1942, itinerant Mexicans. Adapting the most rigorous modern design to highly specific circumstances, they explored a variety of forms. At Yuba City, Woodville, and other settlements, there were special areas for men and women to gather at their respective tasks, pleasant day care centers and schools, community centers for self-government, and familial privacy even in the smallest cabins or mobile trailers. Using photographs as evidence, The Architectural Forum praised the "willingness to experiment," as well as the "quality and thoroughly American character" of the designs.[37]

A respect for difference usually translated into the separation of different groups. The decision to follow existing living arrangements often meant the replication of negative patterns, such as racial and class segregation, without considering alternatives. A professor at Cornell, writing in The Architectural Record, declared emphatically that postwar neighborhoods would likewise "be homogeneous in character. . . [following] the basic principle of democracy—respect for the wishes of the people . . . [and] natural social trends."[38] Most architects sought to create a life of comfortable well-being and familiarity, providing natural amenities and technological benefits. They eschewed the possibility that either architecture or social experiences could be transformative or challenging.

38. Thomas W. Mackesey in collaboration with Gilmore D. Clarke, "Planning the Postwar Community," The Architectural Record 93 (January 1943): 84.

All the same, important modern issues about public space, both formal and cultural, were being addressed, if not resolved, during this era. Three central goals can be stated. The first involved a search for equilibrium: professionally, that between designer, clients, and the public; and formally, between new building, open spaces, and existing surroundings.



Secondly, equilibrium did not necessarily mean conformity. A spirit of experimentation permeated the design process. Antonin Raymond, one of the first architects to build a war housing community, cited the government's "liberal far-sighted program" of "'small laboratories of housing with the architects as chief scientists.'"[39]

39. Antonin Raymond, "Working with U.S.H.A. Under the Lanham Act," Pencil Points 22 (November 1941): 694.

Thirdly, the designers recognized the centrality of experience—perceptual and cultural, personal and collective—as fundamental to architecture. At its best, the writing and the designs of this era sought to explore the nature of experience, rather than dictate a rigid set of beliefs. The aim was that of a conversation, not an indoctrination. Pamphlets and exhibition panels posed questions, asking "Would this be anything like your idea of a pleasant community?" or "Do you like where you work?"[40] Such questions remained open-ended, awaiting a multiplicity of responses.

40. For example, see Elizabeth Mock, "Tomorrow's Small House," Bulletin of The Museum of Modern Art 12 (Summer 1945): 19 (the article describes "The House in Its Neighborhood," a collaborative project of the Ladies' Home Journal and The Museum of Modern Art); the Telesis catalogue, Space for Living (San Francisco: San Francisco Museum of Art, n.d.), unpag.; and Louis I. Kahn and Oscar Stonorov, Why City Planning Is Your Responsibility (New York: Revere Copper and Brass Company, 1942).

If any event closed the door on this discussion it was the symposium called "What Is Happening to Modern Architecture?" held at The Museum of Modern Art in the fall of 1947.[41] Convened in response to Lewis Mumford's praise for the recent architecture of the California Bay Area, most discussants ridiculed this regional style as "neue Gemütlichkeit" or "just a pleasant forgiving of imperfection and an easy-goingness as to precision of thinking."[42] Such mockery implicitly dismissed all aspects of the flexible and responsive urban design which had prevailed during the previous two decades. There again resurfaced a denatured "essence" of modernism, a new manifestation of the International Style which had been canonized in the 1932 exhibition. It turned specifically, once again, to Le Corbusier, taking the Radiant City as a universal model for urban design.

41. Proceedings of the symposium were published under the title "What Is Happening to Modern Architecture?" Bulletin of The Museum of Modern Art 15 (September 1948): 1-21.

42. Alfred H. Barr, Jr. and Marcel Breuer, "What Is Happening to Modern Architecture?" pp. 8, 15.

This architectural vision of modernism soon found enthusiastic political and financial support. Postwar developers wanted dense and profitable urban centers to counter the move outward toward the suburbs. New mayors came to power pledging to rebuild their cities and win back a wealthy tax base. Coalitions of business and labor leaders sponsored a "pro-growth politics" to redevelop dilapidated downtown areas. Primary funding came from the Housing Acts of 1949 and 1954, which introduced urban

43. Only 20 percent of the housing in a proposed renewal area had to be classified as blighted to have the entire area razed.

renewal. Under these provisions the federal government agreed to pay two-thirds of the cost of tearing down "blighted" inner-city housing, replacing it with luxury apartments, office buildings, or government facilities.[43] From California to Connecticut, American cities realized the modernist vision of uniform "towers-in-the-park."

Proposed site plan of Gateway Plaza, Pittsburgh, 1950-53, the first American urban redevelopment project.

The essential design and social premise of postwar modernism aggravated the problems of the earlier design approach, while abandoning its assets. The automobile became a prime determinant of urban policy with the vast highway system funded by the federal government in 1954. New commercial developments were often surrounded by high-speed expressways, facilitating access from the suburbs. Monolithic throughways made access difficult for nearby pedestrians, while their rights-of-way demolished thousands of units of housing in low-income urban communities.

Increasingly, cities were now composed of immense enclaves of single-purpose, single-class buildings, mostly of a uniform style. These autonomous segments were purposefully cut off from each other and from the fabric of the earlier city, whether it was considered "historic" or simply "old." Vast redevelopment projects, inner-city public housing towers, suburban sprawl, shopping malls, and even theme parks sought to order every aspect of life in separate, rigidly zoned categories.



A justifiable reaction, or set of reactions, against the excesses of modernist bravado began to take shape almost immediately, and has gained increasing momentum during the last two decades. There are demands for more humanistic concerns, for history, for social diversity and practicality, for artistic experimentation—demands sometimes at odds with one another, but united in their critique of postwar modernist orthodoxy. A major theme of these criticisms has been the reassertion of urban space as a generator of shared public culture, whether by a large collectivity or a small parochial group. In all these ways architects are raising hopes and concerns that had defined the earlier phase of modernism, before the break at the end of World War II.

44. One book that does an excellent job of making this point about pluralism is Joan Ockman, with the collaboration of Edward Eigen, Architecture Culture, 1943-1968: A Documentary Anthology (New York: Columbia University Graduate School of Architecture, Planning, and Preservation; and Rizzoli, 1993).

There is, of course, no single direction in contemporary architecture, no more than there was in the past.[44] Dystopian efforts proclaim a new sort of abstraction and withdrawal, retreating into an autonomous realm of elegant drawings about chaos and violence, buttressed by erudite statements about the impossibility of understanding one another. In such a negative climate of opinion, one welcomes designers willing to act, to intervene, to confront difference, to combine poetic lyricism with technical prowess.

Their architecture, like its predecessors of fifty years ago, opens up new ways to see the city and react to it. This in turn can generate a public realm of experimentation and debate. It is not necessary to agree, only to acknowledge one another, including the public in its various constituencies. Once again, then, we can engage in a conversation: about continuity and change, public and private, architecture and environment, visions and limits, inventions and interventions.

CHAPMAN'S
VALENCIAS
OLD MISSION
TRADE MARK
BRAND
THIS FRUIT IS
SCIENTIFICALLY GROWN
AND RIPENED ON THE TREE
SUPERIOR QUALITY
AND UNIFORM GRADE
GROWN IN U.S.A.
REG. U.S. PAT. OFF.
GROWN & SHIPPED BY
PLACENTIA ORCHARD COMPANY
FULLERTON, CALIFORNIA
ORANGE COUNTY
OPERATED UNDER PERSONAL DIRECTION OF
CHARLES C. CHAPMAN

# Cannibal City: Los Angeles and the Destruction of Nature

*Mike Davis*



Architectural historians tend to write histories of trees, not forests. There are a dozen good books on the singular, egomanic objects we call "Los Angeles architecture," but only a few pitiful shards of theory—generally too abstract to be very useful—to explain the larger fabrics or deeper structures of our improbable megalopolis. In the absence of synoptic history, we take our bearings instead from simplistic but potent myths.

For example, accounts of Southern California are besotted with metaphysical generalizations about cars and water. The region's infamous sprawling geometry is universally attributed to the automobile (primus mobile) acting upon an oasis conjured from the desert with cheap, stolen water. In noir versions of the story, freeway and aqueduct are equally envisioned as the symbols of conspiracy and power struggle.

This familiar mythography (shades of Chinatown or The Crying of Lot 49) ignores the constitutive role of landscape in the emergence of Southern California. A picturesque conjugation of beach, desert, mountain, and citrus grove—emblazoned on millions of postcards and orange-crate labels—once defined Los Angeles in the imagination of the entire world. Nature, wild or domesticated, provided the essential "use-value" supports for the greatest continuous real-estate boom in history.

Yet Los Angeles's century of hyper-growth (1887-1989, R.I.P.), together with its aggressive municipal empires of water and power (and now waste), have despoiled much of the canonical landscape of Southern California and the Southwest. Since World War II, great glaciers of concrete and asphalt have scoured the valleys of the last traces of orchard and vineyard. This profligate destruction, together with the cumulative underproduction of new public space, has contributed, fully as much as the automobile, to our current crisis of urban form.

At every stage in this inexcusable history, however, Los Angeles has had its demon lovers and luminous prophets. Their forgotten visions still radiate in many of the small utopias exhibited as "Urban Revisions." If contemporary imagination is to have any real purchase on the future, it needs to recover this lost lineage of environmental design.

EDEN WITHOUT A GARDEN?

1. Olmsted Brothers and Bartholomew and Associates, Parks, Playgrounds and Beaches for the Los Angeles Region (Los Angeles: 1930), p. xiv.

In March 1930 the most distinguished citizens' committee in Los Angeles history submitted its final report to city and county authorities. A letter of transmittal, signed by Mary Pickford, John O'Melveny, J. B. Lippincott, Irving Hellman, and others, warned that "the situation revealed by the report is so disquieting as to make it highly expedient to impress upon the public the present crisis in the welfare of Los Angeles."[1]

Public beach at Venice on July 4th, filled to capacity. Photo by Stagg, from Parks, Playgrounds and Beaches for the Los Angeles Region, 1930.

With nearly one-quarter of the city's population out of work in this grim Depression year, it might be presumed that the report's urgency was focused on unemployment relief or soup kitchens for the hungry. In fact, the attention of the 162 prominent members of the Citizens' Committee on Parks, Playgrounds and Beaches was riveted on the "park and recreation crisis." This was less strange than it might otherwise seem.

As the report's authors, the renowned urban-design firm of Olmsted Brothers and Bartholomew and Associates, pointed out, accessible open space was the foundation of an economy capitalized on climate, sports, and outdoor leisure. But the region's scenic beauty was being eroded on all sides by rampant, unregulated private development. Depression or not, Los Angeles's future prosperity was directly threatened by the increasing discrepancy between tourists' expectations and their actual experiences.

2. Ibid., p. 23.

> **The widely-advertised attractions of climate and scenery bring thousands to the Los Angeles Region every year. They find the climate fully equal to expectations but the facilities by which the out-of-doors may be enjoyed often prove a surprise and disappointment. . . . The beaches, which are pictured in the magazines to attract eastern visitors, are suffering from the rapid encroachment of private use; the wild canyons are fast being subjected to subdivision and cheek-by-jowl cabin construction; the forests suffer annually from devastating fires; the roadsides are more and more disfigured by signboards, shacks, garages, filling stations, destruction of trees. . . .**[2]

3. Ibid., pp. xiii, 1-3.

The Olmsteds further observed that "the things that make [Los Angeles] most attractive are the very ones that are the first to suffer from changes and deteriorate through neglect." Although Los Angeles spent more than other cities to advertise its charms, it invested less to preserve or enhance them. The deficiency of parks was "positively reprehensible" and the region fell "far short . . . of the minimum recreation facilities of the average American city." Moreover, as the authors acknowledged, "all this has been realized for years."[3]

Indeed, Charles Fletcher Lummis, famed editor of Land of Sunshine/Out West, had thundered against Los Angeles's Victorian elites for "impoverishing the future" through their reckless alienation of original pueblo lands.

4. Charles Fletcher Lummis, Los Angeles and Her Makers (Los Angeles: Out West Magazine, 1909), pp. 244-45.

> **As late as 1856 the city owned eighty per cent of its area of some 17,000 acres. It gave this priceless heritage away—generally for nothing, and altogether for next to nothing—without even once getting an equivalent or a good bargain. . . . We would have the finest parks in the world, and the finest public buildings—and all endowed beyond the dreams of avarice. As it is, nothing was left the city but the Plaza and some riverbed when we began to take notice.**[4]

By the early 1900s, moreover, even this residual public domain was under threat, as the once arcadian landscape of the Los Angeles River was transformed into a sewer for the city's expanding industrial district. The Rev. Dana Bartlett, pioneer of the local settlement-house movement, battled the corporate "Octopus" of the Southern Pacific Railroad in an unsuccessful crusade to reclaim the riverbed as a nature preserve and playground for the children of the "congested areas" east of Downtown.[5]

5. Dana Bartlett, The Better City (Los Angeles: The Neuner Co. Press, 1907), pp. 33-35.

It was in this context that Charles Mulford Robinson, the famed apostle of the City Beautiful, included a comprehensive plan for parks, boulevards, and a civic acropolis on Bunker Hill in his 1907 report to the Los Angeles Municipal Art Commission. He cautioned that "the tourist metropolis of the country . . . simply cannot afford to stand still, or, rather, with your increasing population, to go from bad to worse in congestion, in city discomfort and ugliness." Robinson hinted that if Los Angeles wavered in its commitment to public space, other "more beautiful" cities would usurp its destiny (was he already thinking of Seattle?).[6]

6. Charles Mulford Robinson, The City Beautiful: Report to the Municipal Art Commission (Los Angeles: William J. Porter, 1909), p. 3.



By the time that the Olmsteds surveyed the same problem twenty years later, the equivalent of the population of Philadelphia (nearly two million people) had moved to the Los Angeles region. The 1930 report was a scathing critique of the twenties boom which, after its collapse in the oil scandals of 1926-28, left 175 square miles of vacant, unsold lots on the city's fringe, but only a few hundred acres of new park land.[7] As the population soared, per capita recreation space had drastically decreased. By 1928, for example, barely a half inch of publicly-owned beach frontage was left for each citizen of Los Angeles County.[8]

7. Nearly one-half million vacant lots imposed huge social costs on Depression-era Los Angeles. The Olmsteds estimated that the carrying charges alone cost $100 million per year. For a more extended discussion, see Constantine Panunzio, "Growth and Character of the Population," pp. 38-39, and Clifford Zierer, "The Land Use Pattern," pp. 56-59, in George W. Robbins and L. Deming Tilton, eds., Los Angeles: Preface to a Masterplan (Los Angeles: The Pacific Southwest Academy, 1941).

8. Testimony of Frederick Law Olmsted, Jr. to Citizens' Committee, Los Angeles Times, 22 February 1928.

With considerable acuity the Olmsteds (with Harland Bartholomew) analyzed why public investment in open space had lagged so far behind the growth of population and regional income. In the first place, new tax revenues were swallowed up by the high municipal infrastructure costs of low-density, often scattered-site, subdivision. Powerful homeowners' associations, meanwhile, opposed every attempt to pass specific assessments for parks and recreation. A selfish, even fanatical presentism ruled Southern California. As the Olmsteds paraphrased the dominant attitude:

> **The benefit of parks bought now will accrue largely in future years and even to future generations. We can get along without them a while longer, anyhow. And if land at those prices is a good purchase, we would rather use our money to get lots on speculation for personal profit than give it up in taxes for our share of a park system.**[9]

9. Olmsted Brothers and Barthomolew, Parks, Playgrounds and Beaches, p. 5.

Speculation—"excessive and fictitious prices for raw land"—was the crux of the open-space crisis. The "high capitalization of future rental values" in even the most marginal or hazardous terrain made a comprehensive program of park-building prohibitively expensive.[10] Ironically, the whole inflationary process was subsidized by local government. The Olmsteds were especially critical of the costly public outlays (roads, sewers, fire protection, flood control, etc.) that encouraged promoters to subdivide scenic canyons, streambeds, and foothills.

10. Ibid., p. 11.

**It costs so much in the long run to adapt rough mountain lands satisfactorily to ordinary intensive private uses that their real net value as raw material for such use is generally far less than their value for watershed protection and for public recreation. Unfortunately in the local speculative land market this fact is often ignored and subdivision sales are made which commit the community to extravagantly wasteful private and public expenditures for converting a good thing of one kind into a poor thing of another kind.**[11]

11. Ibid., p. 10.

The Gordian knot of land speculation, however, could be cut with a single blade: hazard zoning. Since the "burden of wrong development does not fall on the purchaser alone, and scarcely ever on the vendor, but most heavily on the community at large," the municipality could justifiably invoke its powers to exclude speculative development from floodplains and hillsides (as well as, by implication, from earthquake fault zones and chronic wildfire corridors).[12]

12. Ibid., pp. 14-16.

Together with radically enlarged public ownership of ocean frontage, the redemption of Los Angeles's riparian landscapes was the key to the Olmsteds' elegant design for a unified system of public beaches, parks, playgrounds, and mountain reserves. They demonstrated how greenbelts (or "pleasureway parks" in their terminology) could simultaneously solve problems of flood control, recreation, and traffic congestion. Using hazard zoning to force land values downward and "stop the ill-directed spread of the population," they proposed to transform the major flood channels and associated wetlands into a 440-mile network of multi-purpose parkways.[13]

13. Ibid.



The report stressed the importance of embedding regional highways in attractive, tree-lined park corridors screened from adjacent industrial and residential development. "Parkways should be greatly elongated real parks . . . several thousand feet in width," parallel to broad natural flood channels and offering a variety of recreational experiences. Parkways thus conceived would reinforce the role of hydrography in dividing up the monotonous coastal plain into attractive, well-defined local landscapes. Finally, this comprehensive plan would redistribute park and open-space resources to the advantage of the neglected working-class districts south and east of the center city.[14]

14. "Those of lower incomes generally live in small-lot, single-family home districts, and have more children and less leisure time in which to go to distant parks and recreational areas. These families comprise 65 percent of the population, and they should be given first consideration. . . ." Ibid., p. 22.

## DEATH OF THE LOS ANGELES RIVER

The 1930 report is a window into a lost future. A heroic culmination of the City Beautiful era in American urban design, it was also the final fruit of the Olmsteds' intense, decade-long involvement in California open-space planning. (The firm also prepared master plans for Los Angeles County highways, the state park system, and the preservation of watershed in the East Bay hills, as well as designing the acclaimed suburb of Palos Verdes Estates.)[15]

15. In its organization of land use, Palos Verdes Estates (1923) was intended as a model for the rest of Southern California. It dedicated 25 percent of its surface area to recreational and natural landscapes, as compared to the mere two percent in most contemporary Los Angeles neighborhoods.

The Olmsteds were quiet, conservative reformers whose personal utopia was park-rich Minneapolis, not Soviet Russia. Yet if their proposals had been implemented, the results would nonetheless have been revolutionary. The existing hierarchy of public and private space in Los Angeles would have been fundamentally overturned. A dramatically enlarged commons, not the private subdivision, would have become the dominant element in the Southern California landscape. Preserved natural ecosystems (the Olmsteds were passionate proponents of native flora) would have imposed clear boundaries on urbanization. The speculative real-estate market would have been counterbalanced by a vigorous social democracy of beaches and playgrounds.

Needless to say, such extravagant conceptions of public space alarmed guardians of Los Angeles's reputation as the capital of anti-radicalism and the open shop. The Los Angeles Times, in particular, disdained proposals to municipalize almost 100,000 acres of private land and to triple the amount of public beach frontage. The Chamber of Commerce (which originally sponsored the report), as well as leading members of the Citizens' Committee, also took their distance from the Olmsteds' bolder planks.

But even if an encompassing civic consensus had existed, neither the city nor the county had the wherewithal, in the bleak early days of the Depression, to undertake a massive park acquisition program. Only Washington had the requisite resources. Ironically, when New Deal agencies finally came to the fiscal rescue of Los Angeles, local government used federal capital to destroy the riparian landscapes that were so central to the Olmsteds' vision. The death of the Los Angeles River, in particular, was a dismal portent of the future role of the state in reshaping and degrading the regional environment.



The Army Corps of Engineers has often reminded its critics that Los Angeles, sited in an alluvial plain at the foot of a rugged, unstable mountain range, has the worst flood problem of any major Northern Hemisphere city. But, as the Olmsteds emphasized in their Report, flood control could be accomplished by different kinds of public works. Their preference, of course, was to strictly limit private encroachment within the fifty-year-flood corridor. They wanted to preserve broad natural channels for multiple use as spreading grounds, nature preserves, recreational parks, and scenic parkways. An opposite option was to deepen and "armor" a narrow width of the channel in order to maximize potential commercial development within the floodplain. Although beneficial to large landowners, this strategy effectively entombed the natural river in a concrete straitjacket that blighted, rather than enhanced, its surroundings.[16] Unprecedented losses of life in the great floods of 1934 and 1938 made flood control an urgent priority. Everyone agreed that the urban-riparian interface had to be reconstructed to take account of the huge population explosion of the 1920s. But the Olmsteds' greenbelt alternative, with its explicit assertion of the sovereignty of the communal interest, was never seriously debated. Instead Los Angeles temporarily solved its flood problem, and assuaged powerful floodplain landowners (principally, the railroads), by killing its river.

16. The Olmsteds criticized the false economy of investing in a linear, strictly monopurpose flood-control system. "Where flood control alone is dealt with in computing the size of anticipated floods, there is a natural tendency to curtail the area of land to be acquired. . . . Such a policy defeats itself. It compels large outlays for costly construction on narrow rights of way which would not be necessary on wider rights of way." Ibid., p. 16.

In the same period the city also came perilously close to killing Santa Monica Bay. Since the citrus revolution of the 1880s, most Southern California cities had recycled their sewerage to farmers as valuable irrigation water and fertilizer. Los Angeles, by contrast, in 1894 began discharging its raw sewerage into the ocean through a municipal outfall at Hyperion Beach. A primitive screening process was introduced in the early 1920s after a storm of protest against the unspeakable pollution of nearby beaches. But sewerage treatment was unable to keep up with population growth, and, with the huge wartime immigrations, the system broke down entirely. In 1940 the state declared "a gross public health hazard for swimmers and picnickers" and eventually closed twelve miles of beaches.

17. Clarence Dykstra, "The Future of Los Angeles," pp. 5-6; George Hjelte, "Facilities for Recreation," pp. 220, 224; and Ralph Cornell, "The Importance of Appearance," in Robbins and Tilton, Los Angeles: Preface to a Masterplan.

Indeed, a decade after the Olmsteds' report, the "parks and recreation crisis" had become a comprehensive environmental crisis. (The first smog attack in 1943 caused almost as much consternation as Pearl Harbor.) In a historic symposium of the region's leading architects and planners, Clarence Dykstra warned that "the disintegration has begun . . . we have come to the time when old values are being destroyed faster than new ones are being created."[17]

## THE BATTLE OF THE VALLEY

This same 1941 symposium also included a remarkable contribution from Richard Neutra, the architectural representative on the new State Planning Board. "Was this metropolis a paradise," he asked, "or did there exist here a type of blight which fitted none of its classical descriptions?"



18. Richard Neutra, "Homes and Housing," ibid., pp. 189, 194-95.

In answering his own polemical question, Neutra denounced the reckless development of the hillsides, the dispiriting uniformity of most subdivisions, and, above all, the corrosive impact of extreme privatism. "Beautiful and broad views from individual dwellings," he argued, "can hardly atone for the lack of a comprehensive and convincingly landscaped neighborhood design and for lost communal opportunities." Large-scale government housing projects, rather than private developments, offered the best opportunity for integrated community design.[18]

Baldwin Hills Village Green. Photo by Julius Shulman.

Neutra's derisory attitude toward private homes in the hills rings odd today since it is precisely for such projects that he and other first-generation Los Angeles modernists are most popularly remembered. Yet, between the beginning of Lendlease and VJ Day, domestic architecture scarcely made an appearance in (L.A.-based) Arts and Architecture magazine. The war mobilized an unprecedented coalition of architects, planners, and New Deal reformers committed to a common vision of regional planning, slum clearance, social housing, and environmental conservation.

Thus, the famous "case-study homes" of the late 1940s were preceded by the even more important (but less well remembered) "case-study communities" of the early 1940s. In a score of federal war-housing projects, as well as in several exemplary private developments, Southern California's leading modernists attempted to crystallize a new urbanism based on bungalows and garden apartments grouped around dramatic common spaces. If Neutra's Channel Heights project is justifiably remembered as the finest single design of the period, then Baldwin Hills Village has certainly been the most successful as an enduring community.

Completed between 1939 and 1942 after a long struggle to obtain federal financing, the Village was an evolutionary advance on the Radburn garden city ideal. Six-hundred-and-thirty row houses and apartments were arranged in a continuous "S" plan around garden courts opening onto three large greens connected by tree-shaded malls. Uniquely for Los Angeles, automobile traffic was confined to the project's periphery, while the center was an oasis of pedestrian serenity. At every level of organization, the Village's design sustained a superb dialectic between private and communal space. After more than half a century, it remains one of Los Angeles's most vibrant, as well as integrated and ungated, neighborhoods.

In its original context, moreover, the Village was envisioned as a prototype "democratic community" for the postwar era, an alternative urban building-block to the automobile-dominated private subdivision. The most influential contemporary advocate of this new urbanism was Robert Alexander, a member of the architectural team that designed the Village and a future collaborator of Richard Neutra. Appointed to the Los Angeles City Planning Commission at the end of the war, Alexander boldly attempted to use agricultural greenbelts—much in the spirit of the Olmsteds' plan—to deflect postwar suburbanization into a new design path, based on the commons-centered, pedestrian-scaled examples of Baldwin Hills Village and Channel Heights.

Alexander clearly foresaw that the voracious postwar demand for housing, if left to the speculative marketplace, would simply repeat the 1920s boom on a larger and more catastrophic scale. The remaining agricultural areas of coastal Southern California, especially the San Fernando and San Gabriel Valleys, would be transformed overnight into irrational mosaics of monotonous tract homes and vacant lots. The orchards and truck farms that formed the historical matrix for suburban garden cities would be uprooted and new development would coalesce into a single amoebic mass.



Alexander and Planning Director Charles Bennett recognized that the San Fernando Valley, under tremendous pressure from real estate speculators, would be the first and most decisive battlefield. Accordingly, they proposed a zoning strategy that opened the Valley to hundreds of thousands of house-hungry ex-GIs and aircraft workers, but concentrated new development (at medium-density levels) around sixteen already existing suburban nodes permanently separated by eighty-three square miles of citrus and farm greenbelts.

**The planning department staff prepared a master plan for each of the sixteen town centers. . . . Each plan formed a small, compact, self-sustaining community, surrounded and separated from other country towns by agricultural greenbelts. To provide a transition, each urban area was separated from the agricultural zones by a suburban zone in which truck gardening, chickens, rabbits, bees and incidental domestic animals were permitted.**[19]

19. Robert E. Alexander, "The San Fernando Valley," unpublished manuscript, 1990, p. 80; cf. Charles Bennett, "Planning for the San Fernando Valley," an address intended for the war-cancelled convention of the Urban Land Institute, November 1944 (in John Randolph Haynes archives, UCLA Special Collections); and Los Angeles City Planning Commission, Accomplishments—1944, pp. 5-12.

Implicitly, Alexander theorized a virtuous circle where open-space zoning simultaneously preserved landscape integrity, promoted clustered housing, reduced the costs of school and utility construction, and ensured sufficient population densities to sustain rapid transit systems (the existing "red car" system as well as a proposed Downtown-to-Valley monorail).

The proposed greenbelt zoning for the Valley was actually passed into law by the city council at the end of the war, but, as Alexander vividly details in an unpublished memoir, it lacked the broad political support to survive the relentless counterattack of developers.

**With a vast pent-up demand and a sure market, it would have been quite profitable for developers to buy undeveloped lots in any of the existing town centers. They could even acquire adjacent unsubdivided land, applying for changes in zone from R-A suburban to R-1, but nothing would satisfy their greed. Instead, they obtained options for practically nothing to buy the cheapest land zoned for agricultural use and applied for changes in zone to R-1. Sometimes accompanied by a veteran wearing an American Legion hat, they found willing cooperators in the planning director and four of the commissioners who needed no urging to respond to the hysteria of the housing shortage. They gained untold riches as they converted "greenbelts" to densely packed urban town lots.**[20]

20. Alexander, p. 82.

Top, aerial view of the San Fernando Valley, 1949.
Bottom, aerial view of the San Fernando Valley, 1963.
Spence Collection, Air Photo Archives, UCLA Department of Geography.

As politically naive planners were soon shocked to discover, other layers of government were active accomplices in the destruction of Los Angeles's agricultural periphery. The county tax assessor, for example, increased the pressure on farmers to sell out by reassessing their land as prime residential real estate—"a self-fulfilling prophecy which spread like wildfire." The Federal Housing Administration, already notorious for its tolerance of racially-restrictive covenants and white-only suburbs, refused to lift a finger to preserve natural landscapes or to discourage leap-frog development.

As a result, Alexander's virtuous circle was inexorably transformed into the vicious circle that he had warned against: total loss of agricultural landscape, an excessive number of vacant lots, expensive utility and school provision, a dramatic imbalance of homes and jobs, minimal community cohesion, and a low-density population pattern transportable only by private cars. By the early 1960s, instead of a "balanced self-sufficient constellation of communities" bordered by greenbelts, the Valley had become a paved-over "undifferentiated slurb" of nearly one million people.



## ECKBO VERSUS THE URBAN DESERT

In 1958 sociologist William Whyte—author of The Organization Man—had a disturbing vision as he was leaving Los Angeles. "Flying from Los Angeles to San Bernardino—an unnerving lesson in man's infinite capacity to mess up his environment—the traveler can see a legion of bulldozers gnawing into the last remaining tract of green between the two cities, and from San Bernardino another legion of bulldozers gnawing westward." When he reached New York he wrote a famous article for Fortune magazine, describing the insidious new growth-form he called "urban sprawl."[21]

21. William Whyte, "Urban Sprawl," Fortune 57 (January 1958): 102-09.

After the debacle in the San Fernando Valley, there was little political or bureaucratic opposition to the inevitable destruction of the rest of Southern California's picture-postcard landscapes. Although Los Angeles County paid homage in its 1941 Master Plan to the "major importance" of protecting choice agricultural land from subdivision, its actual land-use policies encouraged sprawl. In a 1957 report on the eastern San Gabriel Valley, for example, the Regional [county] Planning Commission affirmed that all the remaining orchards in what had once been the world's largest citrus forest would soon be subdivided. The County's only concern was that "this transition to urban uses should be encouraged to take place in an orderly manner" that minimized the "dead period" between land clearance and home construction.[22]

22. Los Angeles County, Regional Planning Commission, Master Plan of Land Use, 1941; East San Gabriel Valley, 1957.

In the 1950s, "an orderly manner" meant the uprooting of one thousand citrus trees each day. Between 1939 and 1970, agricultural acreage in Los Angeles County south of the San Gabriel Mountains fell from 300,000 to less than 10,000 acres. Hillside landscapes fared little better. Within the city limits of Los Angeles alone, more than 60,000 house sites were carved out of the foothills in the 1950s and early 1960s.[23]

23. Mark Northcross, "Los Angeles County: Biting the Land that Feeds Us," California Tomorrow: 36; and Richard Jahns, "Seventeen Years of Response by the City of Los Angeles to Geologic Hazards," Geologic Hazards and Public Problems: Conference Proceedings (Santa Rosa, Calif.: Office of Emergency Preparedness, Region Seven, 1970), p. 266.

While park-building again lagged far behind population growth, the automobile devoured exorbitant quantities of prime land. By 1970 more than one third of the surface area of the Los Angeles region was dedicated to car-related uses (freeways, streets, parking lots, and driveways). What generations of tourists and migrants had once admired as a real-life Garden of Eden was now buried under one hundred billion tons of concrete and asphalt.[24]

24. Donald Coates, ed., Environmental Geomorphology and Landscape Conservation, vol. 2, Urban Areas (Stroudsburg, Penn.: Dowden, Hutchinson & Ross, 1974), p. 273.

Southern California sprawl became a national scandal. Again thanks to the crusading efforts of Whyte, federal responsibility for the "exploding metropolis" was subjected to unprecedented debate and media scrutiny. Despite fierce opposition from the National Association of Home Builders, the Kennedy administration officially acknowledged the social costs of sprawl and introduced legislation in 1961 to support the conservation of urban open space.

Back in California, the Legislature was prodded by the Sierra Club and California Tomorrow into authorizing a major study of the state's "open space crisis." The consultants were the eminent San Francisco firm of Eckbo, Dean, Austin and Williams, which dominated environmental planning in California during the 1960s and 1970s in the same way that the Olmsteds and Bartholomew had hegemonized park design in the 1920s. Although Edward A. Williams wrote the final report for the State Office of Planning in 1965, the overarching influence of Garrett Eckbo in this and subsequent studies was obvious, and a few words need to be said about his background.



Eckbo is justly regarded as a pioneer of modernism in American landscape architecture. "A green Californian from the frontier," he arrived at Harvard in the late 1930s just as Walter Gropius was starting a mini-revolution. But the Bauhaus has been only one influence in the evolution of a complex personal philosophy. In equal measures he has also been a regionalist, ecologist, and radical democrat who has conspired to turn the aristocratic traditions of landscape design upside down. Since his early days with the Farm Security Administration designing yards and gardens for farmworker housing, Eckbo has been preoccupied with "the contradiction between social relations and individual land use."[25]

25. Garrett Eckbo, Landscape for Living (New York: Architectural Record with Duell, Sloan, and Pearce, 1949).

Thus, in his postwar manifesto for the new environmental design, Landscape for Living (1949), Eckbo decried the "sordid chaos" of "general commercial speculation" and argued that it was "no more than democratic Americanism to say that such forces can be analyzed, exposed and placed under proper public control." Rejecting the reservation of the greenest landscapes for the rich, he evoked the "truly democratic organization of our general community tree patterns" which would replace "the sterile formality of authority" with the "tremendous tree symphony of the future." Indeed, as authentic democracy began to achieve "cultural expression in the landscape . . . the present scale of landscape values will tend to reverse itself."

> **Instead of moving from the ugly city toward the peak of wilderness beauty, it will be possible to move from the wilderness through constantly more magnificent and orderly rural refinements of the face of the earth, to urban communities composed of structures, paving, grass, shrubs, and trees, which are rich, sparkling, crystalline nuclei in the web of spatial relations that surrounds the earth—peak expressions of the reintegration of man and nature.[26]**

26. Ibid., pp. 45, 111-12.

The Urban Metropolitan Open Space Study submitted to Governor Pat Brown in 1965 was resonant with values and motifs from Landscape for Living. Transposed from their original New Deal context, they sounded as radical as any of the contemporary speeches in Berkeley's Sproul Plaza.

> **The traditional view toward private ownership of property that permits the temporary owner a proprietary interest has been outmoded by new knowledge of man's relationship to nature and to the community. This knowledge demands a new attitude toward ownership of land, substituting the concept of trusteeship for exploitation.[27]**

27. Edward A. Williams (Eckbo, Dean, Austin and Williams), Open Space, the Choices Before California: The Urban Metropolitan Open Space Study (San Francisco: Diablo Press, 1969), p. 21. See also Eckbo, Dean, Austin and Williams, State Open Space and Resource Conservation Program for California, California Legislature Joint Committee on Open Space Lands (Sacramento: 1972).

28. Ibid., pp. 22-23.

The study warned that all of California's remaining Mediterranean valleys and foothills, including the Santa Barbara-Ventura coast as well as the Sonoma and Napa county vineyards, were threatened with the same fate as Los Angeles's citrus belt. It criticized county governments for their "weak, timid and unimaginative" use of zoning powers, and denounced a tax system that rewarded land speculators and punished farmers. It also pointed out the profound causal relationship between landscape-destroying sprawl at the urban edge and neighborhood decay at the center.[28]

29. Ibid., pp. 15, 24.

"One of the most significant findings" of the study, moreover, was that "a clearcut crisis situation exists in the Southern California urban-metropolitan area." Postwar suburbanization had entirely outpaced the production or conservation of public space. At minimum, Los Angeles County was facing a 100,000-acre shortfall of regional parks. At the local level the recreation crisis was frequently much worse. Indeed, the open-space situation throughout the Los Angeles Basin—"1,500 square miles of low grade, monotonous suburban construction"—was so hopeless that the study focused instead on stopping sprawl at its outer edges.[29]



30. Ibid., p. 41.

In 1965 significant farm and foothill belts still defended Ventura-Oxnard, San Bernardino, Riverside, and San Diego from engulfment by greater Los Angeles. Although local environmentalists had targeted the Santa Monica Mountains as the most important of these areas, the study emphasized instead the San Jose and Chino Hills which separated the San Gabriel Valley from the suburbanizing west end of San Bernardino County, and the Pomona Valley from northeast Orange County. As "the center of the greatest population pressure within the region . . . they should become the most highly prized and zealously protected open-space resource."[30]

31. Ibid., p. 42.

The second regional priority was "from Conejo to Hidden Hills, between Los Angeles and Ventura, an area of beautiful rolling hills and valleys, peculiarly vulnerable to destruction by careless and indifferent development, yet peculiarly pregnant with possibilities for rich and imaginative design." Other crucial battlegrounds were the undeveloped parts of the Palos Verdes Peninsula, the Oxnard Plain, the Elsinore-Temecula corridor in southwest Riverside County, and the coastal hills and valleys between San Diego and Vista.[31]

32. Ibid., p. 45.

The study also briefly, but prophetically, surveyed the dismal results of urban overspill in the Mojave and Colorado River deserts. "The entire desert seems to be subdivided and covered with a gridiron of graded streets; such development destroys the deserts as landscape and as open space, replacing them with nothing but the empty wasteland of ex-urbanism." Moreover, the elaboration of community designs suitable to the desert appeared to be simply "beyond the capability of [existing] planning processes."[32]

THE SCANDAL OF COUNTY PLANNING

33. "Parklands in the Urban Desert," (originally published in Cry California, 1966), reprinted in John Hart, ed., The New Book of California Tomorrow: Reflections and Projections from the Golden State (Los Altos, Calif.: W. Kaufmann, 1984), pp. 150-53.

The theses of the study (reissued in 1969 as Open Space: The Choices Before California) were amplified in subsequent articles and reports by Eckbo and his partners. In 1966, for example, Eckbo was asked by Cry California magazine (the publication of California Tomorrow) to comment on the issue that the study had deliberately side-stepped: i.e., how to expand open space resources within the congested Los Angeles Basin. After observing that "no comparable urban region in the nation even remotely approaches the basin's inadequacy [in parkland]," Eckbo made a characteristically radical proposal for "greening the urban desert." He suggested that the county could redevelop suburbs into parks by relocating 10 percent of the population ("from various income groups") into new higher-density housing. Estimated cost: seven to nine billion dollars.[33]

34. Ventura-Los Angeles Mountain and Coastal Study Commission, Final Report to the Legislature (March 6, 1972), pp. 6.1, 12B15.1.



Six years later, in 1972, Eckbo, Dean, Austin and Williams produced another major open-space survey; this time an exhaustive study of the Santa Monica Mountain coastline for the state legislature. Saluting the Olmsteds, they reminded readers that the problem of sprawl had first been recognized in the 1930 report, which had also recommended massive public land-banking in the Santa Monicas. Yet, two generations later, 95 percent of "the last major open space resource remaining in the greater Los Angeles metropolitan region" was still in private hands, mostly in large, speculative parcels.[34]

35. Ibid., p. 11.2.

As in the 1965 study, Eckbo and partners insisted on the need to shift land-use analysis from traditional market-centered criteria toward new social and ecological values. In their view, there was a fundamental epistemological conflict between the conception of the mountains as an abstract land unit and as a complex natural environment. They urged the legislature to "treat the area as a total system of air, land and water relationships, not simply as real estate to be developed."[35]

36. Ibid., pp. 9.2, 12B3.1

Given the mountains' incalculable recreational and landscape value, they expressed incredulity at a county general plan projection of a buildout population of 405,000 in the environmentally sensitive Malibu area. They pointed out that Malibu, apart from major problems with earthquakes, flooding, and landslides, also had a fire history "unique in intensity, devastating in effect, and heightened during Santa Ana wind conditions." (The October 1993 firestorm was the fifth holocaust since 1930.) Again echoing the Olmsteds, Eckbo and partners decried the ease with which developers in high-risk areas shifted the costs of fire and flood protection onto the taxpayers at large. They proposed a stringent permit system to keep new construction at a minimum while the legislature evaluated options for expanding public ownership in the Santa Monicas.[36]

The Eckbo reports were seminal moments in the renaissance of regional planning and landscape conservation. The 1965 draft of Open Space was followed the next year by two landmark environmental polemics: Raymond Dassmann's The Destruction of California and Richard Lillard's Eden in Jeopardy. Californians were suddenly forced to confront the cultural and ecological costs of their postwar "golden age," and, from Eureka to San Diego, they were shocked by what they saw.

37. Thomas Kent, Jr., Open Space for the San Francisco Bay Area: Organizing to Guide Metropolitan Growth (Berkeley: Institute of Government Studies, University of California, 1970); and Alfred Heller, ed., The California Tomorrow Plan (Los Altos, Calif.: W. Kaufmann, 1972).

In the Bay Area, a unique heritage of brahmin conservationism provided elite support for successful efforts to protect the Bay's wetlands and create a regional open-space conservancy in the foothills. People for Open Space, with 16,000 subscribers to its newsletter, united the followers of John Muir and Lewis Mumford—environmentalists, planners, and philanthropists—in a common defense of the San Francisco Bay's great natural beauty. With the help of the Ford Foundation, POS developed the first comprehensive "anti-sprawl" plan for any American metropolitan area. Soon afterwards, California Tomorrow—also San Francisco-based—produced a detailed strategic outline for statewide land-use planning emphasizing the preservation of agricultural landscapes and the intensive regulation of suburban development. Both documents reproduced or elaborated core ideas in the Olmsted-Alexander-Eckbo tradition.[37]

38. Robert Fellmeth (project director), Politics of Land: Ralph Nader's Study Group Report on Land Use in California (New York: Grossman Publishers, 1973), pp. 436-55.

Within Southern California, meanwhile, counterpart movements crusaded to stop flagrant tract development in the Santa Monica Mountains and other foothill areas. The successful passage of the Coastal Initiative in 1972 finally codified the principles of public access and controlled beach development that the Olmsteds had advocated back in the 1930s. Ralph Nader's Study Group Report on Land Use in California included a shocking account of the planning system's total failure to regulate speculative development in the Antelope Valley.[38] At the same time, environmental groups sued the County to force it to protect the endangered remnants of Los Angeles's (last) "significant ecological areas."



39. In his scathing critique of the plan, Judge David Thomas accused the Regional Planning Commission of concealing staff reports that showed that 99 percent of the additional urban expansion area consisted of endangered habitats or vital watershed. See The Coalition for Los Angeles County Planning in the Public Interest v. Board of Supervisors, Los Angeles County, Superior Court (C-63218), (12 March 1975).

The Los Angeles County Regional Planning Commission was theoretically the chief custodian of the regional landscape. Yet as critics charged in their lawsuit, the Commission had historically functioned as "expediters for fringe growth" whose planning documents have been little more than "blueprints for sprawl." After soliciting environmental development guidelines from natural scientists in 1970, the Commission brazenly discarded them in order to double the amount of land targeted for urbanization. In response, the Coalition for Planning in the Public Interest organized a successful legal campaign to block the 1973 master plan.[39]

At stake were the remaining fragments of those key open spaces identified by Williams and Eckbo in their 1965 study: the fringes of Santa Clarita, the Ventura Freeway corridor beyond Calabasas, the Hacienda Heights, Rowland Heights and Diamond Bar areas of the San Juan and Chino Hills, and Quartz Hill between Palmdale and Lancaster. The Commission proposed to feed hungry developers another million acres of priceless agricultural and foothill landscape, while the Coalition argued that the population growth could be better accommodated by infill and densification within the existing urban fabric.

40. Los Angeles Times, 3 April 1979.

In 1979, however, environmental controversy suddenly turned into scandal. A grand jury investigation—based on muckracking evidence from the Center for Law in the Public Interest—dramatically exposed the inner workings of a regional planning system dominated and corrupted by development interests. As Commissioner Robert Meeker acknowledged, county officials paid "little more than lip service to restrictions on land use." Indeed, key planning officials had advised developers in the Santa Monica Mountains and the Antelope Valley how to circumvent public hearings and environmental restrictions by illegally partitioning their property amongst relatives and dummy corporations. (An astounding 13,000 individual cases of fraudulent lot division were alleged.)[40]

Robert Adams, Highlands, California, 1985. Gelatin silver print. Courtesy Fraenkel Gallery, San Francisco.

41. Ibid., 16 May 1979, 9 July 1979.

Similarly, when planning staff recommended against environmentally destructive projects in Diamond Bar and Santa Clarita, they were rudely overruled by the Commission majority. Planning Director Norman Murdoch routinely refused to acknowledge memos from Carolyn Llewellyn, the sole critic on the Commission. The independent-minded Mrs. Llewellyn was regularly shouted down by Commission Chairman Owen Lewis—himself a developer appointed by another developer (Supervisor Peter Schabarum).[41]

Although public outrage eventually forced the resignation of Chairman Lewis, it was a very modest, even Pyhrric, victory for the land conservation camp. The brief light focused on corruption within the Regional Planning Commission was never allowed to illuminate the more fundamental conflicts of public and private interests within the County Board of Supervisors (the "five little kings" who are the most powerful and least accountable local officials in the United States). Moreover, once the Commission reformed its most egregious practices, the steam went out of the (largely legalistic) battle to stop the fringe-development juggernaut. The County was finally forced to designate some sixty-five key ecological areas, but no legislation was enacted to ensure their preservation.



As a result, suburbanization has devoured each of the crucial open-space buffer zones prioritized by Williams and Eckbo. Small environmental gains here and there have been parried and checked by new thrusts of subdivision. Unlike the Bay Area, there have been no unqualified victories for open-space preservation, just the continued accumulation of worthless impact reports and impotent environmental plans.

In part, this is attributable to the different political cultures and power structures of California's two major metropolitan regions. County government in Southern California is so hopelessly captive to the land development industry that sweeping electoral reforms, comparable to California's Progressive Revolution of 1911, are probably the prerequisite for transforming land use policy.

Yet 1970s environmentalism in the Los Angeles region was also compromised by its own parochialism and historical amnesia. In contrast both to the Bay Area's People for Open Space, and, especially, to the local precedents of the Olmsteds and Alexander, the mainstream Los Angeles environmental groups fell short of a coherent vision of a stabilized city-nature equilibrium. There was little discussion, in the spirit of regional modernists like Neutra or Eckbo, of the role of parks and open space as the "functional skeleton of the community." More often than not, environmental battles were fought piecemeal without consideration of overall strategy or coalitions with other constituencies. Ecology, in other words, stopped short of the more subversive, but utterly necessary, politics of urban design.

## RETURN OF THE REPRESSED

In his eloquent 1966 jeremiad, Eden in Jeopardy, Richard Lillard warned that it was already one minute before midnight in the battle to save Southern California's most precious natural and historical landscapes. That was nearly thirty years ago. Where are we now?

All the old battles, of course, are still being fought at the megalopolitan frontier. But the bulldozers that so troubled William Whyte are now halfway across the Mojave, and developers uproot Joshua trees with the same mindless zeal with which they once cut down the citrus empire. Suburban sprawl has grown another hundred miles broader in circumference, and Los Angeles smog blights the view at the Grand Canyon.

Meanwhile, Los Angeles's inner-city neighborhoods and blue-collar suburbs, swollen with two million new immigrants, continue to suffer the long drought of recreational and green space. Public action mitigates the environmental crisis primarily for the top 10 percent of the population who benefit from the conversion of wetlands into marinas, and from hidden subsidies for hillside living. Even in the maw of the worst recession since the 1930s, Lillard's "profligate meddling with nature" is unabated, and Southern California remains radically unplanned, undesigned, and out-of-control.

Yet a surprising spirit of ecotopian optimism, not defeatism, currently pervades Los Angeles architecture. For the first time since the 1940s, the focus has returned to the design of public, rather than private, space. Visionary blueprints of past generations are dusted off or, more usually, reinvented.



Thus, an important coalition of architects and ecologists, sponsored by the local AIA, has rediscovered the city-shaping potential of the Los Angeles River. William Fain (of Johnson Fain and Pereira Associates) in his Greenway Plan for Metropolitan Los Angeles has revived comprehensive open-space planning in the grand tradition of the Olmsteds. Landscape architects like Achva Benzinberg Stein are collaborating with residents of South Central Los Angeles to transform vacant lots into community gardens and ecology centers.

On another level, even giant developers like Maguire Thomas have learned to speak impeccable Green—if only, in the cynical view of some, to better despoil the last remaining wetlands. "Neo-traditional" urban design, whether represented by the proposed Downtown Strategic Plan or the Playa Vista general plan, resonates with the environmentally conscious ideas of 1940s regional modernists like Neutra, Alexander, and Eckbo.

These projects and fantasies, of course, exist in a highly ambiguous and compromised socio-political space, somewhere between the onanism of the design world and the street warfare of city politics. Yet some strange beast is slouching toward Bunker Hill, and I suspect it is an authentic fourth wave of environmental design in the lineage of the Olmsteds and Bartholomew (1920s), Neutra and Alexander (1940s), and Eckbo, Dean, Austin and Williams (1960s). This inchoate movement has not yet attained the comprehensive regional vision of its predecessors, nor produced a commanding analysis of Southern California's spatial crisis; indeed it is barely conscious of its historical antecedents. But it has already contributed some breathtaking "urban revisions," and, if I had the temerity to write a manifesto for the new wave, I would single out five core theses:

1 THE FUTURE IS NOT TOO LATE. RADICAL LANDSCAPE RESTORATION IS BOTH POSSIBLE AND NECESSARY.

The audacity of contemporary urban design in Los Angeles owes most to two poets, Lewis McAdams and Gary Snyder. Walking along the wounded banks of the Los Angeles River in 1986, they conceived the crusade of resurrecting the original riparian ecosystem. Like the good Rev. Bartlett long ago, they visualized this "forty-year art work" as a reparation not only of nature, but also of the blighted neighborhoods of east and southeast Los Angeles that have been victimized for decades by noxious dumping.

Like analogous schemes to establish a "Buffalo Commons" in the northern Great Plains or to tear down Hetch Hetchy Dam (or, for that matter, Eckbo's proposal to trade sprawl for parks), the project of greening the Los Angeles River was initially derided as "preposterous" and "fantastic." Yet, through the irrepressible energy of McAdams and his Friends of the Los Angeles River, it has captured the imagination of the entire city. For architects and planners, especially, it has become a "practical utopia" that challenges and redefines the limits of the possible.



2 URBAN DERELICTION IS AN IMMEDIATE RESERVOIR OF COMMUNAL OPEN SPACE. NEIGHBORHOOD SELF-HELP IS A POWERFUL ENGINE OF ENVIRONMENTAL RENEWAL.

These two propositions are profoundly interdependent. Inner-city Los Angeles is not quite the South Bronx or downtown Detroit, but it does contain thousands of parcels of vacant or abandoned land, ranging in scale from the badlands of Crown Hill (just west of Downtown) to the debris-strewn alleys of Watts. Both Fain and Stein have shown how easily neighborhoods, by their own efforts alone or with modest city financial aid, can recycle dead space as greenways, placitas, playgrounds, gardens, and sports facilities.

The city needs legislation to facilitate such reclamation efforts. Property owners who store land-value as dereliction should be obliged to permit temporary communal uses. Moreover, as gang-truce leaders in South Central Los Angeles have repeatedly pointed out, neighborhood conservation could become a moral alternative to gang warfare, reemploying thousands of out-of-work teenagers and young adults in their own communities.

3 URBAN DISTRICTS MUST BECOME MORE ENVIRONMENTALLY SELF-SUFFICIENT. OPEN SPACE IS THE PREREQUISITE TO AN ALTERNATIVE INFRASTRUCTURE.

All urban design, sooner or later, is a critique of infrastructure. In this respect, Playa Vista—the saltwater "edge city" that will soon rise from the Ballona wetlands—is simultaneously the worst and the best of possible "neo-traditionalist" worlds. Extravagant self-praise for its "integration of work and residence at a pedestrian scale" cannot hide the fact that, without mass-transit linkages, it will generate nightmarish street congestion that taxpayers will eventually be forced to ameliorate.

Yet Playa Vista also sets a new regional standard for the on-site treatment of waste water and storm runoff. Fresh-water ponds and a restored section of Centinela Creek provide striking landscape elements as well as an efficient natural system for recycling the effluent of thirty thousand residents. Like Peter Calthorpe's superbly conceived (and rapid-transit-based) projects near Sacramento, Playa Vista offers reassuring proof that new town design can achieve dramatic environmental mitigation through careful

42. See Peter Calthorpe, The Next American Metropolis: Ecology, Community, and the American Dream (New York: Princeton Architectural Press, 1993).

planning of open space.[42] The even bigger question, however, is whether such self-contained "green infrastructures" can be retrofitted to older parts of the city. If so, it may require the re-creation of waterscapes and green areas on the heroic scale proposed by Eckbo in 1966.

### 4 TRANSPORTATION SPENDING IS AN ARCHIMEDEAN LEVER FOR CREATING NEW PUBLIC SPACE.

Los Angeles County's thirty-year, $183 billion mass transit plan, like Playa Vista, is a mixture of good and bad. At a time when public schools and community health care are near collapse, the construction of a $1 billion-per-mile subway system seems a pharaonic misallocation of scarce resources. On the other hand, more socially responsible transit investment—in bus and trolley corridors, as well as an extensive bikeway system—could become a powerful tool for enhancing both the quality and social equity of the urban environment.



Although comprehensive planning of transit-related land use has been discovered late in the day, it has quickly become the new frontier of Los Angeles architecture. Hundreds of local architects, together with planners and artists, have participated in design competitions for a series of proposed Transit Oriented Districts (TODs) along subway and light-rail routes. The best of these designs integrate vibrant public space with affordable housing and clustered neighborhood services. In theory, at least, they are envisioned as dynamic nodes of an alternative, "car-free" urbanism: radical prototypes in the tradition of Alexander's Baldwin Hills Village.

### 5 URBAN DESIGN IS AN ESSENTIAL LANGUAGE OF THE NEW URBAN ENVIRONMENTAL AND SOCIAL-JUSTICE MOVEMENTS OF THE 1990S, BUT URBAN DESIGNERS, BY THEMSELVES, ARE POLITICAL ORPHANS.

One of the leading promoters of the TOD strategy is Nick Patsaouras, a Greek-immigrant engineer who has used his appointed positions on regional transit agencies as bully pulpits to advocate a communitarian "remaking" of Los Angeles. As a dark horse in the April 1993 mayoral primary, Patsaouras translated the new urbanism into a political platform that attracted the support of some of the most well-known names in Los Angeles architecture (Gehry, Rotondi, Fain, Moule/Polyzoides, and so on). For a few months, neo-traditionalists, high modernists, and deconstructivists suspended aesthetic warfare to campaign for their "Shared Vision 4 a New LA."

The platform went back to the future, especially to Eckbo's 1949 Landscape for Living, to retrieve an image of Los Angeles as "a botanical garden on a metropolitan scale . . . a city of trees and open space." Amending the Olmsteds' 1930 master-plan, Patsaouras proposed to use rapid-transit rights-of-way, not automobile parkways, to build a vast greenway system that would bring the "region's natural beauty back into the city itself." Furthermore, he committed himself to a "Bill of Community Rights" that guaranteed good jobs, affordable housing, safe streets, a green environment, and "convenient commuting without owning a car."

Not since the 1940s had anyone dared to bring such a vast reformist vision into the electoral arena. Unable to digest Patsaouras's ideas in a few soundbites, the media, including the Los Angeles Times, ignored him in order to focus on more colorful personalities, like an immigrant-bashing former deputy mayor and a raving maniac from Hollywood. Moreover, the campaign had brilliant design concepts coming out of its ears, but almost no evident organizing strategy or political economy beyond the deus ex machina of the transit budget. There was little attempt to sell the vision where it mattered most—for instance, in the streets of East and South Central Los Angeles. As a result, Patsaouras was able to win little more than one percent of the vote in an election whose immediate backdrop was the worst riot in modern American history.

An underlying problem, of course, is that the current wave of urban revisionists do not know where they fit into the post-liberal political spectrum. Since the 1930s, at least, expansive programs of park building and environmental conservation have been associated with the left wing of the liberal state, if not with social democracy per se. Since the Reagan Revolution and its corollary, the rise of the Democratic neo-liberals, however, urban visionaries have become the New Deal's orphan children. Reinvestment in public space, environmental restoration, and extension of social citizenship rights presume more than goodwill and good design. They assume an epochal renewal of egalitarianism in American life, as well as a profound commitment to end racism, pollution, and poverty in our big cities.[43]

43. On the new political marginality of big cities, see my "Who Killed L.A.? A Political Autopsy," New Left Review 197 (January/February 1993).



In the meantime, today's urban designers have two choices. Like Voltaire, they can seek the ear of sympathetic philosopher-kings—in this case, "progressive" developers and mortgage bankers—in the hope that utopian urbanism can pass the muster of the bottom line. (This is the explicit strategy of most soi-disant neo-traditionalists.) Or, more boldly and self-effacingly, they can enlist as ordinary activists in the grassroots movements to save the city: in Los Angeles, a spectrum that runs from the Green Party and the Friends of the Los Angeles River to Jobs with Peace and the Labor-Community Strategy Center. To these forces of the opposition, architects and planners can bring the invaluable gift of a design tradition that celebrates the relationship between landscape conservation and democratic public space.

Le Corbusier's hand over a scale model.
From La Ville radieuse, 1935.

# The Powers of the Eye

*Richard Sennett*

Urban design is a perplexing art, based on uncertainties. The designs offered in this exhibition, despite their great diversity of form, all seek to address the social lives of people in cities. Can social life as complex as that of the city be designed? Should the architect attempt to do so?



Thirty years ago, in her book The Death and Life of Great American Cities, Jane Jacobs attacked the enterprise of urban design as an exercise in tyranny. She attacked the "megalomania" of architects like Le Corbusier, who, in his Plan Voisin for the Marais in Paris, sought to sweep away, with a simple stroke of the pen, a thousand years of dense urban settlement; she attacked Robert Moses, who sought to gut the economic and social center of New York City by creating a highway system radiating out to the leafy and middle-class periphery of the New York region. She affirmed instead the viability of urban forms which accumulated over time from local uses and historical changes; such messy and unsatisfying shapes of streets, houses, shops, and public spaces were, in her view, socially legitimate and democratic, whereas the artist-designer acted as a dictator.

Her attack has deep roots in the history of the Western city. The same fury at the designing eye's claim to organize society appeared in the ancient world, for instance, in Aristotle's attack on Hippodamus of Miletus, whom Aristotle identified as the designer-culprit of the geometric grid plan for cities. Aristotle asserts that the city cannot be the arbitrary creation or invention of one person, because the rules an artist follows differ from the rules citizens must follow, the citizens learning from mutual conflict how to live together; Aristotle declares:

> **The analogy drawn from the arts is false. . . . It is from habit, and only from habit, that law derives the validity which secures obedience. And habit can be created only by the passage of time; a readiness to change from existing to new and different laws will accordingly tend to weaken the general power of law.[1]**

1. Aristotle, The Politics 73.

The cities we live in are of course nothing like the self-governing city-states of Artistotle's time. Today urban communities form parts of a complicated metropolitan, national, and indeed global economic network; investments made in Tokyo directly affect the work people do in Los Angeles or New York. To celebrate the local community, as Jane Jacobs does, might seem a self-destructive gesture, since the new international network of power certainly has a larger and more powerful design. Yet this critique of the designing eye, from Aristotle to Jane Jacobs, has a dimension beyond the merely local or purely political.

It is the peculiar tragedy of this visual art that the urban designer has far less autonomy than the painter, the sculptor, or the photographer. Urban projects are realized only if the designer can cooperate at every step with banks, investors, and government authorities. Large-scale building projects are today linked to international patterns of investment; they are based on increasingly standardized values in terms of square footage, function, and materials no matter where they are built. The result is that big building projects more and more look like money: they are composed of homogeneous, interchangeable units of value. The shopping mall, office tower, or housing project vary from place to place only in terms of skin treatment or details of decoration.

Critiques of urban design have a particular validity within this context. They ask us to evaluate the urban environment in terms of how much the people who live in it feel aroused by, and so attached to, where they live or work or politic. Yet homogeneity dulls the senses. It diminishes experiences of surprise, the functional replaces the difficult or the challenging. Buildings that function like money, in short, pacify the body.



Yet, just as the urban designer is not a self-sufficient artist, the homogeneous qualities of the urban environment are not simply a result of a single cause like finance. Buildings have come to look like money due to a complex interaction of modern technology, geography, and culture; these factors combine to deaden the bodily sensations of people in urban space.

In this essay, I would like to sketch how these factors produced that result. In turn I hope to give the viewer one critical tool to evaluate the projects presented in this exhibition. How, and how well, would these proposals bring our senses back to life in urban space?

## DEAD SPACE

A few years ago I went to see a film with a friend who had fought in the Vietnam War. A bullet had shattered my friend's left hand, and the military surgeons had been obliged to amputate it above the wrist. Now he wore a mechanical device fitted with metal fingers and thumb which allowed him to hold cutlery and to type. The movie we saw turned out to be a particularly gory war epic through which my friend sat impassively, occasionally offering technical comments. When it was over, we lingered outside, smoking while waiting for some other people to join us. My friend lit his cigarette slowly; he then held up the cigarette steadily in his claw to his lips, displaying the metal hand to others as a provocation. The movie patrons had just sat through two hours of bodies blasted and ripped, the audience applauding particularly good hits and otherwise thoroughly enjoying the gore, but now they seemed afraid to look at this tangible sign of the events that had just given them so much pleasure. People streamed out around us, glanced at the metal hand and moved away; soon we were a little island in their midst.

For nearly a century, modern culture has sought to liberate the human body, to set it free in particular from the sexual phobias, silences, and prejudices of earlier eras. Yet a great chasm exists between modern images of the body and bodily experience. Just as few soldiers taste the movie pleasures of ripping other bodies apart, marketable images of sexual pleasure have very little to do with real lovers' sexual experience. Few films show two elderly naked people making love, nor naked fat people; movie sex is great the first time. The imagery of bodily pleasure in the mass media supposes a flight from one's own body.

It occurred to me at the war film that where we were might have influenced how others reacted to my friend's hand, that the space in which people live has something to do with flight from the body. We saw the film in a vast shopping mall on the northern periphery of the New York region. There is nothing special about the mall, just a string of thirty or so stores built a generation ago near a highway; it includes a movie complex and is surrounded by a jumble of large parking lots. This place dedicated to material consumption seems a fitting home for tasting violent pleasure in air-conditioned comfort and at a psychological distance. Yet I've come to understand that the space makes a deeper impression on those who inhabit it, stamping into them the fear of a real body signifying pain.

The geography of modern society has shifted in our time from densely packed urban centers to thinner and more amorphous spaces, suburban housing tracts, shopping malls, office campuses, industrial parks. These spaces weaken bodily experience in three ways: modern peripheral space dulls the body's sensations of motion, sight, and touch.



Motion: When a Parisian wanted to go from the Place Saint Michel to the Place de la République in the middle of the nineteenth century, the trip through the twisted streets of the old city took about twenty minutes by carriage, fifty minutes on foot. Today, if the traffic is good, a car makes the journey in four minutes; a walker along the straight streets created by Baron Haussmann in the 1850s and 1860s can go between the two points as fast as a carriage once did. Again, at the end of the nineteenth century in New York, it took about an hour by carriage to move up the straight streets of Manhattan's grid from Greenwich Village to midtown; today, even with the fouled traffic in the city, it takes a third of that time. People experience speed today in terms people in the past could hardly conceive. The technology of motion—from automobile engines to continuous, poured-concrete highways—has changed modern geography; thanks to the power of speed, human settlements have extended beyond tight-packed centers out into peripheral space.

Yet speed is a very curious phenomenon. For one thing, anxiety about moving has developed in the same measure as the ability to move fast; people become uneasy if a subway stops for half a minute, and traffic jams bring out the beast in even the most sedate bourgeois. Earlier travelers, harboring no expectation that they would move without interruption, were free of this instant anxiety. The desire for speed has in turn a marked effect on one's sense of space. The moving body does not want to be arrested in space, it seeks pure forward thrust. This dissonance between speed and space again contrasts to earlier eras. For instance, the "Villes Circulatoires" of the eighteenth century sought to organize a city so that people could circulate efficiently through it yet experience its monuments, churches, and parks as pleasurable elements in the process of moving. Washington, D.C. is perhaps the greatest city planned this way; the late eighteenth-century architect Etienne Boullée imagined circulation through such a city as a journey in space, the course of the journey as significant as its origin and its destination.

Today the anxiety about being stopped or slowed down in space prompts urbanists to evaluate and build places in terms of how easy it is to get out of them, how easy it is to quit them. Space is now a means to the end of pure motion. The look of urban space enslaved to motion is neutral, furnished with standard signs, dividers, and drain sewers, streets emptied of street life. This dependency of space upon motion has social consequences. The philosopher Martin Heidegger thought that the modern world weakened the commitment to place, and the rule of motion over space is one physical way that mutual commitment weakens; motion erodes the sense of "being in place," to use Heidegger's words.[2] In terms of bodily experience, the speed of driving through a place as well as the insulation of people inside a modern automobile, bus, train, or subway, erodes the sense of connection to the environment through which they travel.

The physical condition of the traveling body reinforces this sense of disconnection. The actions needed to drive a car, the slight touch on the gas pedal and brake, the flicking of the eyes to and from the rearview mirror, are micro-motions compared to the arduous physical movements involved in driving a horse-drawn coach. Modern cars, buses, and subways do not rock and jolt the way nineteenth-century carriages and trains did. Navigating the geography of modern society requires very little physical engagement; indeed, as roads become straightened and regularized, the voyager need account less and less for the people and the buildings on the street in order to move, making minute motions in an ever less resistant environment. The modern moving body is thus a pacified body; we move both passively and rapidly through space.

One reason the crowd at the war film watched so uneasily my wounded friend smoke is suggested by this disconnection of motion from place. Of course, out there, on the periphery of New York, we were far from the grim realities of violence in the center of the city, but more, the film had some of the same qualities of release from circumstance as modern travel. My friend's metal hand created something like traffic jam anxiety—the hand which stopped the flow of fantasy, demanded a human connection, displayed the impediment of reality.

**Sight**: Modern geography dulls our sensations in a second way, through its effect on the operations of the eye. As cities have spread out and diffused, the eye has been obliged to do a kind of sociological work that formerly was also done by the voice, for though the modern environment is full of mechanical noise it is also a landscape of human silences.

The pre-industrial, dense urban center was a place in which strangers talked openly to one another, on the street as in coffee houses, cafes, shops, and government buildings. More than sociable impulses moved strangers to talk to one another; in an age without mass communication, talk was the most important means of gaining information, especially among the large mass of people who could not read. Some critics have argued that the growth of mass literacy began the process of eroding discussion among strangers, so that people increasingly read about others rather than talked to them, but this was not the case. The advent of the modern newspaper in the eighteenth century sharpened, if anything, the impulse to talk; displayed on racks in cafes and bars, the newspapers served as points of discussion for the people who read them in public. Throughout the nineteenth century, men felt free to speak to others on the street,

2. Martin Heidegger, "Making, Being, Doing," in Poetry, Language, Thought, trans. Albert Hofstadtler (New York: Harper and Row, 1975).

intervening when something untoward occurred or striking up casual conversations; women, surprisingly, had more verbal contact with other women in public places than we might suspect in retrospect.[3] Throughout the nineteenth century the authorities feared the political consequences of strangers gathering together to talk, knowing that social revolt could be ignited by the sparks of discussion. In Chicago and New York as much as in London, Paris, and Berlin, a police system of spies and repressive laws operated throughout much of the nineteenth century, attempting to keep people from talking too much to each other in bars, pubs, and in public squares.

3. Jürgen Habermas, The Structural Transformation of the Public Sphere: An Inquiry into a Category of Bourgeois Society, trans. Thomas Burger, with Frederick Lawrence (Cambridge, Mass.: The MIT Press, 1989; Darmstadt, 1962); Mary P. Ryan, Women in Public: Between Banners and Ballots, 1825-1880 (Baltimore and London: The Johns Hopkins University Press, 1990). See also my The Fall of Public Man (New York: Knopf, 1976).

The geographic dispersion of the city, the driver's detachment, and the rise of television accomplished what the nineteenth century police could not. The density of talking bodies has thinned out, and physical contact between them has weakened; watching television is a more passive experience than reading. Of course, people today still talk sociably to strangers in bars or on airplanes, but the talk lacks a space in which it can become collective action.



As the city has fallen silent, the eye has become the organ through which people now get their direct information about strangers. What social knowledge comes to the eye, looking around in silence?

Under these conditions, the eye can be tempted to organize information about strangers in a repressive way. It may make use of what the critic Roland Barthes has called "an image repertoire of representations."[4] Scanning a complex or unfamiliar scene, the eye will try to sort out rapidly what it sees in terms of images that fall into simple and general categories, drawing on social stereotypes. Encountering a black man on the street, many white people will register only threat. The urbanist Kevin Lynch has shown how an image repertoire can be used to relate to buildings and places as well as strangers; carrying a snapshot of "home" in the mind, a person compares the building fabric of a new place to the snapshot of home: the less the two correspond, the less connected the person feels to his or her surroundings. In a study of how people walk on the street, the sociologist Erving Goffman described the bodily result of seeing via an image repertoire; after that initial classifying glance at another, people walk or otherwise manage their bodies so that they risk as little physical contact as possible.[5]

4. Roland Barthes, The Fashion System, trans. Matthew Ward and Richard Howard (New York: Hill and Wang, 1983; Paris, 1967), pp. 100-110.

5. Kevin Lynch, The Image of the City (Cambridge, Mass.: The MIT Press, 1960); Erving Goffmann, Relations in Public: Microstudies of the Public Order (New York: Basic Books, 1971).

An image repertoire is just the opposite of an explorer's binoculars. By scanning their surroundings with an image repertoire, subjecting the environment to simple categories of representation, comparing likeness to difference, people diminish the complexity of their visual experience. The image repertoire filters out visual information. Socially, this means that the operation of the eye deadens experience of the other, the new, and the unknown. Moreover, the experience of rapid movement so deeply impregnated in modern bodily experience encourages the eye to use an image repertoire to classify and judge immediately. Just as rapid motion disconnects the moving body from place, so here the computer-quick operations of the image repertoire dull connection to and stimulation by one's surroundings. People made this use of the image repertoire at the movie theater when they looked for a moment at my friend, then averted their gaze and gave us a wide berth. One glance was enough to see that he was alien, even though he was alien because he was a living war-ravaged body.

6. For a succinct statement of his work, see Melvin M. Webber, "Revolution in Urban Development," in Housing: Symbol, Structure, Site, ed. Lisa Taylor (New York: Rizzoli, 1982), pp. 64-65.



In the last few years we have learned how profound a role politics and economics play in shaping experiences of sight. One of the first analysts of the modern urban periphery, Melvin Webber, laid the groundwork for understanding how the image repertoire operates in these modern spaces, due to new forms of labor. Most modern work, he remarked, consists of office and service tasks which do not need to be conducted in a dense urban core; the process of manufacturing a radio or automobile may take place in many sub-factories, not in a single place; electronic communication systems make it possible to disperse workers; the advent of large numbers of lower-level women workers has pulled such jobs out closer to where they live.[6] The result, a good Marxist would argue, is that the working classes are no longer visible to each other.

Curious about this "de-centered economy," I recently spent some time watching a woman imprint, via a computer screen, a company logo on auto tires in a suburban factory. A prompt appeared on her screen when each tire was ready to be stamped, on an assembly line far from where she sat; if the tire was not exactly in position she pressed a button marked "align," an action performed by a robotic pair of arms; then she pressed a button called "stamp," an action performed by another robotic device. Hour after hour she pressed these two buttons; if by chance the mechanical arms failed, rather than sort matters out herself she pressed a third button marked "malfunction," and a maintenance worker near the assembly line manually adjusted the tires so that the line could move again.

This ordinary use of a computer followed some of the rules that govern the automobile. Speed rules in making tires, as in driving on them, and speed is correlated to spatial dissociation; in front of the computer screen, a worker makes micro-movements which trigger mechanical actions in another place. Even more powerfully, the program built into the machines constituted an image repertoire of the most severe sort, radically restricting what workers see hour after hour. Indeed, in this factory the woman had never seen the stamping machine she operated.

Much had been gained, via this computerized labor, in terms of the safety of the worker and the efficiency of the work, but the labor process evinced some of the same deadening consequences for the body as does modern geography. Boredom was acute, made worse in this factory by the company rule forbidding workers to talk to each other when at their screens; an eerie silence reigned, punctuated by faintly clicking keyboards. Since attachment to the work was low, carelessness was high, and sometimes I observed the woman make a breathing space for herself by pressing the "malfunction" button even though the screen prompt said "stamp"; she then had a minute or two to take her eyes off the screen. The best the managers could do to alleviate boredom was rotate the mass of workers every few days between tasks organized in a similar way. As one of the executives observed to me, the freedoms of high technology labor belong only to the people who control the programs.

**Touch**: In 1751, William Hogarth made a famous pair of engravings, Beer Street and Gin Lane, meant to depict images of order and disorder in the London of his time. Beer Street shows a group of people sitting close together drinking beer, the men with their arms around each other's shoulders, or touching the women's forearms. For Hogarth, bodies touching each other signaled social connection and orderliness, much as today in small southern Italian towns a person will reach out and grip your hand or forearm in order to talk seriously to you. Gin Lane displays a social scene in which none of the bodies touch, each person catatonically withdrawn into him or herself, drunk on gin; the people in Gin Lane have no corporeal sensation of one another, nor of the stairs, benches, or buildings in the street. This physical isolation was Hogarth's image of social disorder.

Some of the body contact depicted in Hogarth's Beer Street might look today, to puritanical modern viewers, like sexual harassment. Touching another person's body contains an undertow of intrusion, possibly of violation. We would not, I think, be as likely to measure social order in terms of body contact as did Hogarth and his contemporaries, for modern forms of geography have altered the modern experience of touch.

As a commercial and labor market, the eighteenth and nineteenth century city inevitably concentrated and forced into contact a great variety of people. The economic dispersion of modern urban settlements has undone the necessity for contact. Thus, while a city like New York is today as a whole as ethnically diverse as it was a century ago, that diversity is spread out, and the urban region has become a landscape of discontinuous communities with little material contact or linkage between its parts.



The way urban planners deal with this stretched-out geography reveals a certain attitude about the sensation of touching. Modern planning seeks to create social order in distended space by deadening possible points or places of contact between different kinds of people. In siting highways, for instance, the river of traffic will often be located to seal off a residential community from a business district, or run through residential areas to separate rich and poor, or ethnically divergent sections. In community development, planners will concentrate on building schools or housing at the center of the community rather than at its edge. More and more, the fenced, gated, and guarded planned community is sold to buyers as the very image of the good life. Contact seems to these planners, contrary to Hogarth, to be a source of unruly conflict or unmanageable disorder.

The makers of these closed communities defend themselves by saying that sealed space simply responds to a real fear of physical contact with outsiders. The mayor of Paris recently declared that he sympathized with native Parisians' aversion to the armpit smell of foreigners impregnating their clothes, that he too was disgusted by the dirtiness of most foreigners on the buses and in the subways; he shocked some people but sounded a deeply resonant chord even in that once most open of cities. Playing on fears of physical contact is good politics as well as economics; both draw on an analogy to bodily violation. To deaden the places where different groups meet is like de-sensitizing the skin. The inward center, the "heart," of a community can then be shielded from the disturbing stimulations of difference.

If class and ethnic politics play a large part in deadening human zones of contact, culture also plays a role. The vocabulary of freedom does not demand contact between different groups—mutual toleration, perhaps, but not touch, not visceral contact. In cities like London, New York, or Los Angeles, which contain many different ethnic groups, the boundary streets are often neglected and amorphous zones; few people cross from one side to the other to shop or walk with their children. Fear justifies all. I suppose this is what most struck me at the movie theater, the fear that my friend's metal hand might reach out for someone's lips or eyes.

William Hogarth, *Beer Street*, 1751. Engraving.
Courtesy of the Print Collection, Lewis Walpole Library, Yale University.

William Hogarth, *Gin Lane*, 1751. Engraving.
Courtesy of the Print Collection, Lewis Walpole Library, Yale University.

LIVE DESIGN

As this sketch may indicate, making urban designs that rouse people's senses is a far more complex matter than giving people a sense of ease in the environment. A good city, Aristotle declared, is a place that lets people confront all of life, its pains as well as its pleasures, its difficulties as well as its comforts. In terms of modern cities, a design full of life would be based on the following three principles:

First, it would privilege space over motion. This is far more than a matter of creating pedestrian zones for shopping, as inside a mall. Being in space—the sort of experience Heidegger imagined—requires attachment to the spaces in which people live. The automobile breaks those attachments by making everything in the mobile environment instantly legible, known at a glance. People become attached to space when it is puzzling or unfamiliar, when it requires interpretation, not when it is familiar.



This principle takes us back to Jane Jacobs, for the kind of environment that engages people in this way contains a great deal of indeterminacy. Rather than its functions being laid out clearly and at a single stroke, an urban design following this principle has the capacity to change, thanks to the presence of the people who inhabit it. It is an environment that can grow more convoluted in the course of time. To take a concrete instance: many modern urban designs establish rigid boundaries between public and private zones, so that people immediately know where they do and do not belong. To make those boundaries more flexible, as in the classic pattern of the courtyard which mediates between private and public space, means that in time the space becomes more arresting; in a city like Jerusalem you need to look at different courtyards in order to know where you are, where you can and cannot go. You must interpret the space; it engages you; you move in it rather than just through it.

This first principle leads to a second. A live urban space must break down the power of the image repertoire. It can do so through containing diversity, but diversity of a specific sort.

Almost all planners today pay lip service to the principle of diversity but don't take it seriously, socially or economically. The diversities that stimulate people are disruptive; they would involve, for instance, putting a hospital or welfare center in between the shops in a mall. They require desegregation of the eye. This kind of diversification in space is obviously no easy matter. It means that space focuses the tensions in a society, rather than isolates them from one another.

In American cities, we have become so accustomed to the regime of fear which inspires isolation that cities like Naples or Bombay seem unthinkable to us. In Naples, the pressure of housing has mixed the classes together, and over the course of time a certain equilibrium has been established; in Bombay, the lack of housing among the poor has mixed together religious and ethnic groups who hate one another but have similarly established a *modus vivendi*. No planner engineered either of these equilibriums, which is Jane Jacobs's point. Yet so strong is the image repertoire in our society that the planner who believes in diversity can make it work only by insisting on the concentration of dissonance as an urban value—the most political statement a modern planner can make.

Because fear of crime—a lightly veiled fear of race—so dominates modern thinking about cities, other diversities in American society are often overlooked. If we have long segregated the races, increasingly we segregate people of different ages, or the well from the sick. The growth of peripheral fragmentation and edge cities has separated places of work from schools, schools from housing tracts, government offices from non-bureaucratic activities. Mixing any of these elements would prove threatening or jarring—but it is exactly in that disturbance that people become aware of one another.

Where could this arousal occur? That question puts forward the third, and perhaps most challenging principle of urban design contained in our bodily sensations. Almost all of the thinking we do about the values of community gives greater value to the geographical centers of community life than to the boundaries between communities. The community seems strengthened, its identity revealed, by defining the center. The center as a place of life, and the edge as a weak zone, seems indeed a kind of natural order. Yet in the ecology of most natural systems, the greatest biological activity occurs where different zones meet, as in a swamp or a forest; species congregate at the boundaries where they interact with other species.



To strengthen that sense of touch and contact, an urban design has similarly to focus on the edge as a scene of life. In practical terms, this means finding ways to use the dead space on the fragmented periphery separating housing projects from malls, malls from office campuses, office campuses from hospitals or schools. It may well be that the American downtown is dead, but the urban problem of connection and contact has not therefore disappeared; it too has migrated to the periphery.

Of course a planner could make pretty and profitable places ignoring these three principles. But at a price. The isolation and climate of fear that rules American society would not be addressed. The possibilities for living in difference—which are the very essence of urban culture—would not be explored. Urban design is urban to the extent it tries to confront the difficulties we have living with each other. The gain of confronting our difficulties is a more vivid bodily awareness of our environment, and of ourselves.

# Projects in the Exhibition

*Time Present (rendering of proposed light rail).*

*"CHANGE OVER TIME.*

*Trees planted in visible cycles which display constantly the changes from seedlings to mature specimens."*

*Diana Balmori*

***Balmori Associates, Inc.***

FARMINGTON CANAL GREENWAY

NEW HAVEN

*Time Past (site along the canal).*

# PLANNING STUDY for CENTRAL ARTERY CORRIDOR BOSTON

***Chan Krieger & Associates***

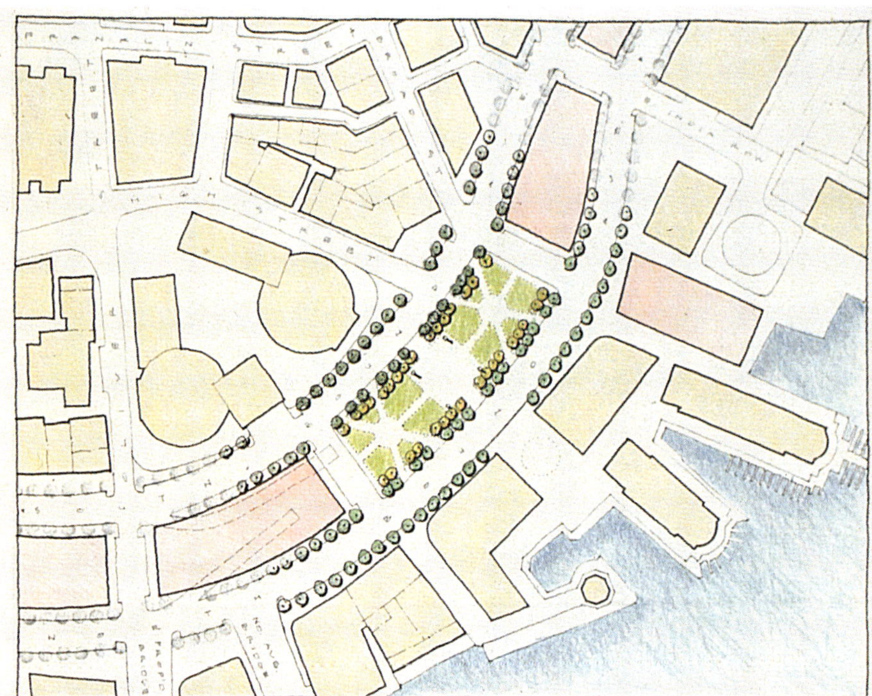

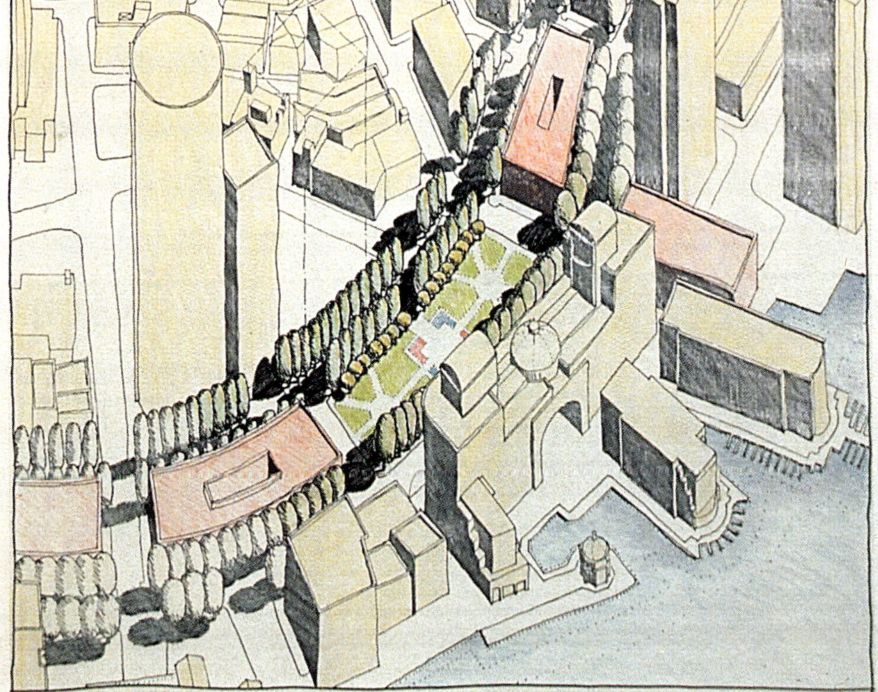

*Drawing of proposal for Fort Hill Square, plan and axonometric.*

# A GREENWAY PLAN for METROPOLITAN LOS ANGELES

*Johnson Fain and Pereira Associates*

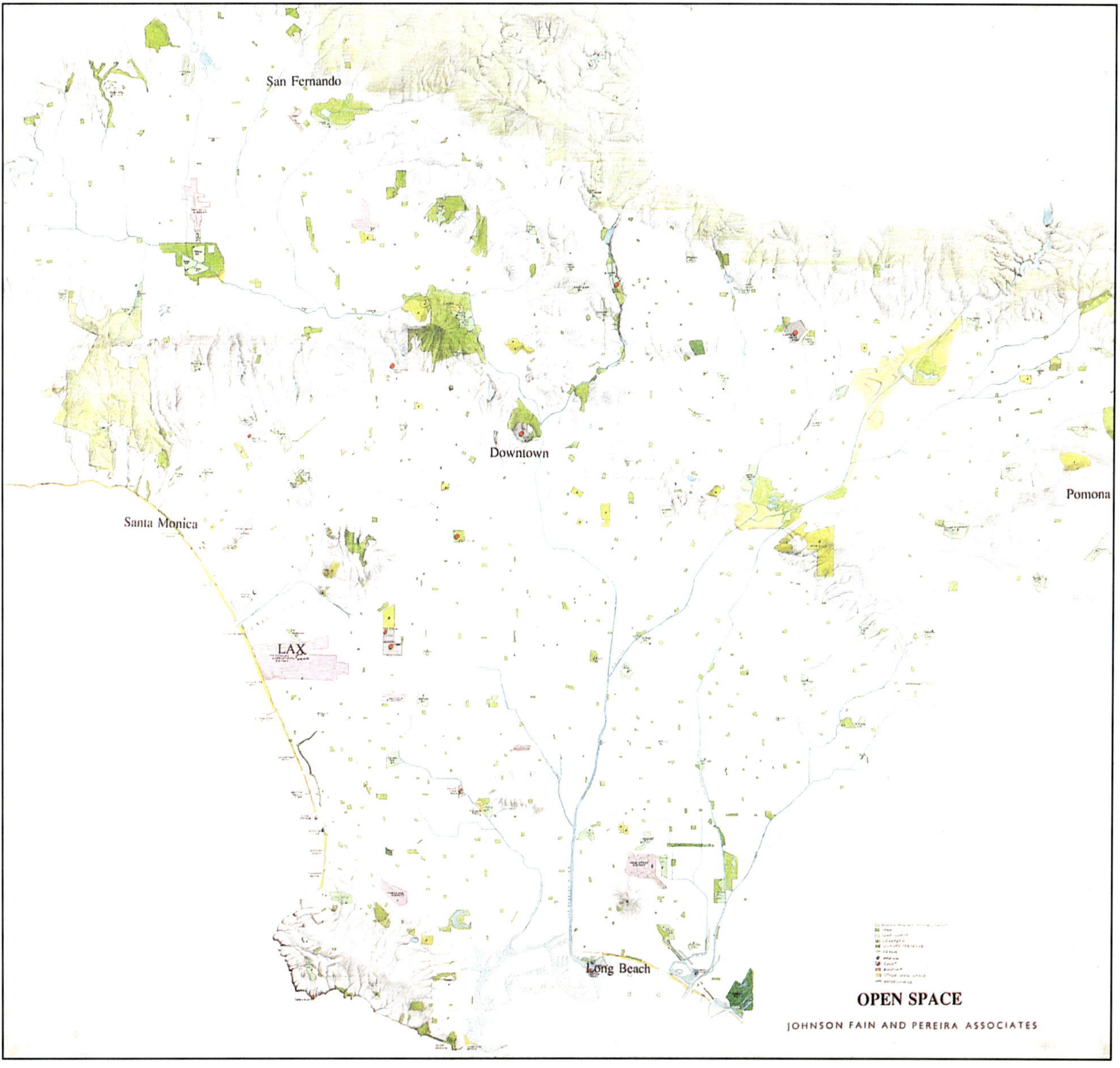

## THE MASTER PLAN for FAUBOURG QUEBEC MONTREAL

*The linear belvedere of rue Notre-Dame (Rendering by Saucier Perrotte/Roper).*



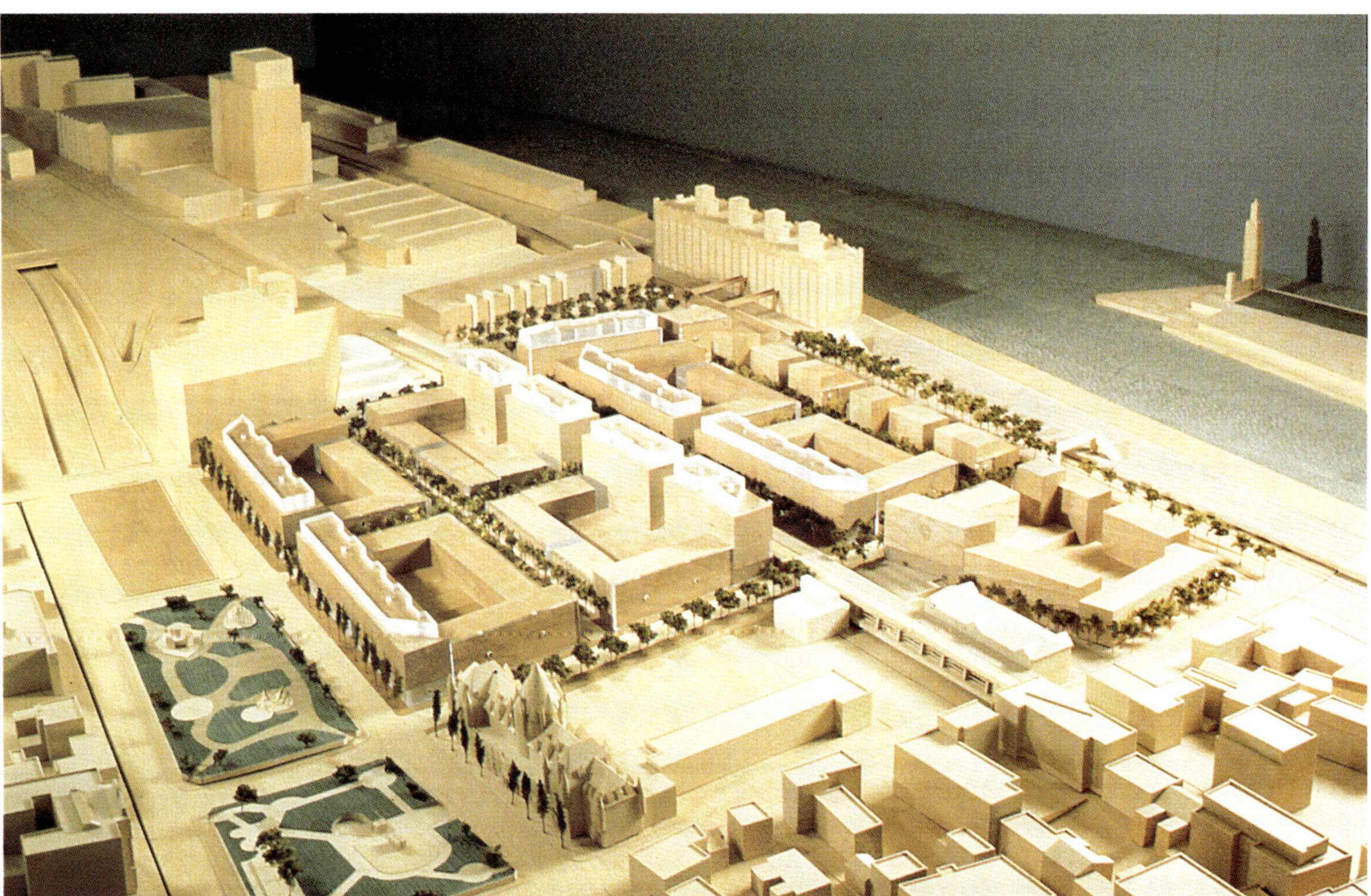

*Site model.*

*First phase plan—west end.*



## PLAYA VISTA, LOS ANGELES

***Andres Duany and Elizabeth Plater-Zyberk, Architects and Town Planners; Hanna/Olin, Ltd.; Legorreta Arquitectos; Elizabeth Moule and Stefanos Polyzoides, Architects and Urbanists; Moore Ruble Yudell***

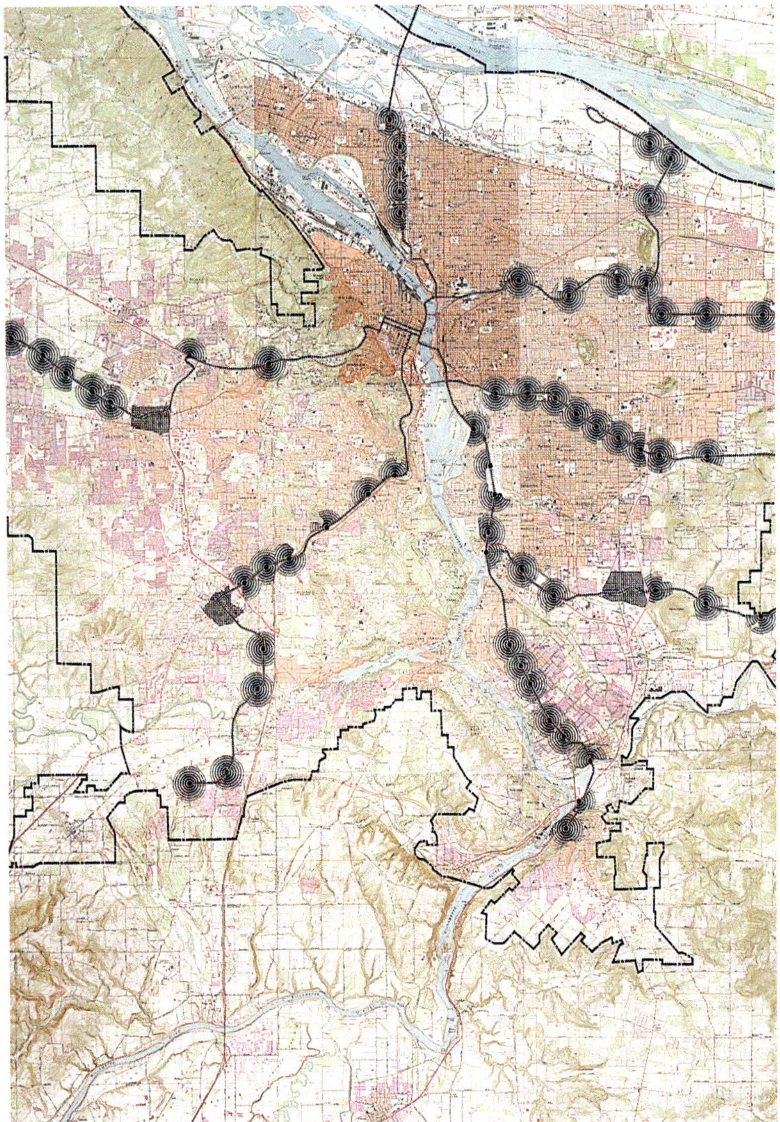

*Portland Region: Urban Growth Boundary, Transit System, and Walkable Neighborhoods.*



REGION 2040 STUDY

PORTLAND, OREGON

***Calthorpe Associates***

Site plan.



## SUSTAINABLE ARCHITECTURE: TOWN CENTER FOR ESSLINGEN, SWITZERLAND

*Angélil / Graham Architecture*

*Michael Sorkin Studio*

## PROPOSAL for a MILITARY BASE CONVERSION, SOUTHWESTERN UNITED STATES

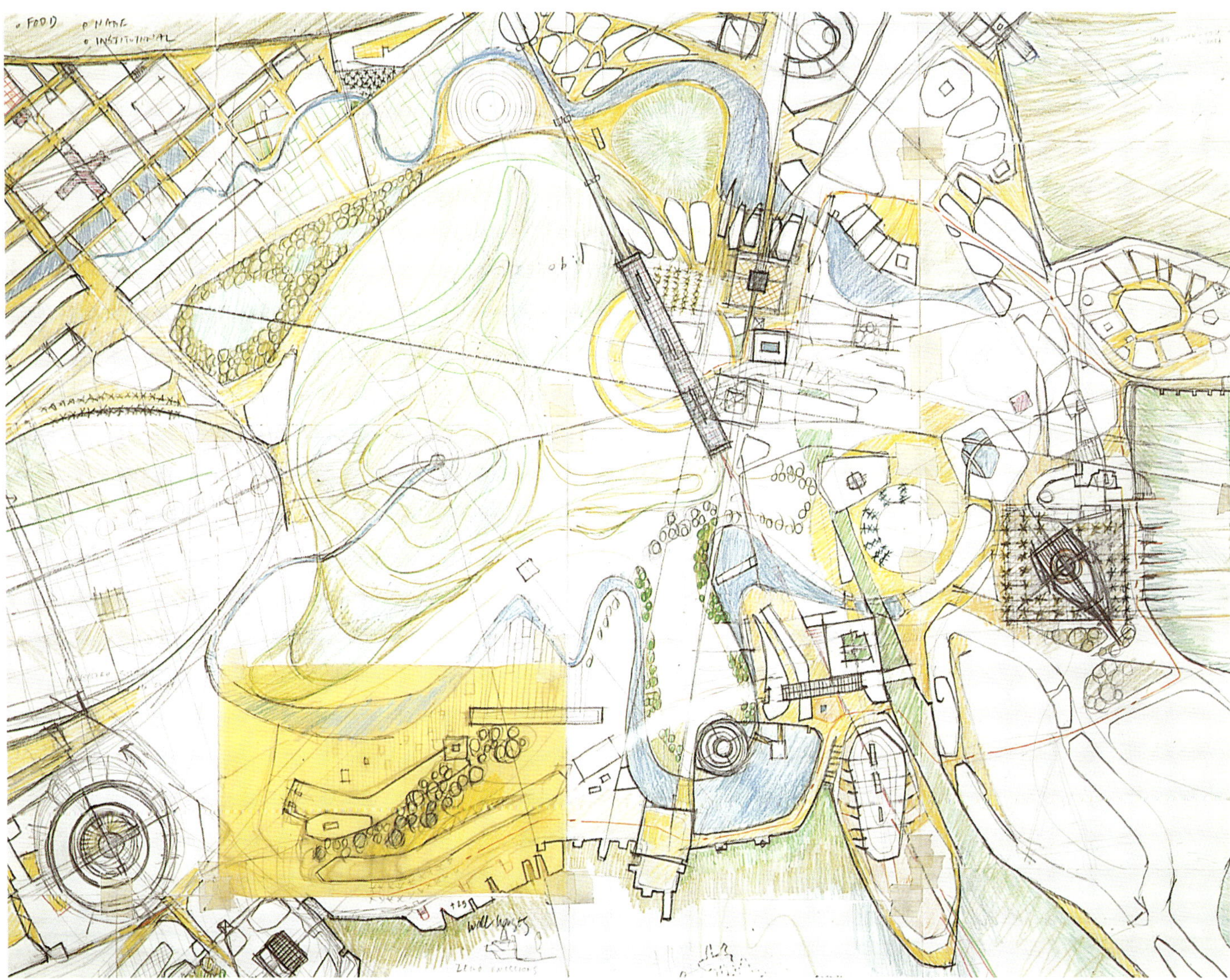

*Weed, AZ: Sketch.*

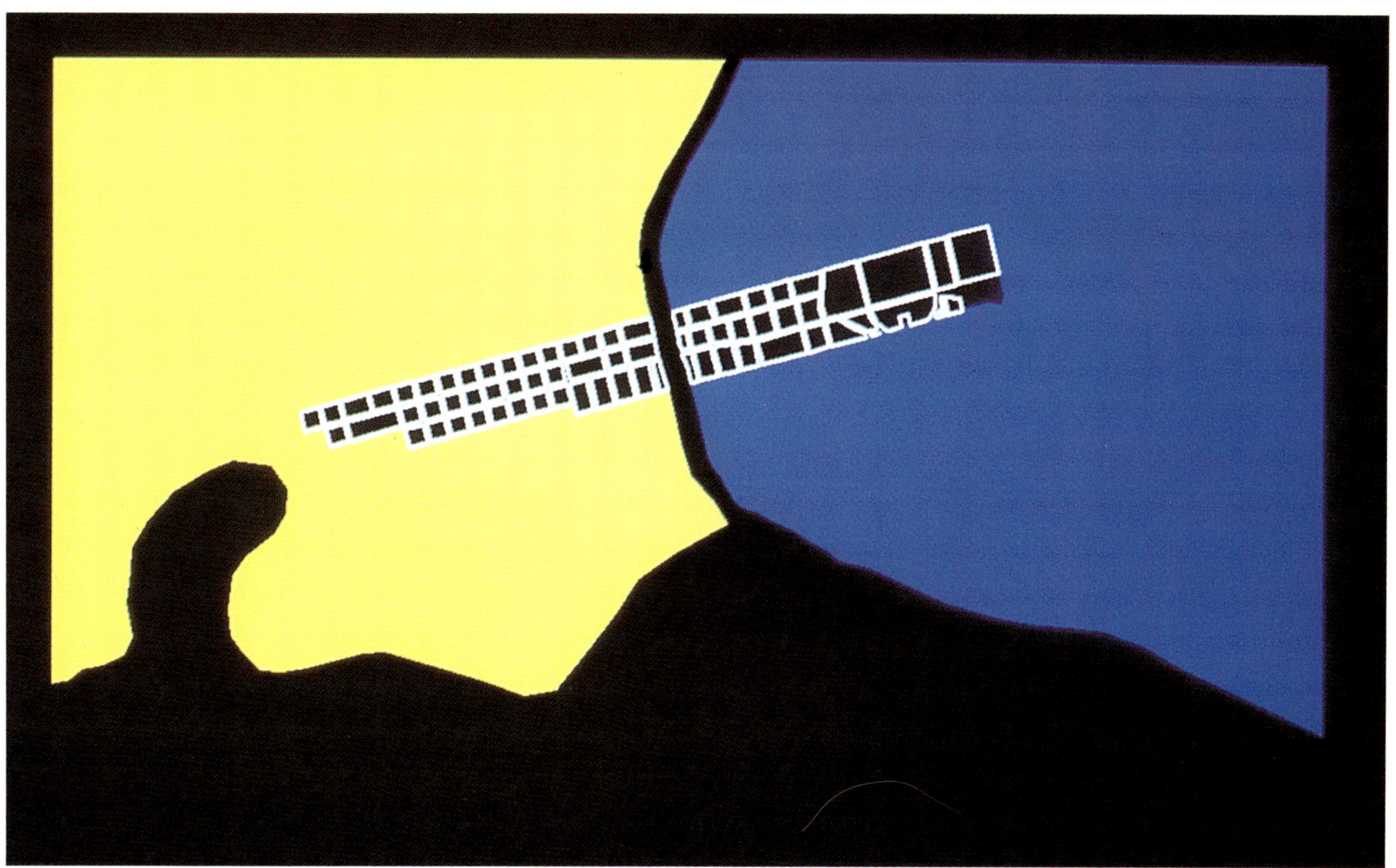

*The East side and West side are physically separated by the Des Moines River–symbolically as the City (West side) and the State (East side)–and linked by the downtown corridor running from the Gateway to the Capitol.*

***Agrest & Gandelsonas, Architects***

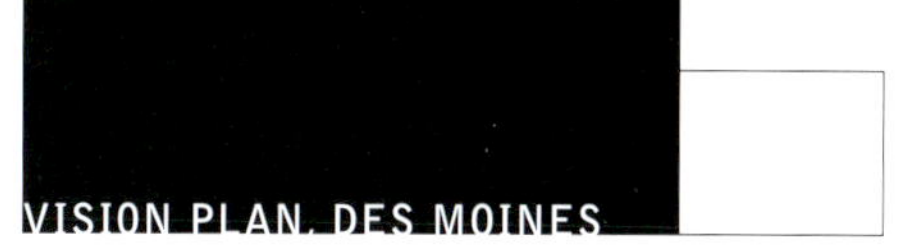

VISION PLAN, DES MOINES

# DOWNTOWN STRATEGIC PLAN LOS ANGELES

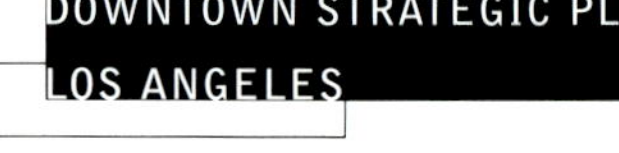

*Elizabeth Moule and Stefanos Polyzoides, Architects and Urbanists*

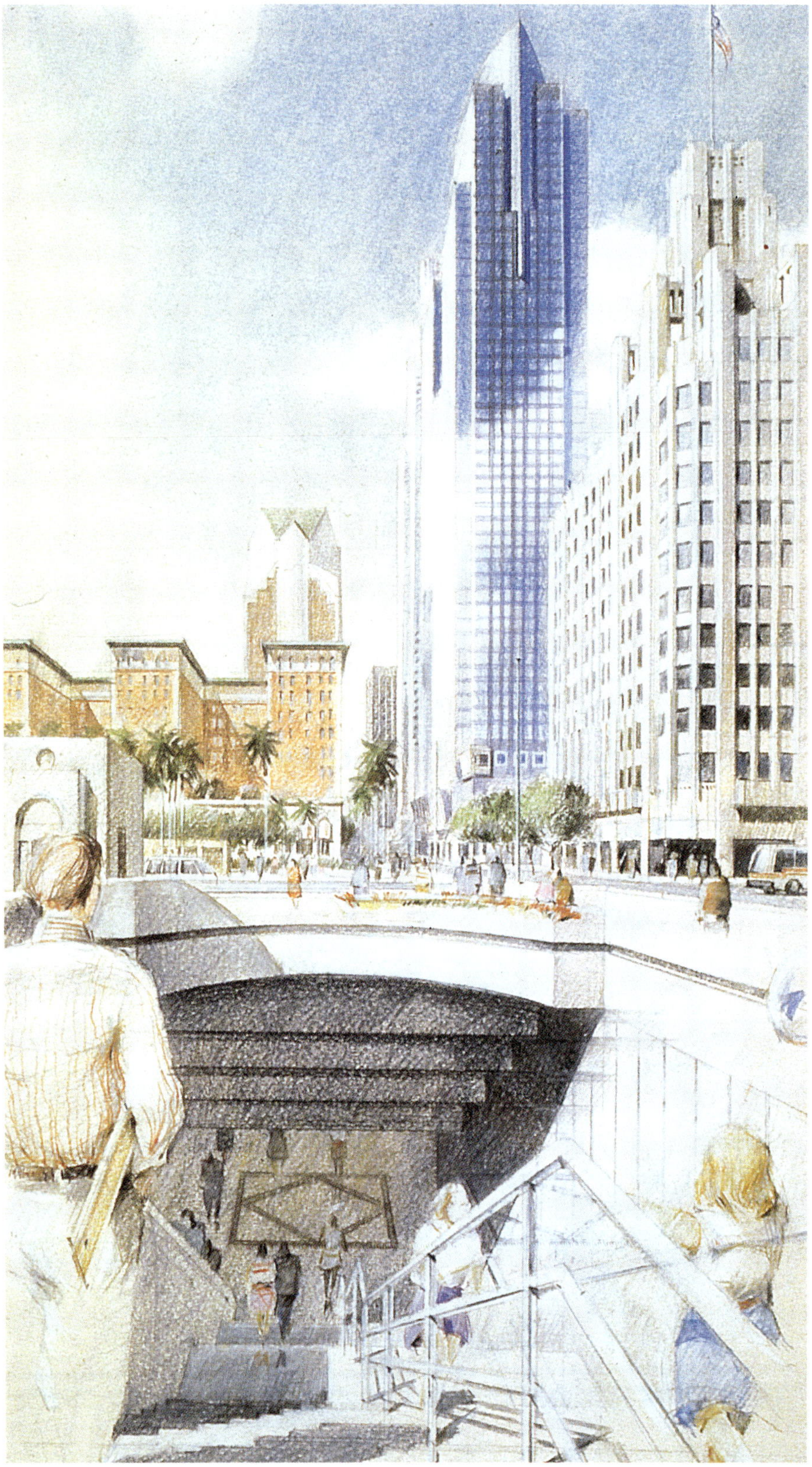

*As development occurs over time, three interrelated physical frameworks will regulate the urban form of Downtown: Open Space, Built Form, and Access. The Access Framework will resolve Downtown's internal transportational requirements and its regional accessibility.*

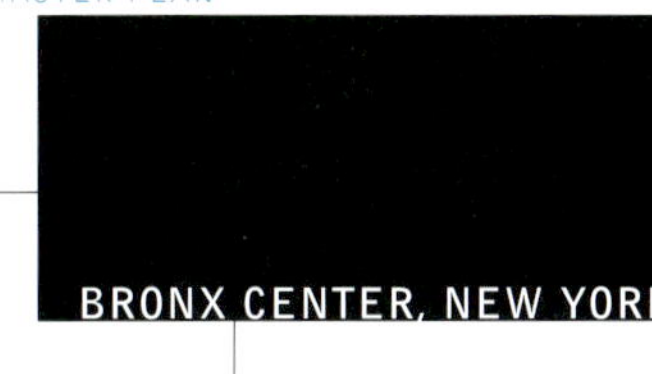

*Street corner.*

## IMPERFECT UTOPIA: A PARK FOR THE NEW WORLD. SITE PLAN FOR THE NORTH CAROLINA MUSEUM OF ART, RALEIGH

*Smith-Miller + Hawkinson Architects; Barbara Kruger; Quennell Rothschild Associates*

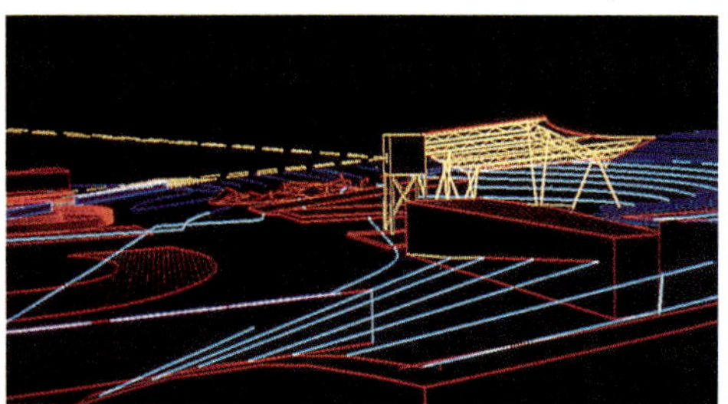

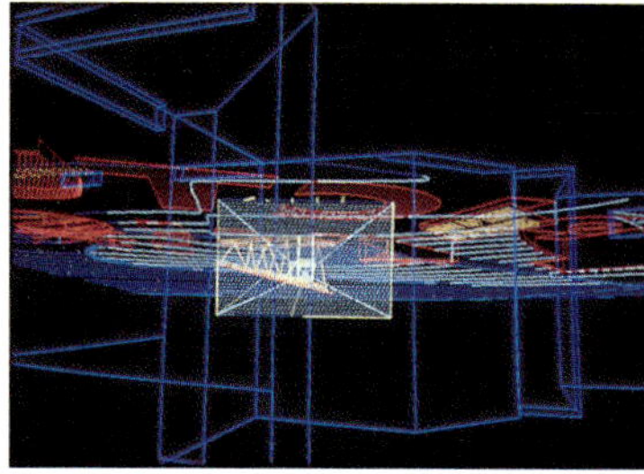

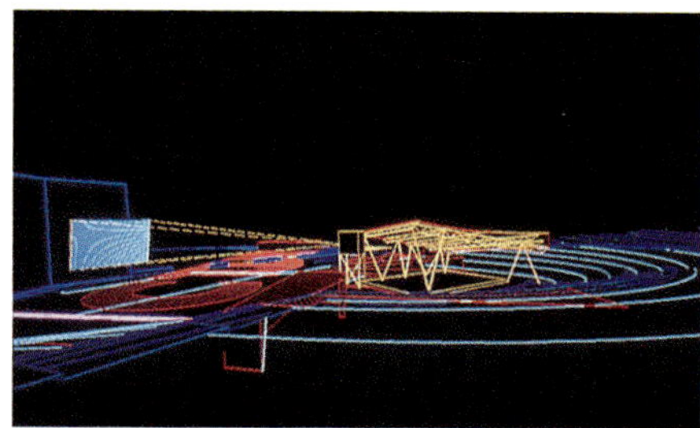

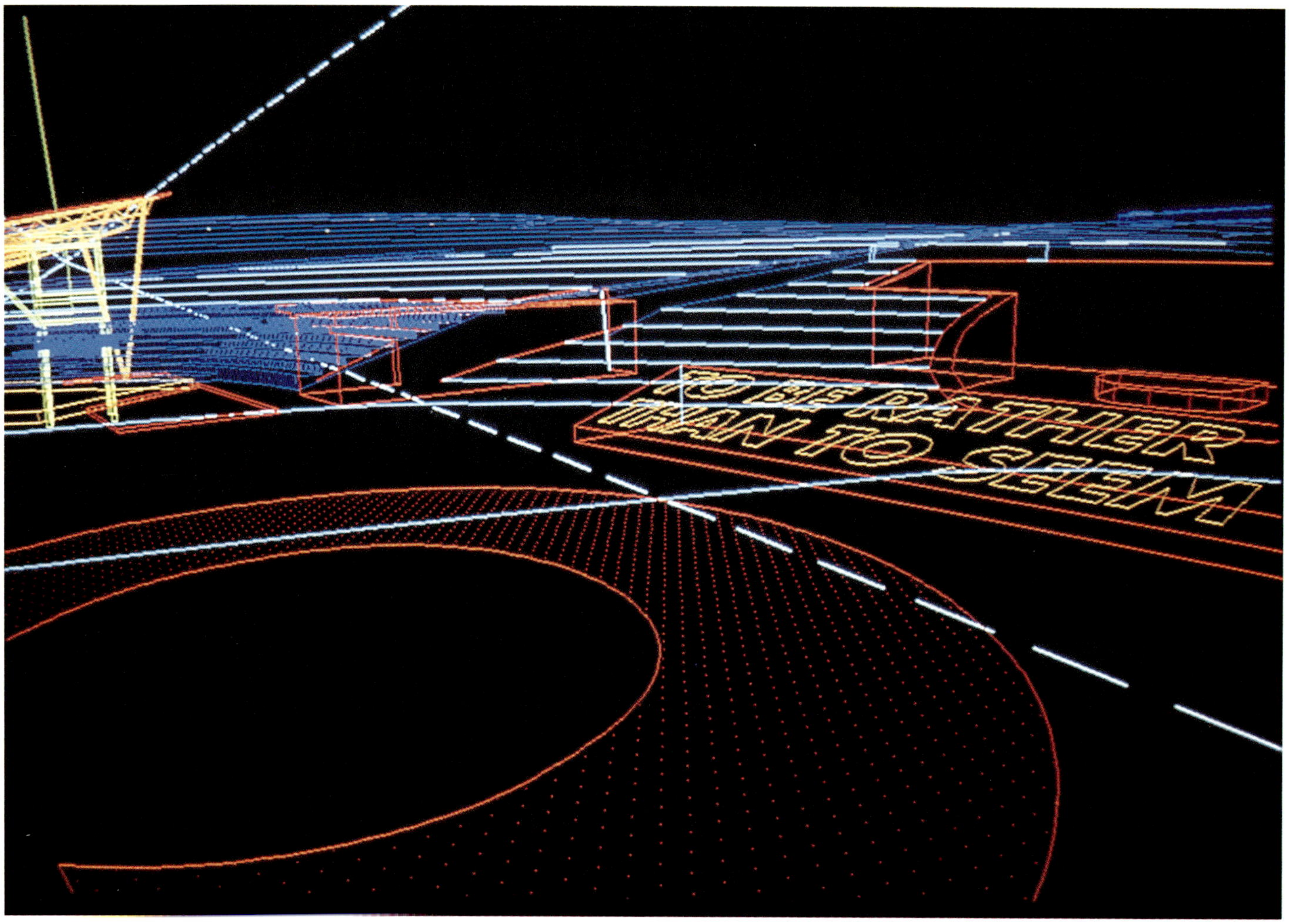

*Computer-generated drawings (by John Conaty).*



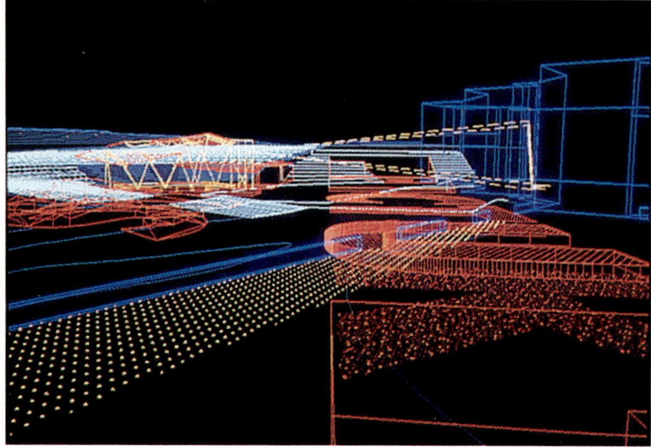

*Z Building and Wendy's Wall.*



## CONCEPTUAL MASTER PLAN FOR GRAND CENTER

ST. LOUIS

***STUDIO WORKS in collaboration with Trivers Associates, Mary Miss, and James Turrell***

## "STEEL CLOUD": WEST COAST GATEWAY, LOS ANGELES

*Rashid + Couture / ASYMPTOTE*

*Detail of the motion cinemas: rear projection screens and viewing units situated above the Hollywood Freeway.*

The garden reconnects residents with both nature and history, offering an alternative within the city.

UHURU GARDEN
WATTS,
LOS ANGELES

*Achva Benzinberg Stein,*
*BLS Environmental Planning*
*& Design, Los Angeles*

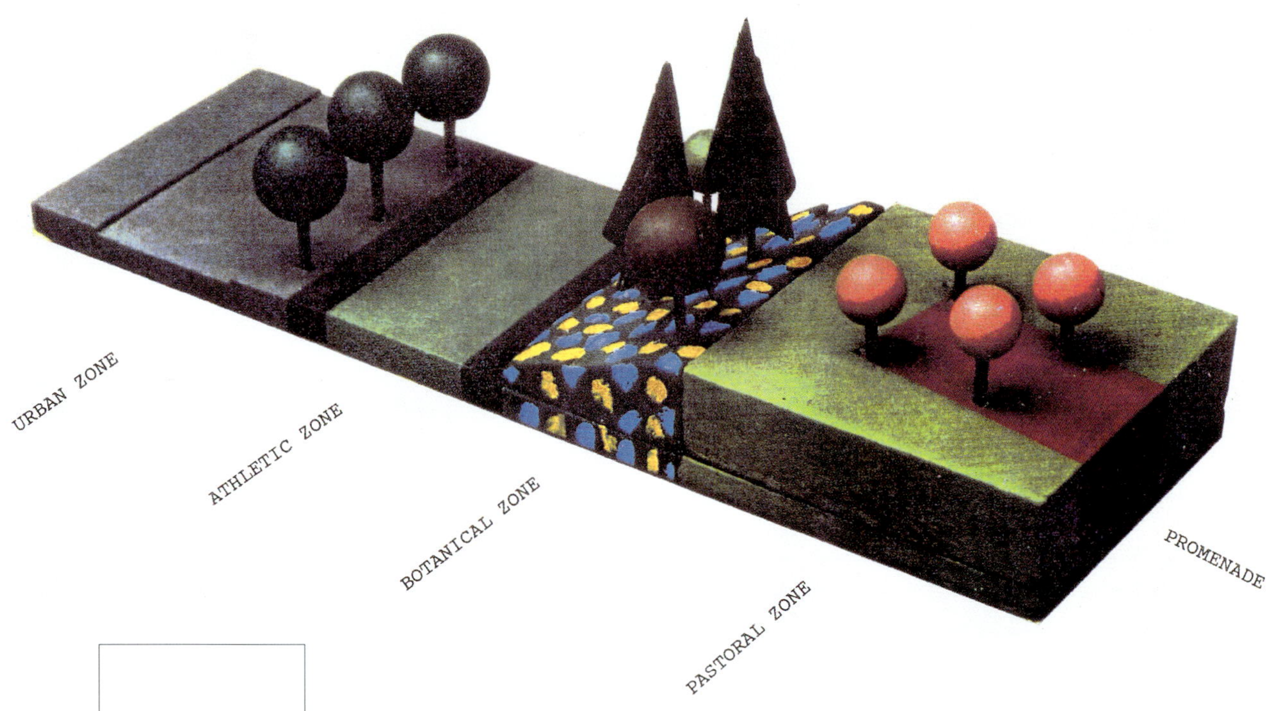


## TERRITORIAL IMPERATIVE: MASTER PLAN for BATHGATE AVENUE COMMUNITY PARK, BRONX, NEW YORK



*Baratloo-Balch Architects*

*Sectional model and site plan.*

# Urban Revisions : Current Projects for the Public Realm

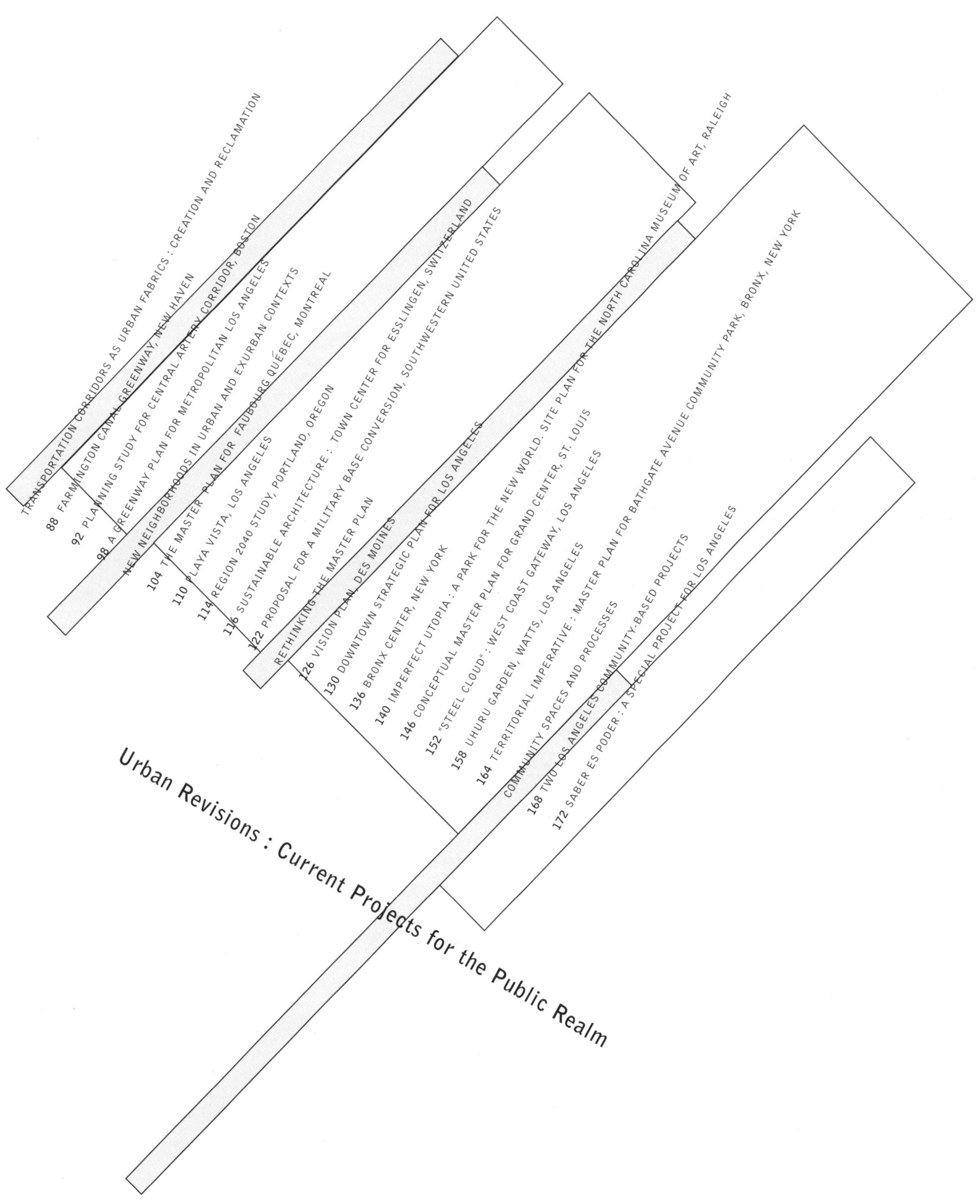

# FarmingtonCanalGreenway

*Balmori Associates, Inc.*

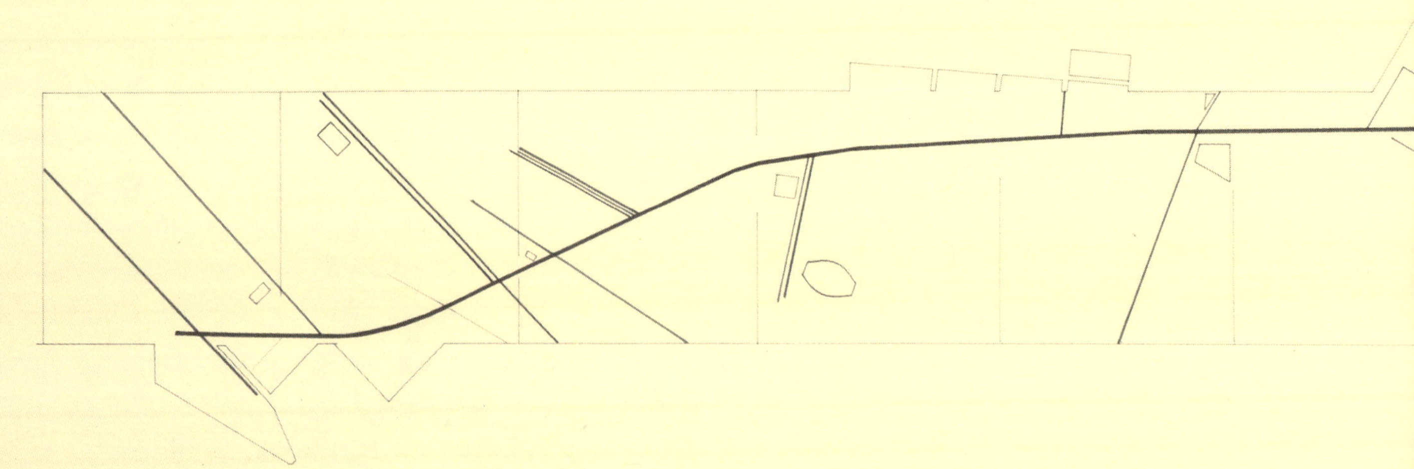

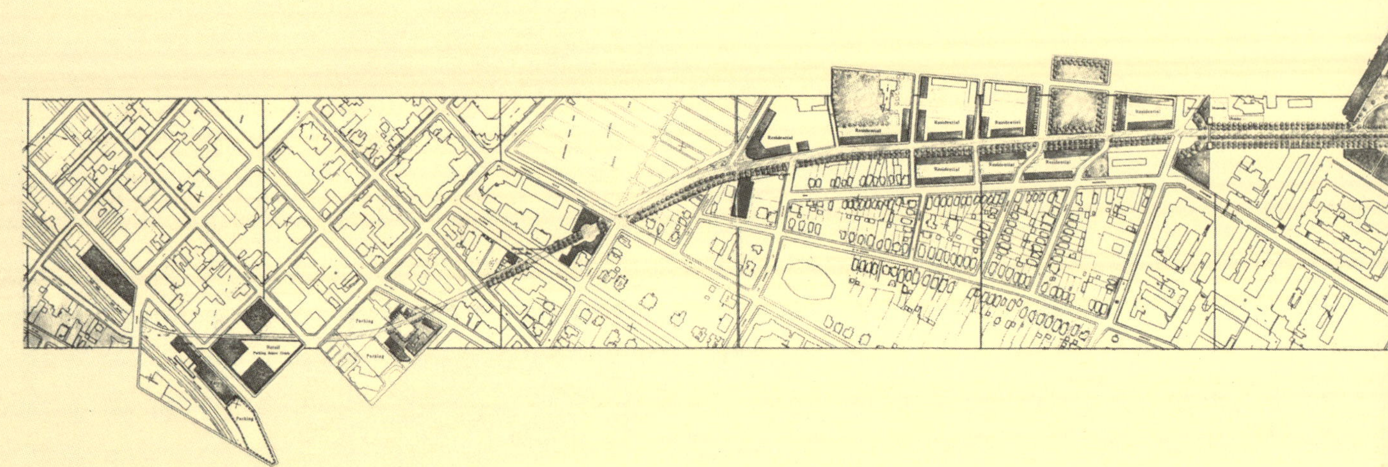

# NewHaven

New Haven-based landscape architect Diana Balmori's design for the **Farmington Canal Greenway** takes as its site an abandoned canal and railroad corridor running from New Haven through the town of Hamden, Connecticut. Initially commissioned by the Farmington Canal Rail to Trail Association to develop a master plan for reuse of the site as a pedestrian and biking corridor, the study evolved into a collaborative design for a nine-mile linear park including pedestrian bridges and bicycle paths along a twenty-five-foot-wide swath of land. While construction of the Hamden portion of the Greenway will start this fall, New Haven has just purchased the land for its section and will proceed to the next stage of design by summer 1994.



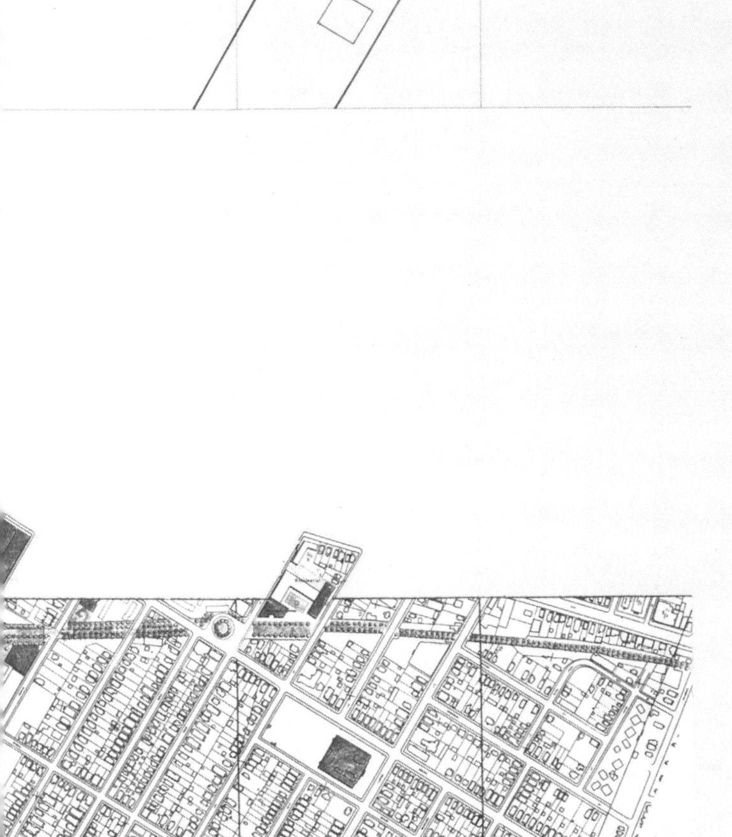

"A MODEST PROPOSAL
for remaking the American City

LINEAR CORRIDORS TRANSFORMED
from defunct canals and abandoned railroads

A DESIGN IN THE FOURTH DIMENSION : TIME
A design never finished but evolving
layers designed
over layers
like living things always complete
yet always changing."

Diana Balmori

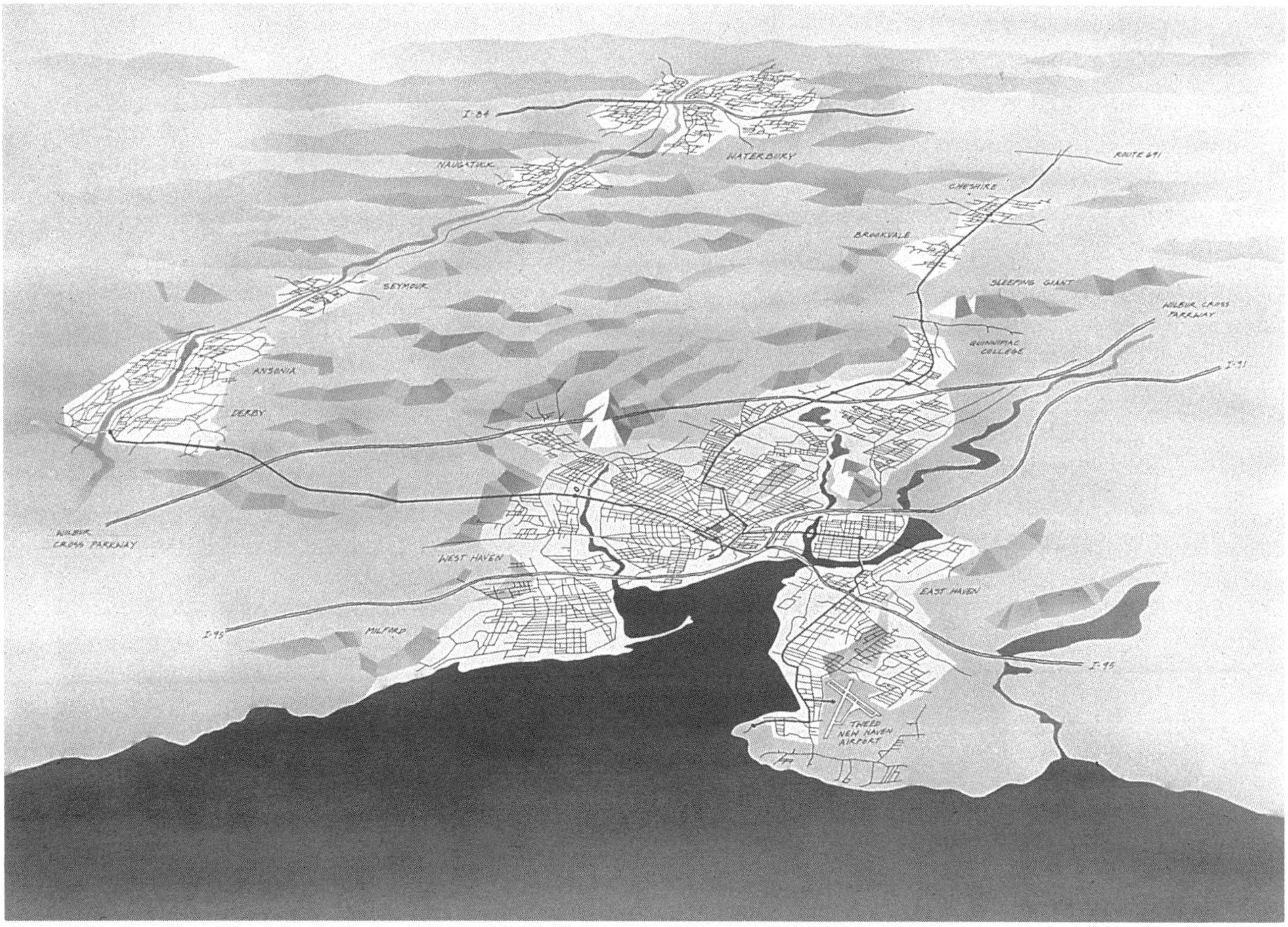

Aerial plan showing light rail corridor.

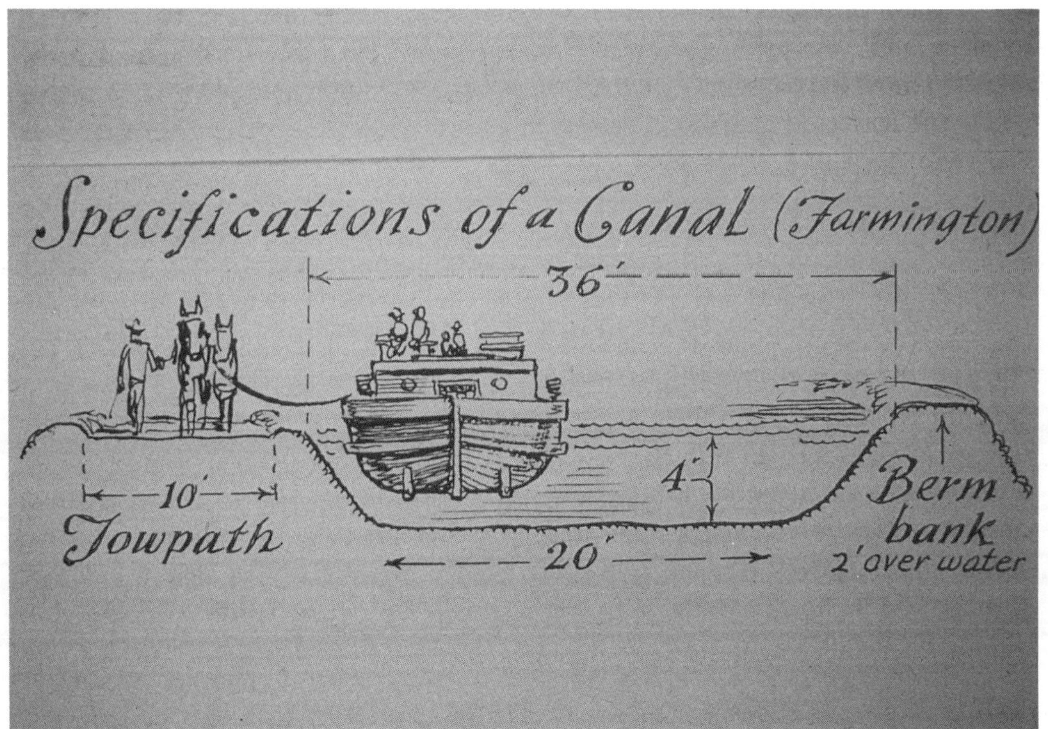


Historical drawing showing specifications for a canal.

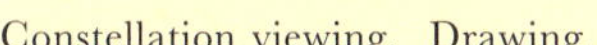

Constellation viewing. Drawing.

Site.

Site.

**Design Team**

Diana Balmori, Principal
Mariko Masuoka
Robin Cash
Christopher L. Siefert

**Urban Design Consultant**

Alan J. Plattus

**Participants from the following community groups**

Q. House Community Center, Dixwell
Dixwell Neighborhood (and Peter Gray, Director, Dixwell Development Association)
Newhallville Neighborhood
William Ginsberg, Director, Science Park

**Exhibition Design Team**

Ana Maria Torres, Design Team Leader
Hillary Quarles
Mihaly Turbucz
Martha Burgess

**Video**

Ana Maria Torres
Hillary Quarles
Jonathan Horowitz
Music by John Cage, "Music of Changes"

In New Haven, Balmori conceived an expanded greenway on the site of the former canal and rail line, with the goal of unifying and connecting diverse neighborhoods in a city beset by sharp social, racial, and economic differences. Her vision includes the introduction of a light rail system in the below-grade section of the corridor to reconnect New Haven's Union Station with the Yale University campus and with the rest of the city beyond (an area bisected under the urban renewal program of the 1960s), juxtaposed with a series of linear greenways and park-like interventions responsive to the character of each urban segment or neighborhood through which they pass. Beyond the downtown light rail section, the corridor traverses the low- and middle-income community of Dixville; Science Park, a research and light industry complex; then passes through another residential community, Newhallville. This public transportation connection would facilitate access to possible sources of employment within the city and around the region by providing increased mobility for many of its inhabitants. The tram and light rail connection also represents a tangible way in which to reintegrate the important physical relationship between Union Station and the rest of the city.

Public involvement in the design of the greenway surrounding the rail system has been substantial. Representatives of the community of Dixville, for example, have requested that the greenway take the form of an urban boulevard, providing a greater sense of urbanity and reinforcing the street life of the district, while representatives of Newhallville have voiced their preference for grassy, park-like open space. Balmori is keenly interested in the idea of physical and social heterogeneity implied by alterations in the greenway's visual presence and function within different districts, even as it constitutes a physical and conceptual whole within the city.

Challenging the idea of urban disjunction—between various parts of the city and between communities and constituencies—Balmori's design considers current problems as economic, environmental, and regional opportunities: economic, as Greenway construction based on simple, non-highly technological design is a possible source of jobs for the least skilled communities; environmental, in its vision of this corridor as a place that values air, soil, water, plants, animals, and humans (no vehicles that use gasoline will be permitted, no petroleum-based materials or paving through which water cannot percolate will be used); regional, in its integration of the different populations along the canal line and regeneration of elements of the region, such as the American chestnut tree, which will be returned to the Eastern deciduous forest through its use in the corridor.

# Planning Study for

*Chan Krieger & Associates*

Central Artery ( Route 93 ) through Boston.

# Central Artery Corridor Boston

Boston's **Central Artery** project is an immense highway reconstruction effort intended to reclaim a pivotal downtown area bisected by an elevated expressway under a previous era's urban renewal program. As a planning consultant to the Central Artery project, architect Alex Krieger and his associate Tom Sieniewicz, of the Boston firm Chan Krieger & Associates, proposed a complex linear pattern of alternating blocks of buildings of various uses and small parks or squares marking sites of historic significance. The resulting checkerboard of infill development and sequential open spaces bordered by a pair of new avenues was one of four proposals that focused the local debate about the best use of the land to be reclaimed from the existing highway. The plan ultimately adopted by The Boston Redevelopment Authority reflects Krieger's design only in part, modifying his balance of open to built areas in order to preserve seventy-five percent of the site for open space. Final engineering of the tunnel is currently underway, along with major reconfigurations of the traffic flow in the surrounding area. It is estimated that this infrastructural work will require five to six more years before significant alterations to the above-ground urban fabric can begin.

Three-dimensional view of overall project.

Krieger has long concerned himself with the problem of reconciling the demands of contemporary planning with the traditional patterns of American city-making. His work strives to reflect the identity, or urban archaeology, of a particular environment while satisfying present circumstances, economic imperatives, and civic policy, though not necessarily conventional wisdom. Challenging the assumptions of city officials and various special interest groups that the Central Artery corridor should either be entirely reserved for open space or faithfully rebuilt to its historic scale and character, Krieger's design seizes instead on the potential of this two-mile-long by four-hundred-foot-wide highway scar to become a discernable new fabric in the city. A new district is created, which in the character of its individual squares reflects both its immediate surroundings and such local spatial antecedents as the form and proportion of Boston's historic Copley Square.

Collage of seven Copley Squares.



Besides its rejection of the kind of modern planning that brought highways and other auto-dominated usages into the heart of the city, the Central Artery corridor reclamation project raises a number of issues regarding present urban values. Among them are questions about the most meaningful forms of restoration and preservation, the viability and utility of large amounts of urban open space, and the interface between complex, multi-layered, innovative planning practices with equally complex bureaucratic and public processes.

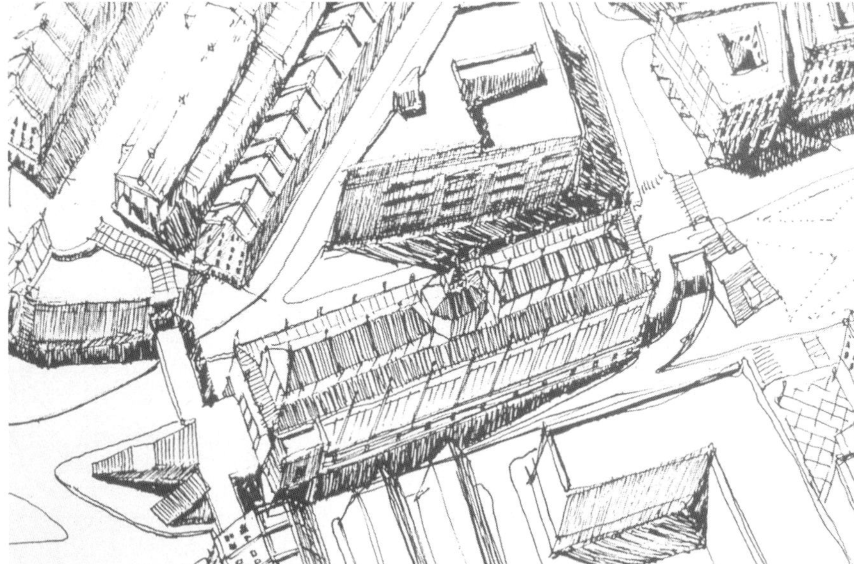

Faneuil Hall ramp parcel. Axo-sketch.

Existing Central Artery through downtown Boston, looking north. The Customs House Tower can be seen to the left center of the picture.

**Design Team**

Alex Krieger, Project Director
Thomas Sieniewicz, Project Urban Designer
Lawrence A. Chan
Peter Osler
Alex Anmahian
Clement Van Buren
Matthew Vanderborgh
Elise Adibi
Robert Rink
Ingrio Strong
June Eames
Eurico Francisco
Todd Fulshaw
Neil Harrigan
Nancy Kramer
Amy Lin
Chris Scovel
Willie Wong
Dan Donavan
Kathryn Clarke
Pat Cooleybeck

**Participants from the following organizations**

The Boston Redevelopment Authority
Vanasse Hangen Brustlin, Inc.
Boston Transportation Department
Massachusetts Executive Office of Transportation and Construction
Massachusetts Department of Public Works
Massachusetts Bay Transportation Authority North Station Team
Bruce Campbell & Associates, Inc.
Martin Sokoloff Associates
Artery Business Committee

Boston Redevelopment Authority proposal for the site. 1/100 scale model.

# A Greenway Plan for Metropolitan

*Johnson Fain and Pereira Associates*

Huntington Drive, El Sereno ( East Los Angeles ).

# LosAngeles

Only four percent of the total area of metropolitan Los Angeles is dedicated to public open space and recreational facilities, contrasting with San Francisco and Boston's nine percent and New York's seventeen percent. **A Greenway Plan for Metropolitan Los Angeles** envisions a four-hundred-mile linear, public, open space system that would use recreational biking, jogging, and equestrian trails to link parks, beaches, historical and cultural sites, schools, universities, transportation hubs, and other important public facilities throughout the region. Created by the Los Angeles firm of Johnson Fain and Pereira Associates, the plan uses available land resources to create a grid of connecting public open space from the river and flood control channels, utilities rights-of-way, and abandoned rail rights-of-way that have until now been isolators and barriers.

Abandoned rail corridor in Watts ( South Central Los Angeles ).

Proposed community garden plots; plaza at the Towers; and a new community services building behind.

Flood channel easement and high school in background ( West San Fernando Valley ).

Improved bike path and Farmers' Market, connected to high school ( West San Fernando Valley ).

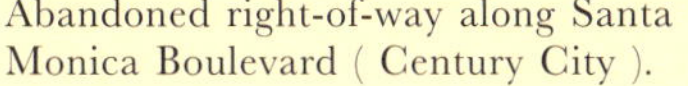

Abandoned right-of-way along Santa Monica Boulevard ( Century City ).

Proposed promenade along Santa Monica Boulevard.

Although many perceive Los Angeles as a modern autopia, there are in fact hundreds of thousands of people without cars, living primarily in central city locations with only limited access to local or regional recreation and employment opportunities. Currently, residential districts are dominated by the single-family detached home; and open space consists primarily of streets and private yards, rather than public parks, plazas, and parkways. But there have always been rich Mexican-American, African-American, and Jewish cultures in Los Angeles, with distinctly different appreciations for the incorporation of streets and plazas into public life. These cultures are now being joined by large numbers of immigrants from Central and South America, Asia, the Middle East, the Pacific, and Eastern Europe. These cultures have long-standing traditions of active use of public open space. For them, promenades, plazas, parks, and streets are important extensions of private living space. The new face of Los Angeles is one that will look toward increased respect for public open space in the life of the city.

The Greenway Plan proposes to synthesize a grid of public open space from existing infrastructural elements. It capitalizes on the implementation of the MetroRail transit system and offers a new organizational structure for future land-use decisions. New green transit corridors will give added structure to the city, with commuter and recreational bike paths, windbreaks, and jogging paths. Abandoned rail rights-of-way that are not included in future transit schemes will join the nationwide Rails to Trails program. River and flood control channels already used by equestrians will be improved with landscaping and additional park uses. Electric power rights-of-way now used by nurseries and Christmas tree farms will continue to provide "green" income-producing sites that can be incorporated into the public greenway system and support local commercial development. Furthermore, by identifying opportunities for multi-family housing along open space corridors and near public facilities, the Greenway system will help offset increased density in Los Angeles.

Proposed new transit and pedestrian allée for Huntington Drive, El Sereno.

| Design Team | Client |
|---|---|
| William H. Fain, Jr., FAIA, Principal | Beth Rogers, Pacific Earth Resources, |
| Robert P. Shaffer, AIA | Camarillo, California |
| Patric B. Dawe, AIA | |
| Donna Vaccarino, AIA | |
| Mark R. Gershen | |
| Juan C. Begazo | |
| Katherine W. Rinne | |
| Lori Gates East | |
| Neil Kritzinger | |



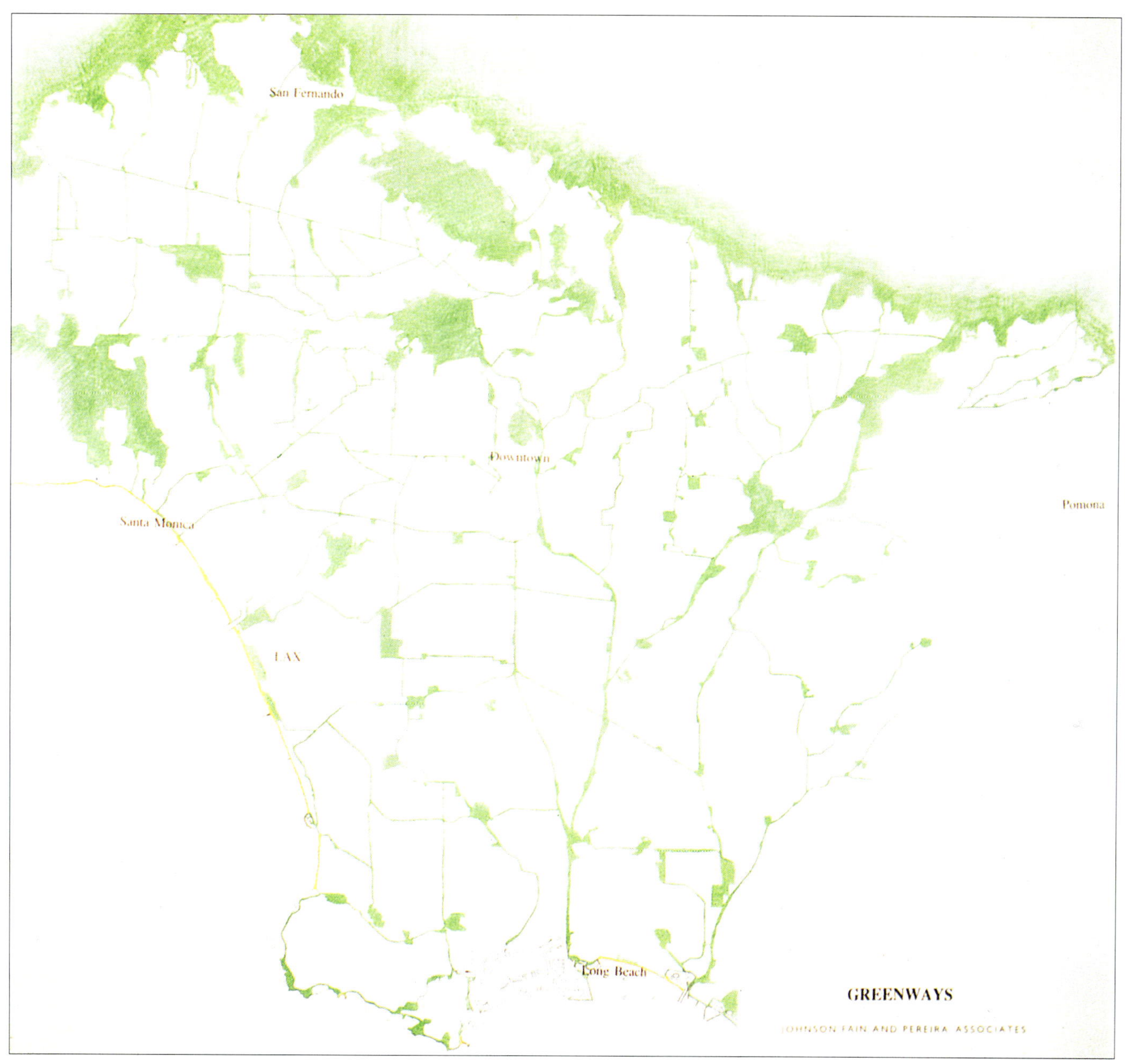

# The Master Plan for Faubourg Québec

**Faubourg Québec** is a major urban redevelopment project on the site of a former railway yard bordering the St. Lawrence River and the old city and port of Montreal. Conceived as an intervention within the existing urban fabric, the project reflects the urge to create a substantial new community of housing in close proximity to the

# Montreal

Massing model.

View along waterfront esplanade.
( Rendering by Saucier Perrotte/Roper )

city center to respond to a broad range of social, cultural, and economic objectives. Among these are providing public access to the waterfront, increasing the urban housing stock as an alternative to suburban sprawl, and creating a variety of housing types to support a diverse social mix.

Typical residential courtyard. ( Rendering by Saucier Perrotte/Roper )

Proposed cafe under the viaduct of rue Notre-Dame. ( Rendering by Saucier Perrotte/Roper )

Of particular interest to an understanding of the physical revision of cities is the process whereby the design guidelines for Faubourg Québec were established. Under the aegis of the SHDM (Société d'Habitation et de Développement de Montréal/ Housing and Development Society of Montreal), several distinct groups of local and foreign architects were invited to participate in the conception of the project over a three-year period, building upon one another's work and ideas about the appropriate development of the site. Close attention was paid to the character of the surrounding area as a starting point for all aspects of the project, rather than adopting a "tabula rasa" approach lacking in sensitivity to the historical and morphological basis of the city.

The articulation of an undervalued or even "invisible" site within a broader urban context underlies the first phase of planimetric studies of the project. Emerging from the explorations of these initial proposals were a related set of more detailed studies of key structuring elements of the site. An additional series of pictorial studies of the evolving project served to communicate the identity and reality of the proposed urban environment.

The project for Faubourg Québec inverts the conventions of urban design by first establishing a coherent and permanent public domain. It responds to the memory of the city at three distinct scales—the city (the waterfront esplanade), the neighborhood (Viger Square and the bridge building of rue Notre Dame) and the individual block (the network of residential streets and courtyards). It also responds to the reality of current development practice by providing a self-critical flexibility and evolving definition in the creation of built form.

| Design Team | Architectural Consultants | Additional Consultants |
|---|---|---|
| Bureau de projet Faubourg Québec (SHDM- Société d'habitation et de développement de Montréal) | Melvin Charney | Georges Adamcyzk, Professor |
| Pierre Desjardins, Director | Peter Roper | Robert Galarneau, Urban Planner |
| Pierre-Luc Dumas, Architect, Assistant Director-Planning | Jacques Rousseau | Mark Poddubiuk, Architect |
| Berridge Lewinberg Greenberg Ltd., Urban Planners | Peter Rose | |
| Cardinal Hardy et associés, Architects | Saucier & Perrotte | Poullaouec-Gonidec, Jacobs et St-Denis, Landscape Architects |
| Dupuis et Le Tourneux, Architects | Herman Hertzberger | Arkéos Inc., Archaeologists |
| Poirier, Dépatie, Architects | Hildebrand Machleidt | Lavalin, Engineers |
| Provencher Roy et Associée, Architects | Daniel Solomon | Nicolet Chartrand Knoll, Structural Engineers |

Plan of the proposed street grid and public space.

From among these many investigations, both parallel and sequential, as well as from numerous feasibility and market analyses conducted to ascertain the viability of this major addition to the urban fabric, the SHDM project staff crafted a master plan for the development of the site. This plan addresses such issues as overall organization of the thirty-acre area, its hierarchy of public space and urban landscape, circulation and movement, land use (residential, commercial, cultural / recreational), and zoning (building heights, proportions, and density), providing cohesion and definition, yet also a high degree of flexibility to what will later be built in Faubourg Québec. Forming the basis for a subsequent architectural competition for the project's first phase under the joint sponsorship of SHDM and private developers, the master plan is intended to frame rather than to predetermine the architecture of the individual buildings that will be realized over the next ten years.



Claude Beaulac, Economist
CAMI, Market Analysts
Jules Hurtubise, Economist

Service d'habitation et de développement urbain-Ville de Montréal
Service des loisirs et de développement communautaire-Ville de Montréal
Service des travaux publics-Ville de Montréal

Study model of the bridge building at rue Notre-Dame.

Aerial view of site, looking east.

The Los Angeles community of **Playa Vista**, a privately-sponsored project intended to house 25,000 people on the largest undeveloped tract of land in the city, represents the most ambitious attempt to date to offer new standards of density and infrastructural self-sustainability in the American urban context. Surrounded by residential, commercial, and industrial uses, as well as waterfront

# PlayaVista LosAngeles



Master plan organizing neighborhoods within a system of streets, open spaces, and parks.

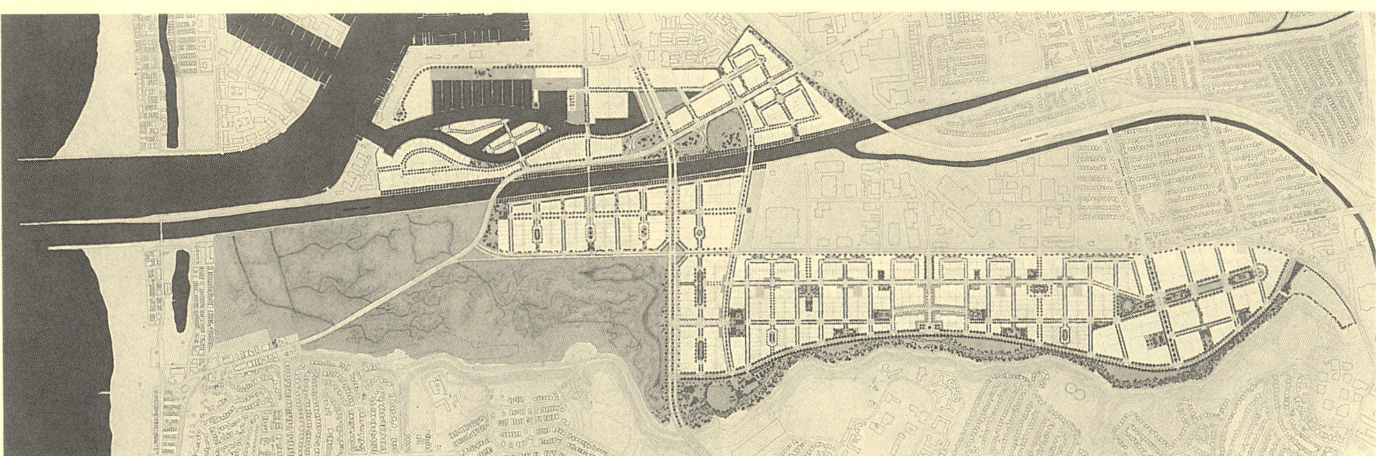

Housing prototypes.

and wetlands, its current master plan departs significantly from several previous plans that had emphasized intensive commercial development. Planned for Maguire Thomas Partners by a team of principals from the architectural firms of Andres Duany and Elizabeth Plater-Zyberk, Hanna/Olin, Ltd., Legorreta Arquitectos, Elizabeth Moule and Stefanos Polyzoides, and Moore Ruble Yudell, it is envisioned as an urban infill project oriented to the pedestrian and including a mixture of offices, commercial and recreational facilities, and housing types.

Typical neighborhood park and mixed-use fabric.

Master Planning Team

Andres Duany and Elizabeth Plater-Zyberk, Architects and Town Planners
Ricardo Legorreta, Legorreta Arquitectos
Laurie Olin, Hanna / Olin, Ltd.
Elizabeth Moule and Stefanos Polyzoides, Architects and Urbanists
Buzz Yudell, Moore Ruble Yudell



A clear hierarchy of street and open space shapes the physical structure of Playa Vista's neighborhoods. While most are residential in character, each provides the elements necessary for daily life within comfortable walking distance. Intended to create a more vital social and economic community, its plan also seeks to endow Playa Vista with a greater sense of place and responsiveness to the region's historical urban context. These elements stand in opposition to the physical and social character of the typical planned community and seek to counter and redirect the rampant manifestations of suburban sprawl and "edge cities" that have emerged in the post-World War II period.

Neighborhood park framed by medium-density residential buildings.

| Developer | Consultant Team |
|---|---|
| Maguire Thomas Partners - Playa Vista | Psomas and Associates, Civil Engineering |
| Nelson C. Rising, Partner-in-Charge | Latham and Watkins, Legal Counsel |
| Douglas J. Gardner | Barton-Aschman Associates, Inc., Transportation Engineering |
| Joel H. Stensby | Sharon Lockhart, Environmental Counselor |
| John T. McAlister | June Kailes and Bill Jordan, Disability Consultants |
| Randy S. Johnson | |
| Thomas S. Ricci | |

Conceived to be implemented in several phases, Playa Vista has been hailed as a model for urban growth and a kind of social ecology in its complex mixture of usages and its emphasis on sustainability. Noteworthy features include the containment and treatment of its own waste water and the restoration of the adjacent Ballona Wetlands, one of the few remaining tidal marshes in Southern California. In addition to the integral presence of transportation networks linking the area with the rest of the city, the project also incorporates measures to mitigate the impact of anticipated future traffic on the surrounding communities. While the political processes surrounding approval of the first phase of Playa Vista, scheduled to begin in 1995, are extensive and have been controversial, it is clear that this project will be closely watched by proponents and critics alike for its impact on the future of managed growth in the American urban landscape.

# Region2040Study

*Calthorpe Associates*

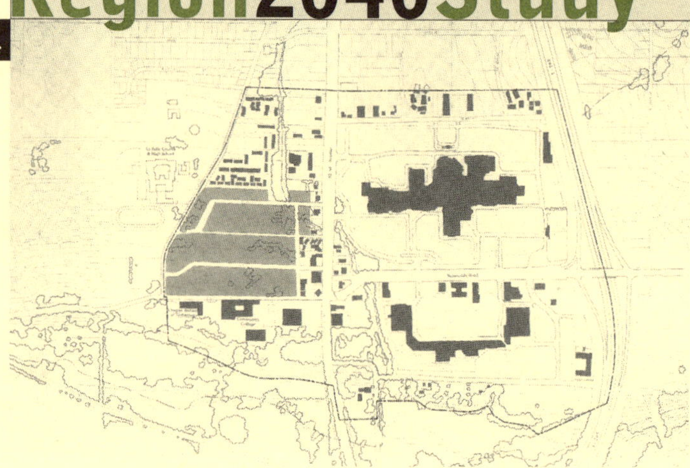

Plan of existing conditions.

Clackamas Town Center.

Two different concepts of linearity are fundamental to a new vision of regional form and urbanism—they are the skin and bones of the regional city. The first line is the Urban Growth Boundary, which sets a definable limit to regional sprawl. The second group of lines, an expanding set of transit corridors reaching out from the urban center to the suburbs, shapes the internal form of the region. In Peter Calthorpe's view, the viability of walkable neighborhoods and the quality of the public realm are intimately linked to such regional policies.

Complementing the urban growth boundary at the regional scale is the use of transit as the organizing armature of growth within the boundary. Instead of freeways, light rail and transit form a framework for an expanded pedestrian domain. Requiring walkable origins and destinations along the system, this almost remedial urbanism has at its center the pedestrian—the need for humanly scaled streets, mixed-use neighborhoods, diversity of population, and formative public space.

The Region 2040 Study of Portland, Oregon, works with the two lines at both regional and neighborhood levels to tackle the question of how the region should expand. It introduces the necessary questions of how to convert existing sprawl into urban communities and how to configure new neighborhoods in developed and undeveloped areas. Anticipating a population increase of one million over the next fifty years, Portland's regional government sponsored the development of several growth concepts to explore the trade-offs of "growing up or growing out." Calthorpe Associates was commissioned to examine eight sites within the region and to illustrate how they would look fifty years from today. Two of the plans adjudicate these disparate goals by examining alternative redevelopment strategies for both a large regional shopping mall and a declining suburban downtown neighborhood to the west, as well as exploring the urban design implications of bringing the light-rail line to the two sites along northern or central alignments.

# PortlandOregon

Client

METRO ( Portland Metropolitan Regional Planning Authority ),
John Fregonese, Mark Turpel, and Dave Ausherman

Design Team

Peter Calthorpe, Principal Urban Designer
Shelley Poticha, Principal Planner and Project Manager
Canan Tolon and Mark Mack, Perspectivists
Matt Taecker, Phil Erickson, Senior Urban Designers
Catherine Chang, Regional Graphics and Urban Design



Design and Graphics

Joe Scanga, Sue Chan
Maya Foty, David Arkin
Isabelle Duvivier, Donald Moffat
Peggy Chan, Tom Ford

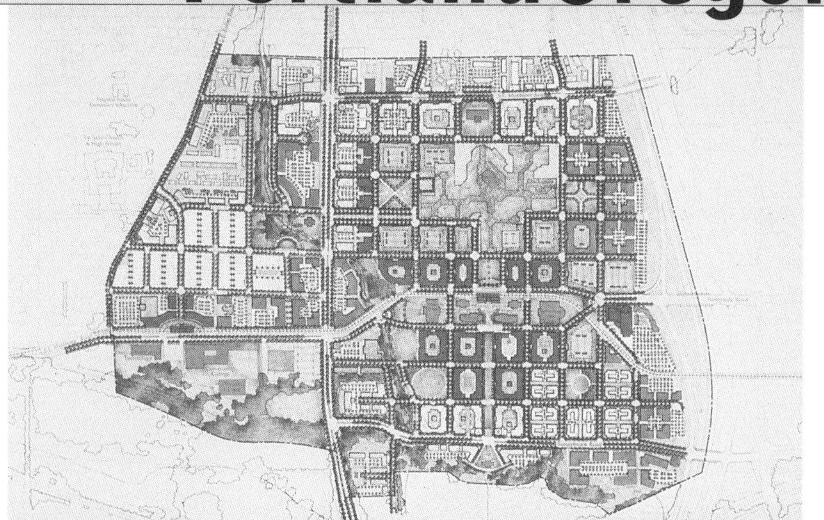

Plan of proposed alterations.

The Clackamas Town Center Plan takes a new approach to "place-making" within the context of a regional mall. In this scheme, the scale of the downtown Portland street-grid is applied to the surface parking lots and the southern portion of the shopping mall. New mixed-use buildings are placed within this grid, combining retail, office, and residential uses to foster a diversity and intensity that replicates a classic downtown. The seven-lane barrier of Sunnyside Road is removed and replaced with a one-way couplet and a central transit station/civic corridor that can now become a community focal point.

The second of these investigations, a plan for the moderately-sized suburban community of Central Beaverton, looks at the potential to create distinct urban places out of a predominantly commercial strip district. Three planned light-rail stops are used as the spark for new development and the need to provide ridership within walking distance. Each stop will have a different character and purpose. The western station becomes a civic center, with a performing arts center, library, community college, and town green; high density housing and convenience retail dominate the plan for the central station; and the eastern station serves as an employment node, with intensive office development. New development is placed on vacant and underutilized properties to create different types of walkable neighborhoods.

These alternate futures are intended to demonstrate the potential of the site, both responding to the creation of transit in the area and to the differing effects of moving the urban growth boundary. Although pedestrians will not displace the car anytime soon, their absence in our thinking and planning is a fundamental source of failure in our new developments. To plan as if there were pedestrians may be a self-fulfilling act; it will give children some autonomy, the elderly basic access, and others the choice to walk again. To plan as if there were pedestrians will turn suburbs into towns, projects into neighborhoods, and networks into communities.

# SustainableArchitecture:

*Angélil / Graham Architecture*

Site model.

# Town Center for Esslingen

Aerial view of Esslingen, Switzerland.

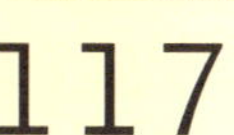

The design of Los Angeles-based architects Marc Angélil and Sarah Graham for a new **Town Center for Esslingen**, a small community ten miles from the city of Zurich, Switzerland, explores the integration of technology and alternative energy use. In the zone between the city and the countryside, this town center consists of fifty housing units, office, retail, and light industrial space, a train station, post office, station restaurant and cafe, farmers' cooperative market, and underground parking. Like the transit-oriented development being investigated and applied in the U.S., the project seeks to provide the components of a viable pedestrian-oriented community around a light-rail connection to an adjacent city. Yet unlike the transit-oriented developments planned in the U.S., the appearance of the buildings in Esslingen town center is decidedly not contextual in terms of historical or vernacular references. The project instead attempts an architectural integration with the existing conditions of the rural landscape, its topographical formation, the predominant natural vegetation, and the open fields of existing farm land. In their general scale and disposition, the buildings of the town center recall the kind of density and topographically-responsive configuration characteristic of the traditional European town, but do not mimic traditional building types.

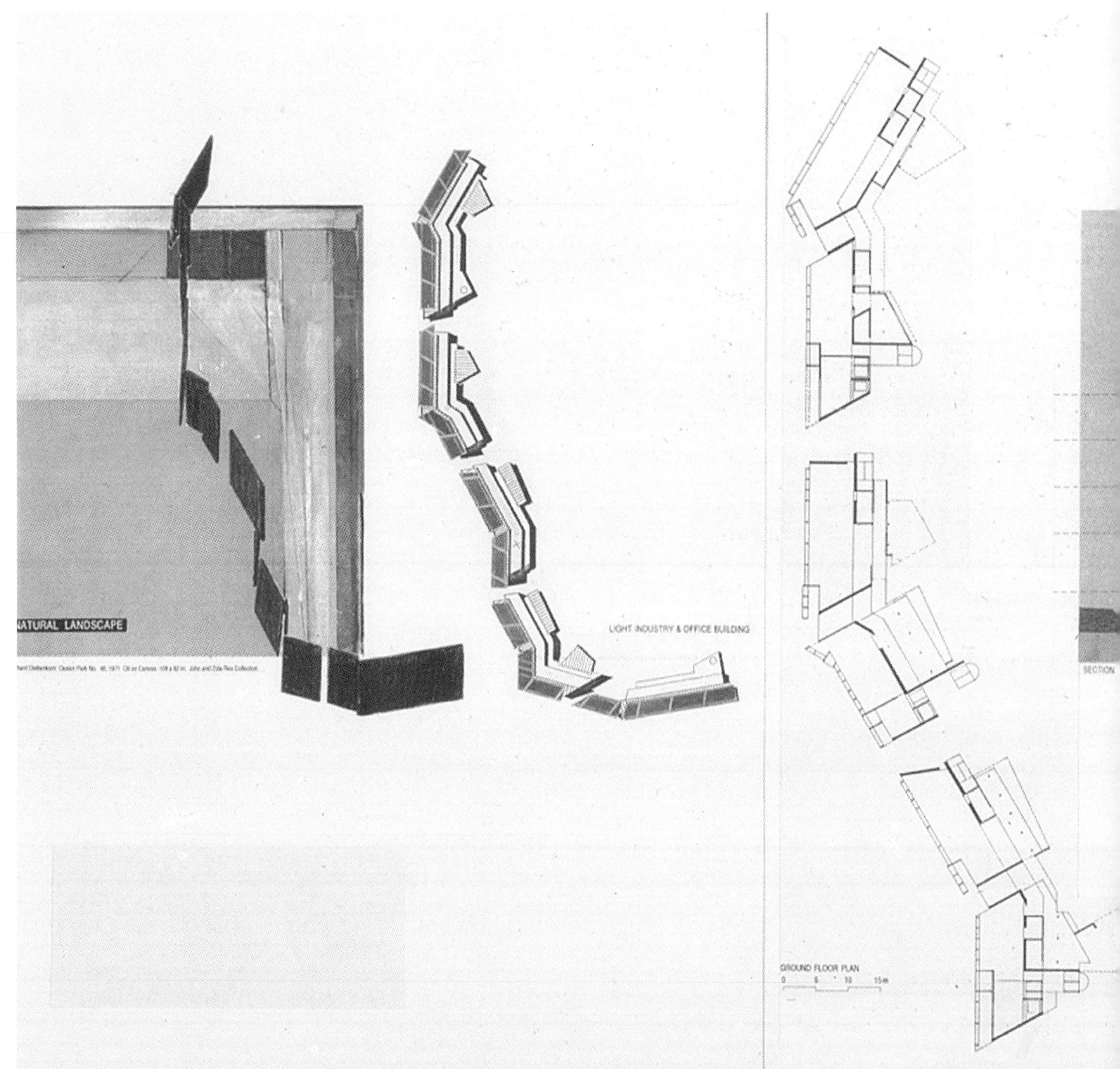


The Wall Edge : light industry, office, and commercial buildings.



This project's design reflects a conviction that a coexistence between the natural and the man-made can be attained by careful integration of the required buildings into the existing built and natural landscape. Undertaken as a kind of case study project sponsored by the local authorities and the engineering firm of Basler & Hofmann, it seeks to encourage dense building and efficient land use. A small river crossing the site allows for division of the project into two distinct areas. On its south side are situated freestanding public buildings and open spaces. Along its north side, a penetrable wall of office, retail, and light industrial buildings is delineated, its face utilizing the southern exposure of the water's edge with a solar collector wall of passive and active energy elements. Behind this zone stands a dense residential fabric of row housing and courtyards.

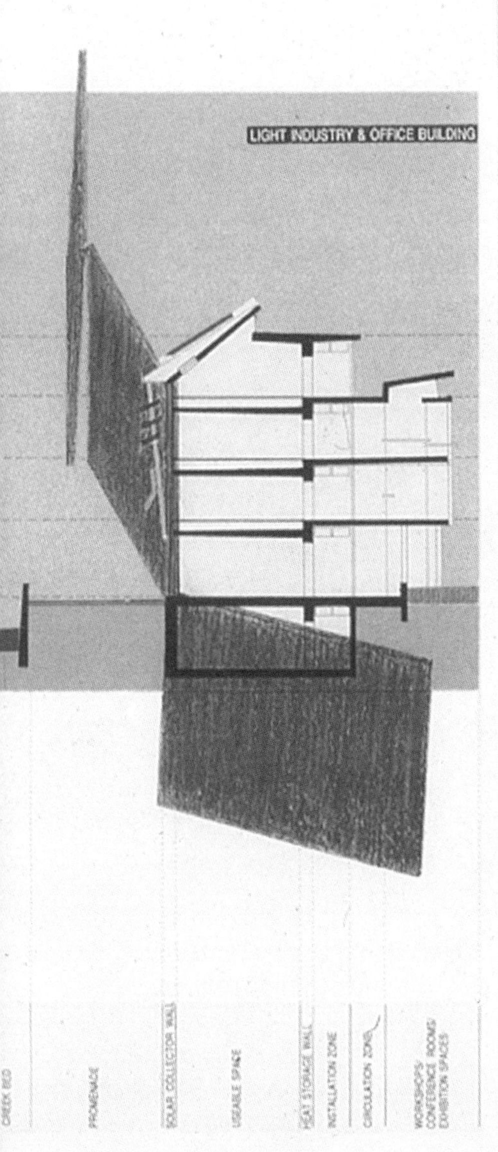


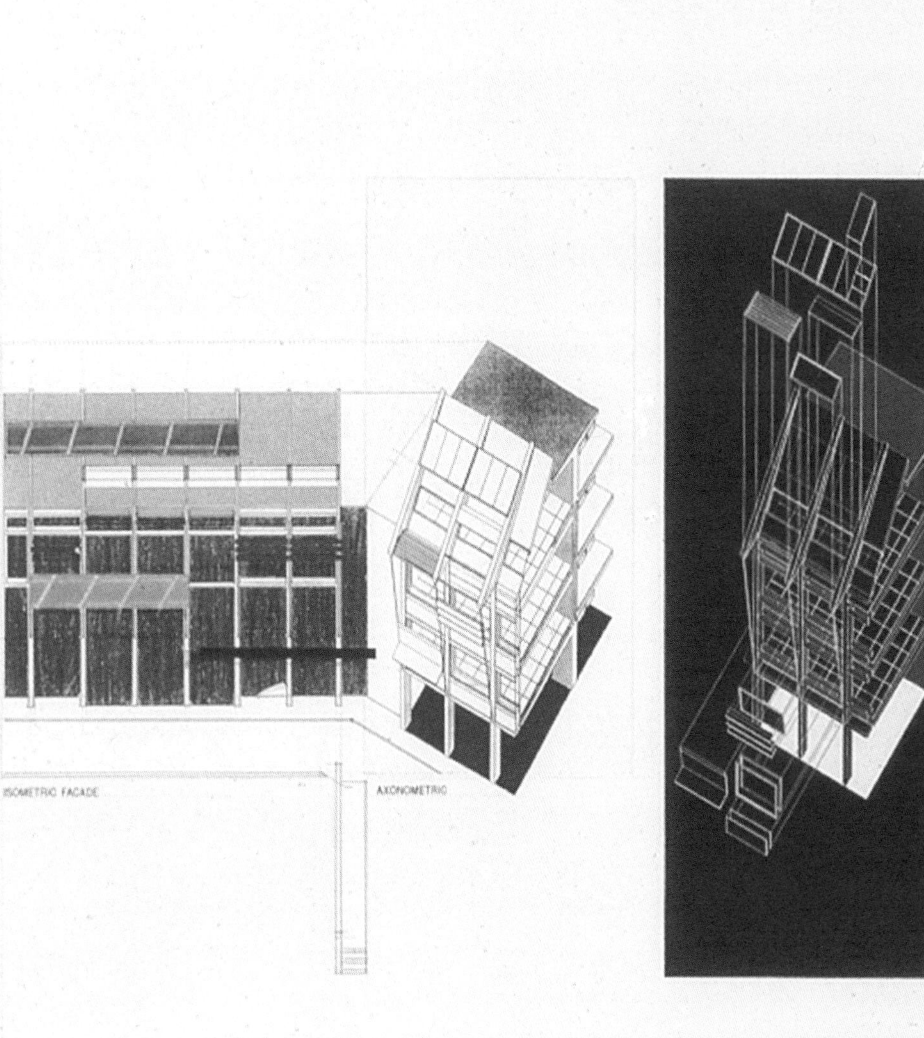


Solar collectors and photovoltaic panels form sloped roof elements on the housing and adjacent office buildings. When producing more power than utilized, the excess is designed to feed back into the utility system which will function as an energy bank.

Experimental on many fronts, the planning and design of Esslingen Town Center establishes the basic conditions for intensive solar energy application and for a multiplicity of uses. Further environmentally sensitive elements such as recyclable building materials and development of measures to prolong the life span of structures are being investigated by the project's clients. Their goal is to achieve ways to reduce energy use in the building sector by forty percent by the year 2020.

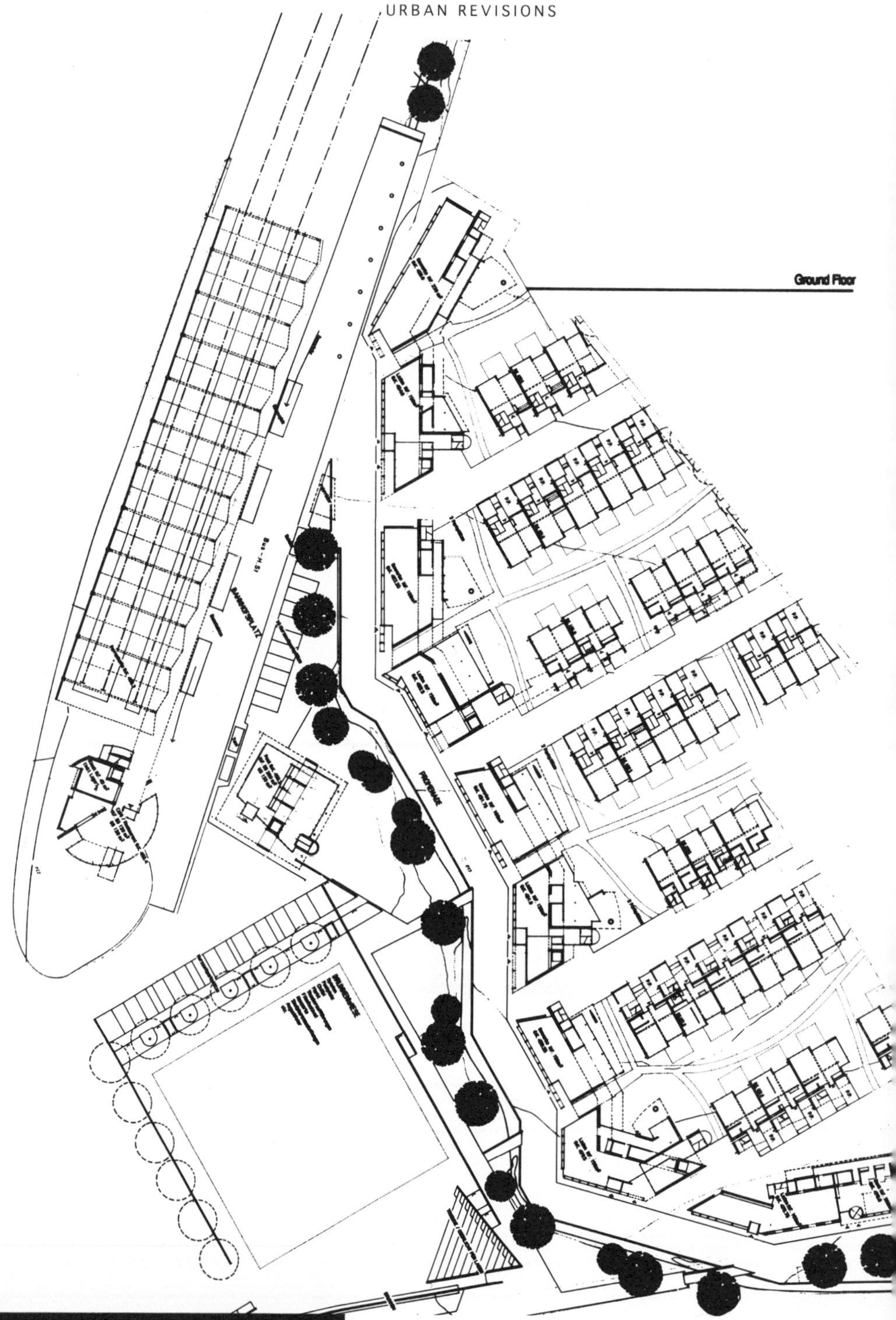

Ground Floor

Working model : The Public Realm.

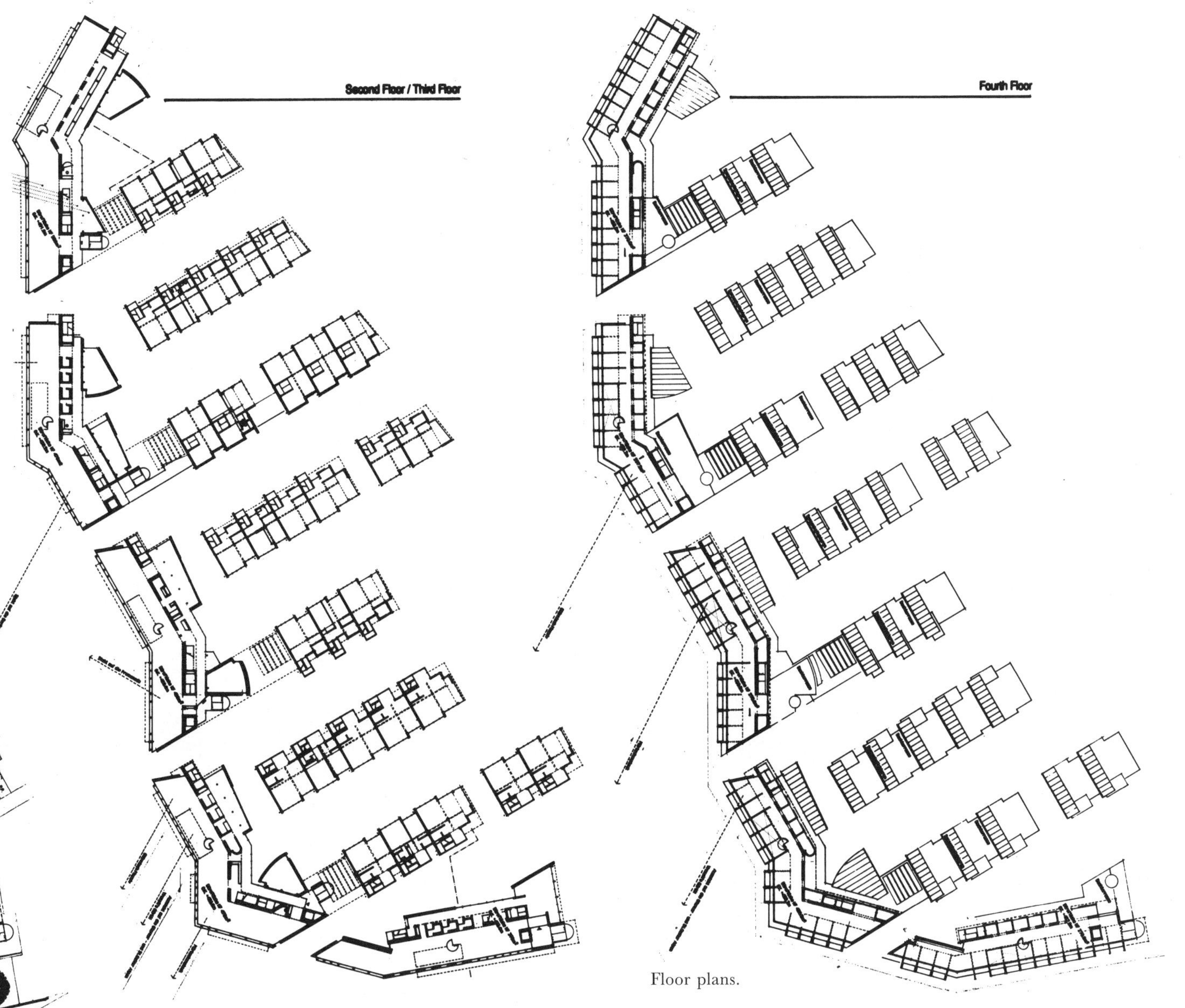


Floor plans.

| Design Team | Consultants | Structural Engineer | Mechanical Engineers |
|---|---|---|---|
| Marc Angélil, Principal<br>Sarah Graham, Principal<br>Manuel Scholl, Principal<br><br>Reto Pfenninger<br>Matthias Kobelt<br>Lukas Felder<br>William Paluch<br>Anthony Paradowski<br>Richard Douglass<br>Thomas Schwendener<br>Ryan Smith<br>Leslie Sung | Basler & Hofmann Consulting Engineers, Zurich<br>Konrad Basler<br>Ernst Hofmann | Basler & Hofmann Consulting Engineers, Zurich<br>Sandro Spadini<br><br>CAD Presentation for Exhibition<br>University of Southern California<br>Karen M. Kensek<br>Douglas E. Noble<br>Victoria Turkel<br>John Cornelius<br>Tim Eilers | Basler & Hofmann Consulting Engineers, Zurich<br>Charles Filleux<br>Fritz Nünlist |

# Proposal for a Military Base Conversion

Working drawing.

# Southwestern United States

*Michael Sorkin Studio*

Design Team

Michael Sorkin, Principal

Andrei Vovk
Peter Kormer
Doug Bergert
Patrick Clifford

Detail of study model.

New York-based architect and writer Michael Sorkin has long used the form of the city as a basis for theoretical investigation. Strongly committed to the idea of invention rather than to approaches based on tradition and recollection, Sorkin's highly speculative and even utopian work proceeds from a number of key assumptions about the relationship between physical space and public life. These assumptions include the idea of the "rephysicalized" city of many centers rather than of one primary center, the notion of an urbanism accommodating the widest variety of choices about ways to live, the primacy of transportation and human movement, and the desirability of the city as a site of distinctiveness and autonomy yet also of propinquity.

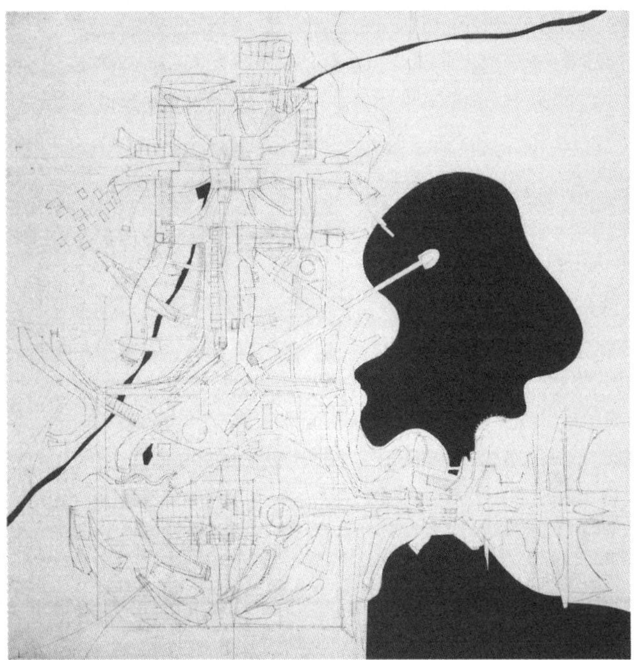

Study drawing.

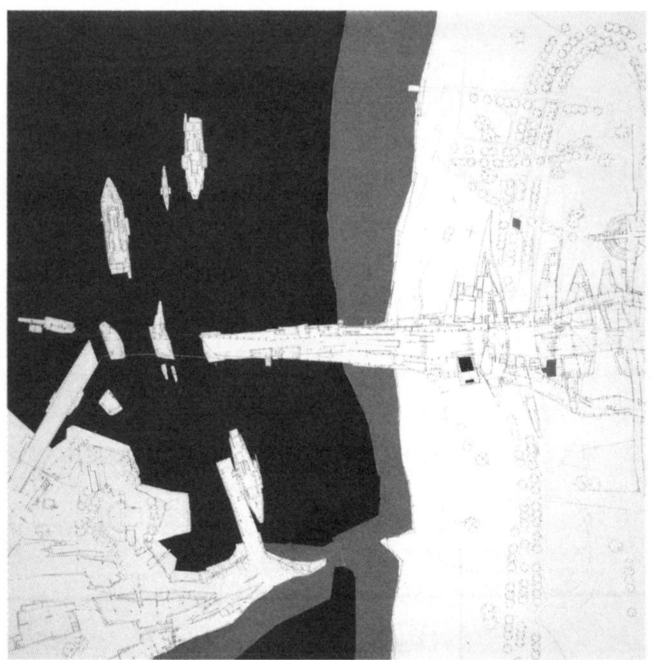

Plan at grade.

As the one purely theoretical project included in Urban Revisions, Sorkin's design for the transformation of a site in the southwestern United States, on property currently occupied by the military, is emblematic of a visionary sensibility about the redesign of public space. The project investigates formal arrangements made possible in a city that privileges human locomotion, in which the free juxtapositions of electronic space have a liberating effect on the physical relations of urban space, and in which ideas about sustainability—both ecological and economic—are pervasive.

Sorkin envisages the city of "Weed," located on the site of the Yuma Proving Ground along the Colorado River north of Yuma, Arizona, as a utopian community combining futuristic and agrarian ideals. Juxtaposing innovative and extensive public transportation networks, designed by converted military engineers from the old base, with green, terraced hillsides and a patchwork of fields and ponds laced with irrigation canals, Sorkin's city is organized around diverse and intimate neighborhoods, in which carpenters and artists work alongside engineers and scientists. The project is informed by an optimistic view of the city as a means of national renewal, as a bulwark of democratic culture, and as a site of special pleasure.

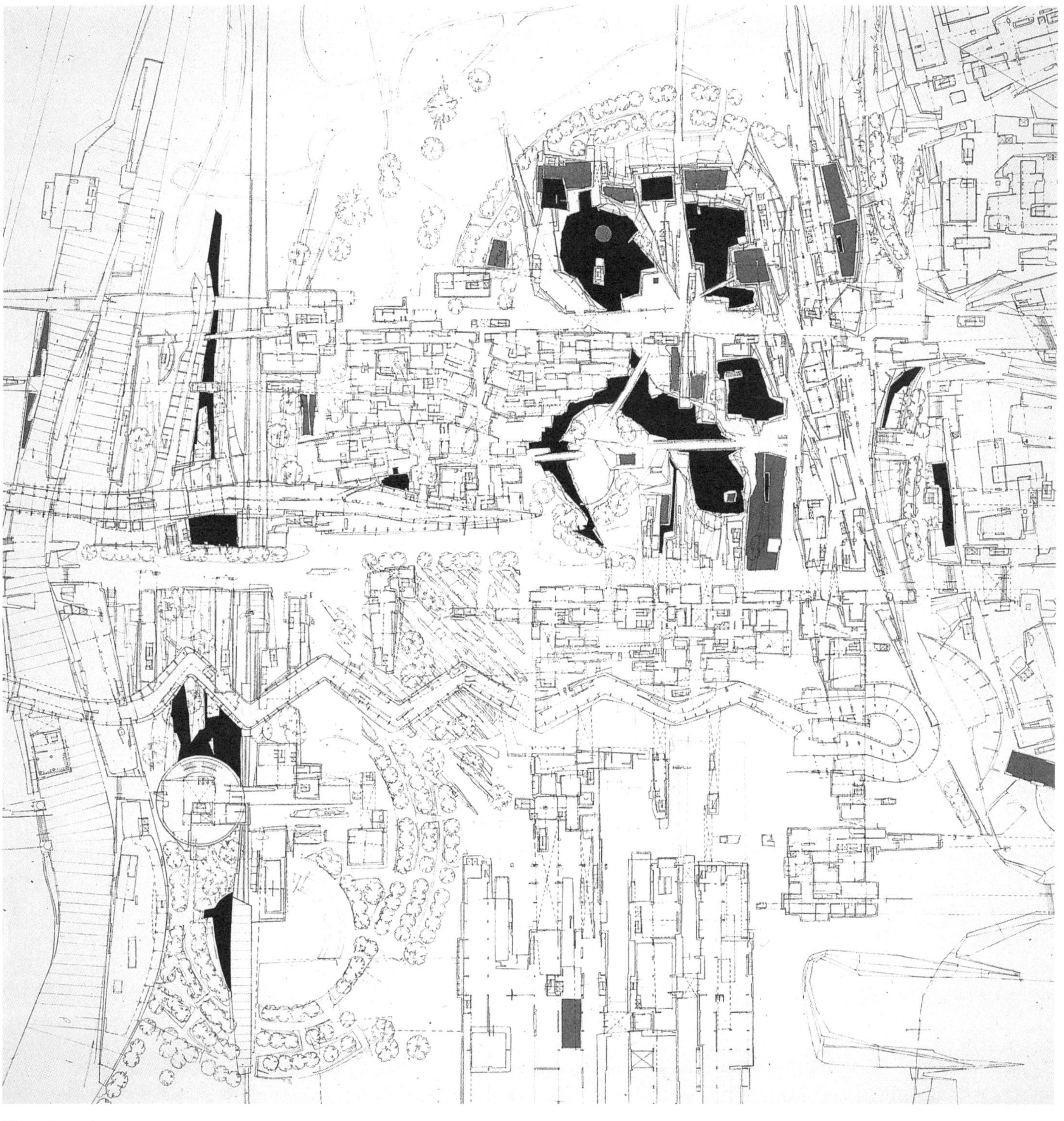

Plan at grade.

# VisionPlan

*Agrest & Gandelsonas, Architects*

Aerial view of site.

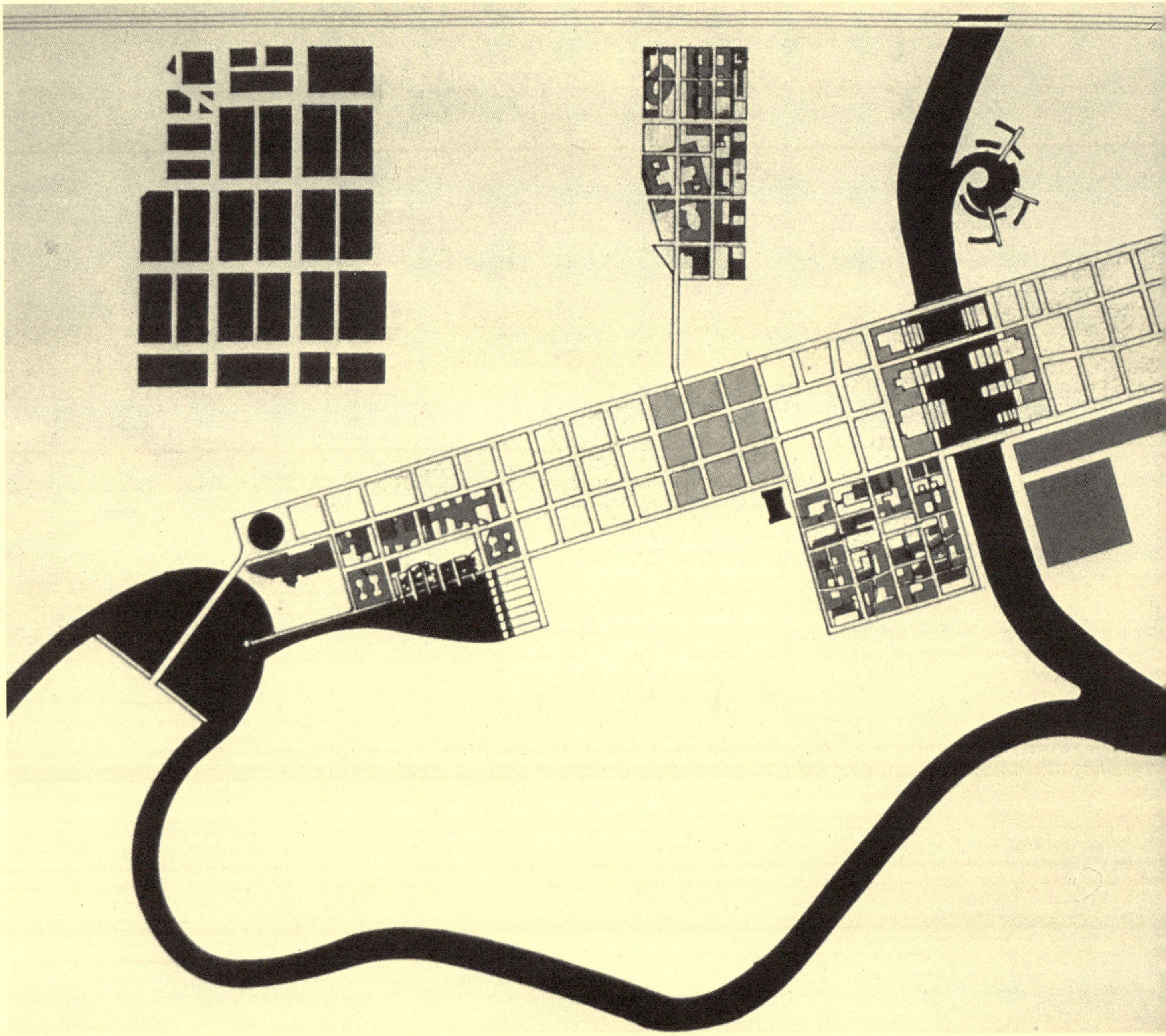

Proposed residential neighborhoods depicted in figure / ground.

Des Moines skyline.

# DesMoines

Architects Diana Agrest and Mario Gandelsonas have undertaken an extensive planning and design study for the city of Des Moines, Iowa. Begun in an academic context, the **Vision Plan for Des Moines** was established as a concerted physical planning effort in 1990. Extending investigations developed throughout much of their work into the textual analysis of urban form, their readings of Des Moines reveal points of connection and overlay which in turn become the bases for potential new physical relationships. Instead of the traditional "Master Plan," the Vision Plan has developed strategies that range from restriction to freedom, from determinacy to indeterminacy, from order to chaos, that focus on moments and not on a rigid plan. The process provides a menu of alternative design strategies and tactics that leaves room for market forces to influence the final configuration of the projects. The Vision Plan incorporates such specific proposals as terrace-like connectors to enhance the relationship between the river and an updated Civic Center; a cohesive and appropriately-scaled pattern of landscaping to create a visual and physical transition from the airport to the downtown core; the creation of a lake from a section of the river at the entrance of downtown, both marking it and creating a new landmark for Des Moines; a checkerboard configuration of parks and buildings as a formal and economic revitalization of the East side; and the introduction of several residential neighborhoods into the existing downtown urban fabric. Besides reconstitution or reevaluation of such linkages, Agrest and Gandelsonas's study of buildings as both fabric and object addresses massing and mediations of scale in the urban context. The plan reflects and responds to the concerns of many constituencies within the city, ranging from its Chamber of Commerce and business interests to residents of underserved neighborhoods seeking to upgrade their housing stock and become more fully integrated with the life of the city.

Hillside terracing concept for the development of outdoor spaces.

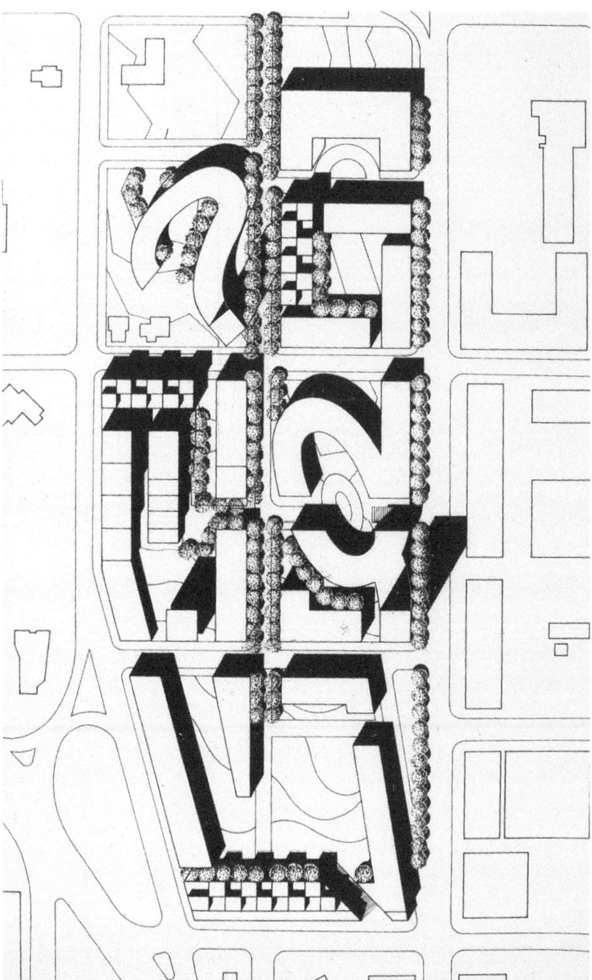

Plan of hillside neighborhood, depicting massing and trees.

Vision Plan

Agrest + Gandelsonas, Architects
Diana Agrest, Design Director
Mario Gandelsonas, Project Director
Claire Weisz, Project Manager
Nick Arne
Evan Donglis
Tom Fletchner
Yoko Hiroshi
David Ruff
Mark Yoes

Exhibition

Joseph Rosa, Design and Coordination
Juergen Mayer
Jasmit Singh Rangr
Cameron Wu, Computer

Des Moines Planning and Zoning

James M. Grant, Director
Patricia Zingsheim
Robert Nickle

Vision Plan

Chairman
John Pat Dorrian, Mayor, City of Des Moines

Richard Brannan
Melva Bucksbaum, Vice Chair
James Cownie, Vice Chair
Mark Feldman
Robert Houser
Andrew Mooney
Mark Putney
Sarah A. Matthews, Administrator

Hillside II

Environmental Design Group
William Ludwig, Architect
Allen Bowman, Architect

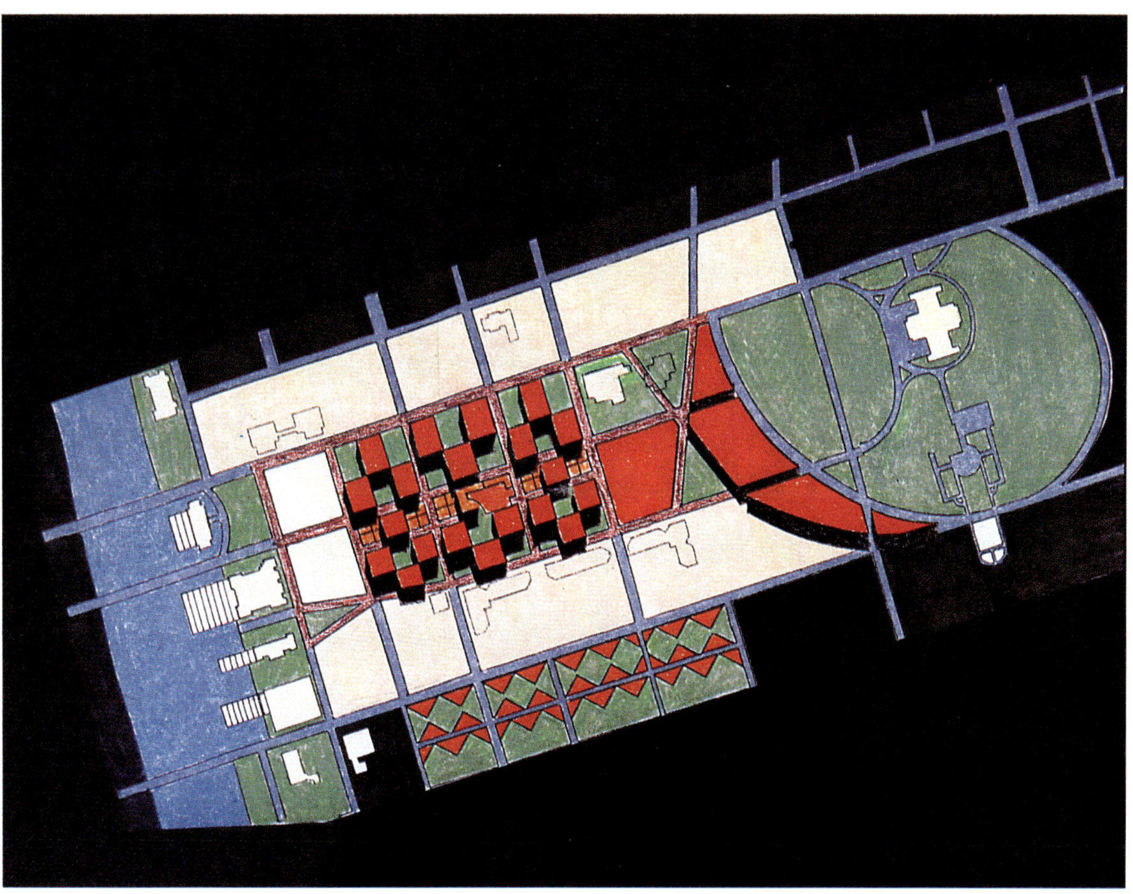

The East Side: Plan of mixed use development between the River and Capitol.

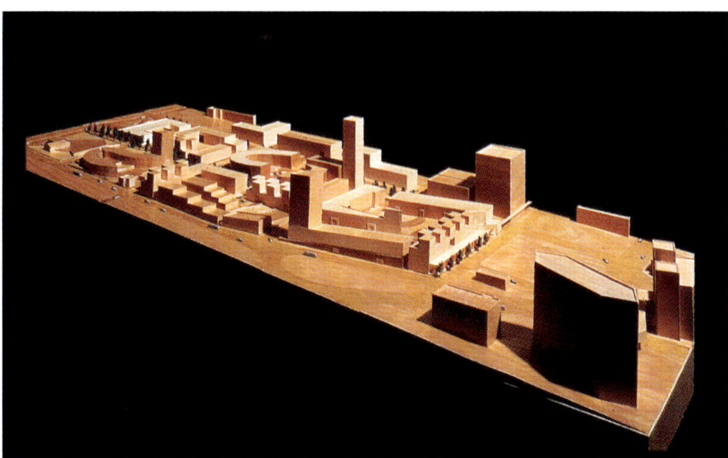

Hillside neighborhood model, with massing and program to conform with design guidelines of the Vision Plan.

During the Vision Plan's development, Agrest and Gandelsonas employed a formal, abstract method of concretizing and presenting their ideas through an ongoing process of dialogue with the "client," a ninety-member steering committee chaired by the mayor and involving every sector of the community. Explication of their diagrammatic, apparently cryptic, drawings initiated a fresh kind of discussion about the physical properties of urban form as the basis for specific economic development opportunities. Using the aesthetic as a way to initiate consideration of the social, their analysis of links, connections, splits, and divisions helped to generate ideas about refinement and reactivation of ill-defined or underused areas of the city.

The Vision Plan's goals include the genesis of a physical environment that reflects a deepened understanding of the specific aesthetic character of the American city. In the architects' view, recognition of the urban processes and formal structures of the American city as determined by political and economic forces radically different from those of Europe is crucial to the successful analysis and reconstitution of the urban fabric.

*Elizabeth Moule and Stefanos Polyzoides, Architects and Urbanists*

Aerial view of downtown Los Angeles.

# Downtown Strategic Plan for Los Angeles

Los Angeles-based architects Elizabeth Moule and Stefanos Polyzoides, commissioned by the city's Community Redevelopment Agency, have created and headed a team of urban designers to develop a Downtown Strategic Plan for Los Angeles. Envisioned as a guide to the next twenty-five years, the Downtown Strategic Plan departs significantly from the premises of earlier approaches to the structure of an urban business district. With the goal of reconstructing a pedestrian, mixed-use, safe, clean, and green center for the Los Angeles metropolis as an economic and cultural necessity, the plan grew out of a five-year-long public process directed by a sixty-five-member committee representing a wide range of interests. Its conceptual structure organizes downtown into three principal parts: "the City," an area of intensely mixed office, retail, civic, residential, and entertainment uses; "the Markets," dominated by a large, diverse concentration of wholesale businesses with clusters of housing, retail, and a range of social services; and in between, "the Center City," the historic core of downtown, as well as its theater, garment, and jewelry districts. Within these, the plan pinpoints several distinct physical frameworks in need of enhancement and vitalization, some the products of urban renewal and some with historical architectural importance. To enable the visualization of potential within each district, the architects generated designs for sixteen "catalytic projects," presenting a microcosmic view of potential alterations consistent with the plan's emphasis on seeding growth rather than imposing a fixed end vision.

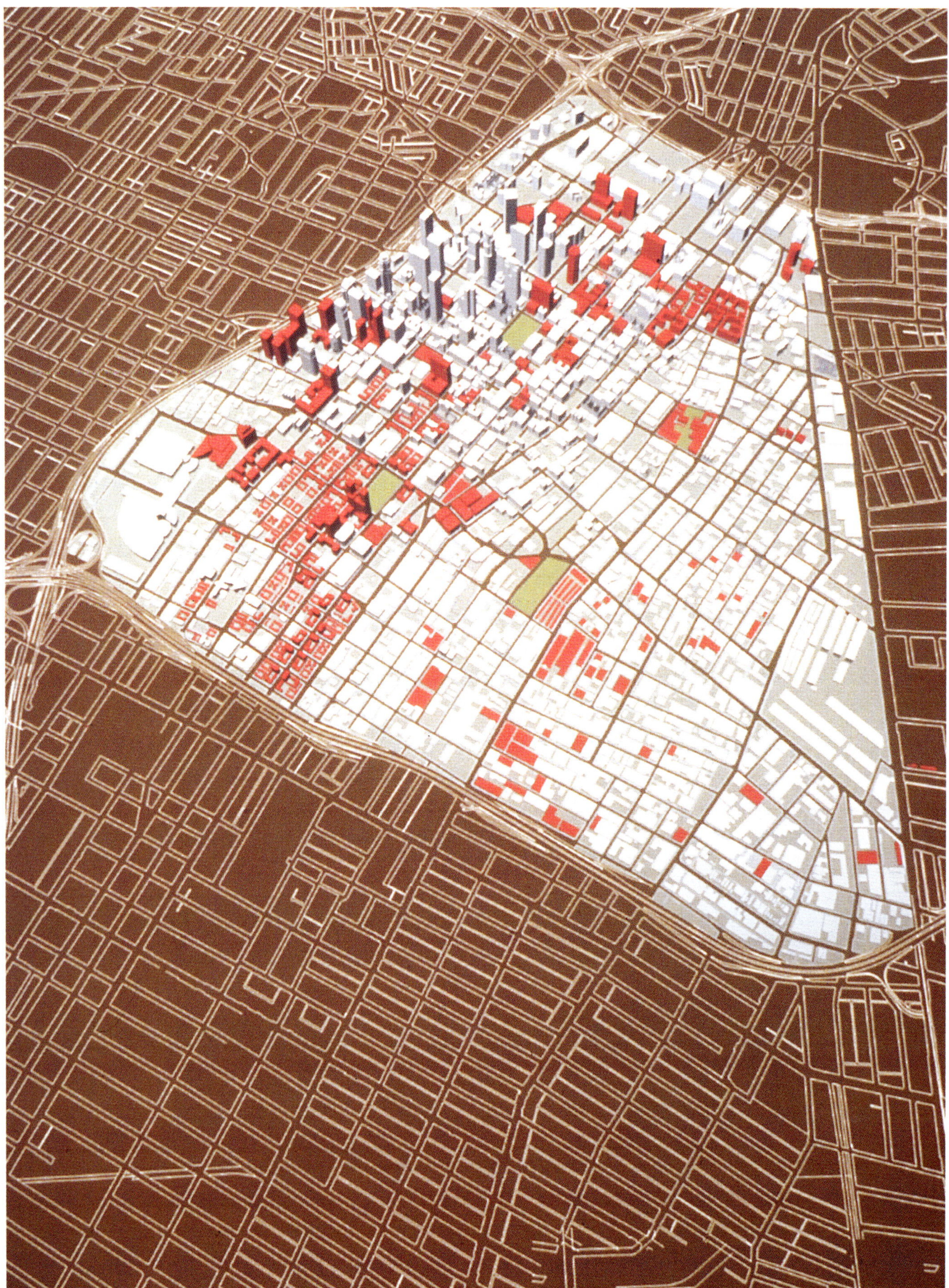

Axonometric plan of the downtown area.

Site.

Site.



Committed to an incremental, combinatorial approach to the urban fabric rather than to the idea of sweeping change, the Downtown Strategic Plan is based on the creation of linkages between networks of transportation, open space, and built form. The architects' identification and elaboration of a vision for these districts arose not only from a desire to improve the physical workings of city life and urban form, but also as an informed response to a host of historical, social, cultural, demographic, economic, and technological research about the character of the city center and its increasingly economically–and culturally–diverse future. By recognizing and emphasizing the heterogeneous character of downtown Los Angeles, the plan demonstrates an urge to preserve the old and encourage the new, and to accomplish the integration of the various social and spatial fabrics that comprise this complex city center. Additional goals include the stabilization of the historic core alongside the densification and increased urbanization of the newly-rebuilt areas. The plan seeks to structure and define the individual identities of each neighborhood, but at the same time emphasizes their connection and interdependence within a larger whole.

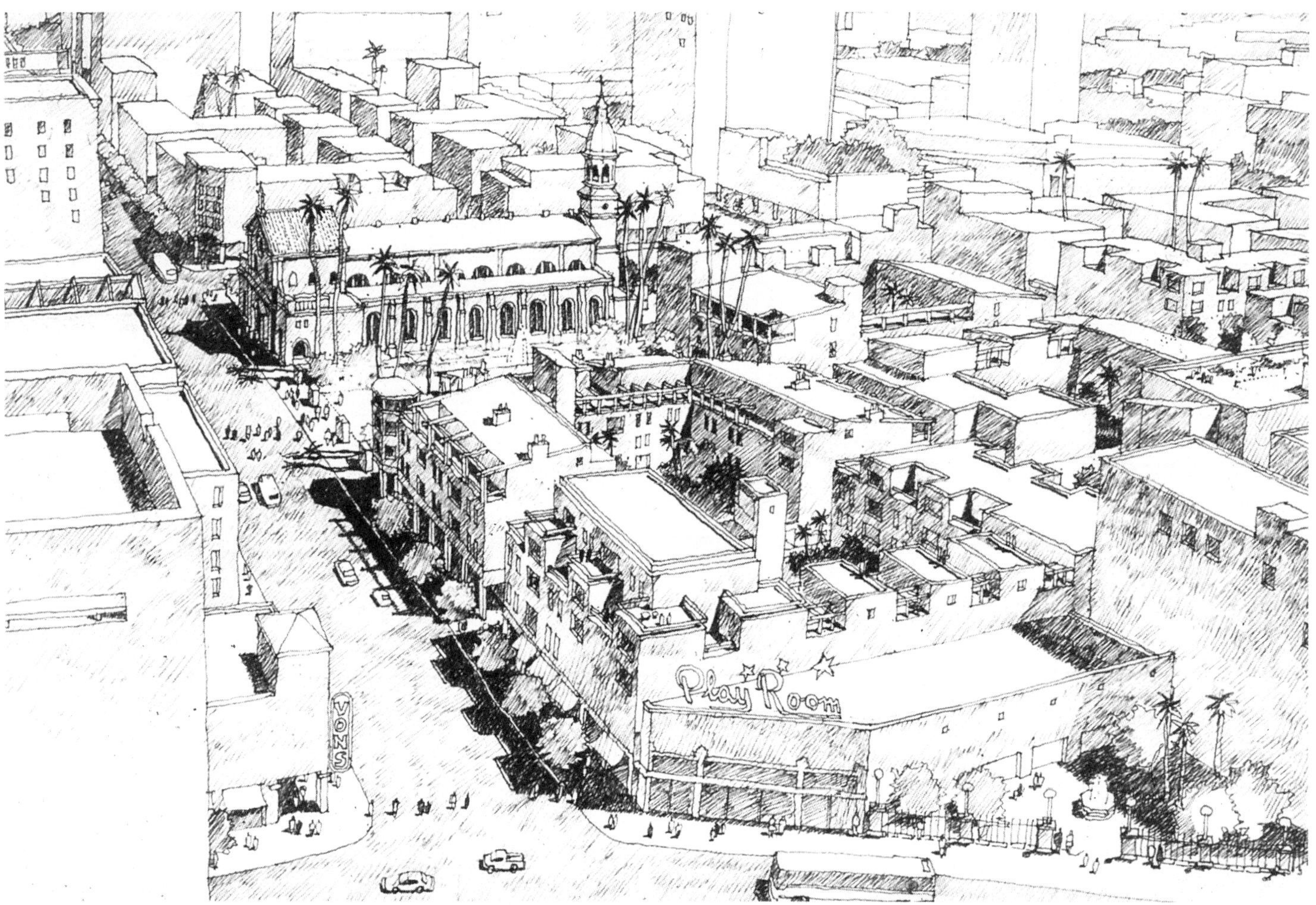


Drawing of proposed housing cluster adjacent to St. Vibiana Cathedral.

| Lead Consultants | Collaborating Firms | Sponsoring Organization |
| --- | --- | --- |
| Elizabeth Moule and Stefanos Polyzoides, Architects and Urbanists | Andres Duany and Elizabeth Plater-Zyberk, Architects and Town Planners<br>Solomon Architecture and Planning<br>Susan Haviland, Architect<br>Peter deBretteville, Architect<br><br>Hanna / Olin, Ltd., Landscape Architecture<br>Kaku Associates, Inc., Transportation<br>Barton Aschman Associates, Transportation<br>Korve Engineering, Transportation<br>Will Fleissig, Implementation<br>Cordoba Corporation, Economic Planning<br>Michael Dear & Jennifer Wolch, Homelessness and Social Services<br>Carson Anderson, Historic Preservation<br>Terry Hayes, Environmental Planning | Downtown Strategic Plan Advisory Committee |

Proposed truck staging area.

The Los Angeles Theater in the proposed Broadway Theater Entertainment District.

Community meeting showing Comité Nos Quedamos / We Stay Committee member with sign.

# BronxCenterNewYork



In New York City's South Bronx, a 300-block area known as **Bronx Center** is currently being reshaped by an intensive community planning process that is emerging as a model for connections between and among community residents, elected officials, and the public and private sectors. The Bronx Center is guided by a steering committee chaired by Richard A. Kahan, President of The Urban Assembly, a non-profit, international network of urbanists. In concert with a broad-based group of civic and community organizations, the Bronx Center effort is one of the most ambitious and comprehensive community-based planning projects to be undertaken to date.

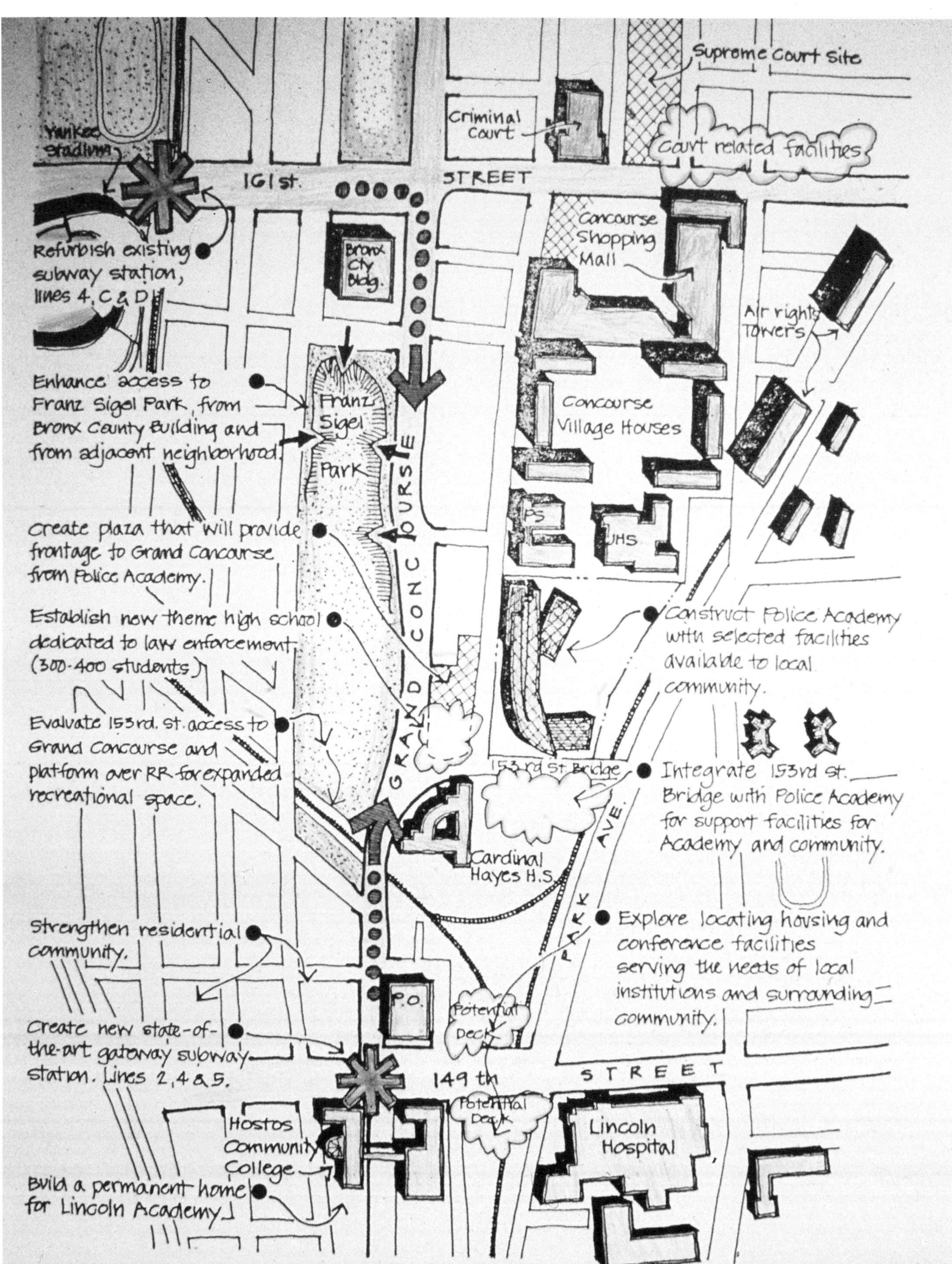


Plan diagram of the community's recommended alterations to the site.

Site.

Site.

Organized as a way to coordinate, maximize, and rationalize the planned public expenditure of over $2 billion, and to engage local residents and businesses in the development of comprehensive plans for the revitalization of the community, the project has developed into a formidable grass roots effort. Since 1992, a neighborhood group calling itself the Comité Nos Quedamos / We Stay Committee has actively participated in the development of existing plans for physical and social alteration of the community. After successfully stopping an urban renewal plan prepared by the city without community input, they developed an alternative plan that minimizes relocation of residents and businesses.

Even at this early stage of the project, a number of successes are attributable to input by Bronx Center residents. Foremost among these, to date, is the community's proposal of alternatives for the proposed new Police Academy, for which a competition had been won by the firm of Ellerbe Becket prior to the community's involvement in defining the area's master plan. Focusing attention not on the architecture of the building but on its provision of services and its social and physical relationship to the surrounding vicinity, the community's suggested changes ranged from reorienting the building's entrance to establishing a magnet high school for police training that would provide an important link between the neighborhood, its youth, and the police. The accomplishment of Bronx Center will be the successful promotion and integration of community concerns as a crucial component of the urban planning and design process, informing whatever future changes take shape in the area, be they social, cultural, economic, political, or spatial and physical.

The success of Bronx Center is credited to engaging the energies and imaginations of Bronx citizens, institutional and political leaders, city officials, community activists, academicians, and professionals who continue to contribute hundreds of hours to this project, among them

The Office of the Bronx Borough President Fernando Ferrer
Genevieve Brooks, Deputy Borough President

The Urban Assembly
Richard Kahan, President
Catharine Cary, Executive Vice President

The Parodneck Foundation
Harry DeRienzo, Vice President and Chief Executive Officer

The Pratt Institute Center for Community and Environmental Development ( PICCED )
Ron Shiffman, Director

The We Stay Committee / Comité Nos Quedamos
Yolanda Garcia, President

Municipal Art Society
Kent Barwick, President

*Smith-Miller + Hawkinson Architects ; Barbara Kruger ; Quennell Rothschild Associates*

# Imperfect Utopia:
# A Park for the New World Site Plan

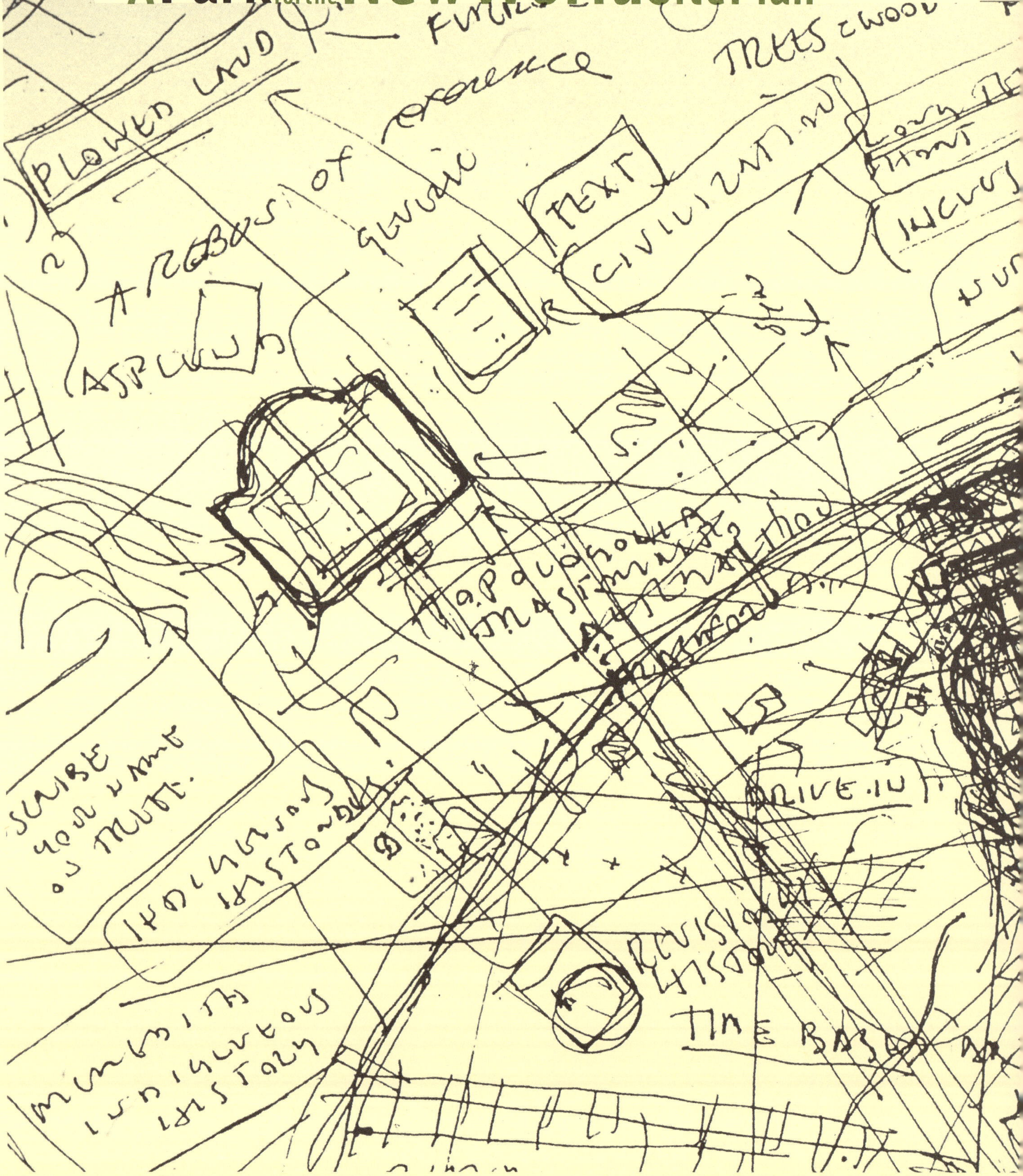

Preliminary sketch.

# Raleigh
## for the North Carolina Museum of Art



The New York-based team of architects Henry Smith-Miller and Laurie Hawkinson, artist Barbara Kruger, and landscape architect Nicholas Quennell has designed a plan for a 160-acre park surrounding the North Carolina Museum of Art in Raleigh entitled **Imperfect Utopia: A Park for the New World**. Commissioned in 1987 by the museum as the result of a national competition, this collaborating team's proposal rethinks the master plan and the master planning process. The important distinction of this project relative to others of similar ambition and scale is its insistence on questioning the accepted ideas and operations traditionally invested in the overarching, fully-realized, and finished nature of a master plan.

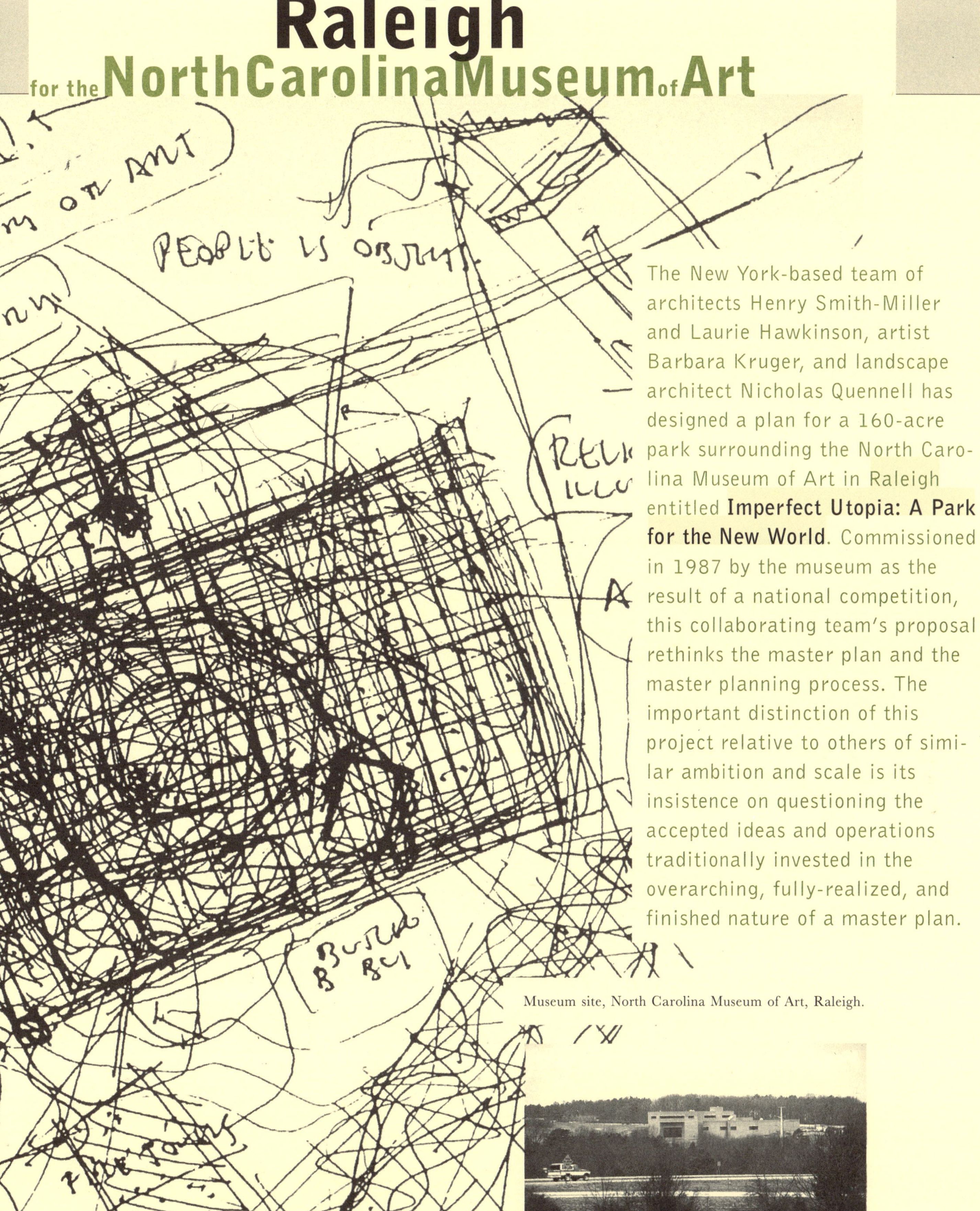

Museum site, North Carolina Museum of Art, Raleigh.

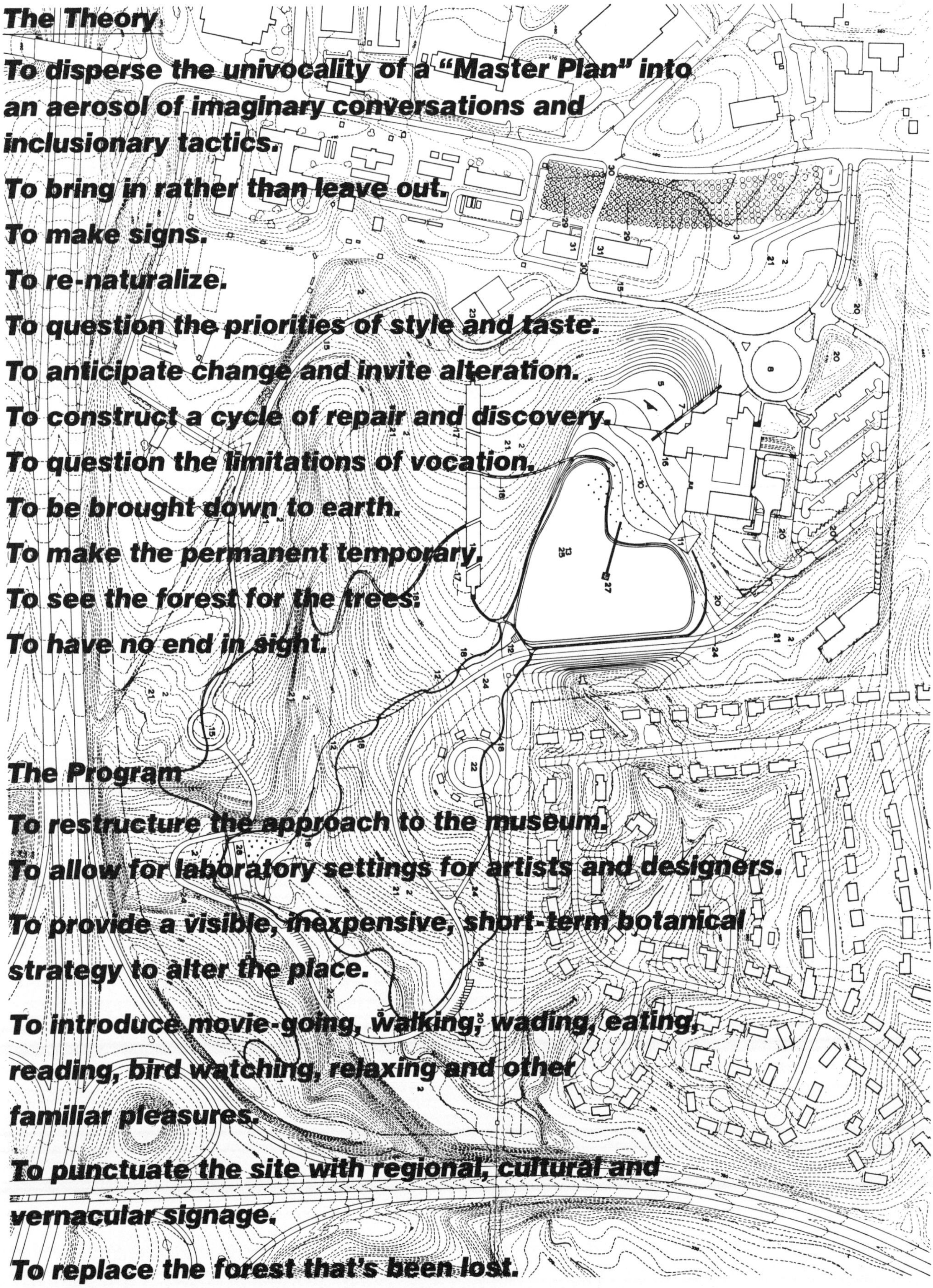

**The Theory**

**To disperse the univocality of a "Master Plan" into an aerosol of imaginary conversations and inclusionary tactics.**

**To bring in rather than leave out.**

**To make signs.**

**To re-naturalize.**

**To question the priorities of style and taste.**

**To anticipate change and invite alteration.**

**To construct a cycle of repair and discovery.**

**To question the limitations of vocation.**

**To be brought down to earth.**

**To make the permanent temporary.**

**To see the forest for the trees.**

**To have no end in sight.**

**The Program**

**To restructure the approach to the museum.**

**To allow for laboratory settings for artists and designers.**

**To provide a visible, inexpensive, short-term botanical strategy to alter the place.**

**To introduce movie-going, walking, wading, eating, reading, bird watching, relaxing and other familiar pleasures.**

**To punctuate the site with regional, cultural and vernacular signage.**

**To replace the forest that's been lost.**

The Theory & The Program. Text written by the collaborating team which served to "guide" the project. This open-ended series of planning scenarios became a substitute for the traditional master plan.

Drawing by John White, circa 1558. This early drawing near Roanoke, Virginia, shows the sowing, harvesting and celebration of corn. The drawing is pivotal to the concepts of "Imperfect Utopia" as it clarifies that the land was manipulated years before, and that an original condition of the landscape is indeterminate.

The team expands the field of architecture to include landscape design, art, and engineering. Rather than hinging the plan on an overreaching formal device, the project addresses the existing contingencies of this suburban, posturban landscape and uses an open-ended series of planning and program scenarios to engage ideas of history, culture, geography, and topography. Two texts—The Theory and The Program—are utilized by the team as procedural tools to guide their collaborative vision. In addition, the common planning apparatus of zoning is used, but in this case to provide inclusivity rather than exclusivity.

Phase I of the project, The Textualized Landscape, is presently under implementation by the North Carolina Museum of Art. Encompassing approximately two and one-half acres immediately adjacent to the museum's entrance, this particular zone for "Active Culture" expands the museum's capacity for outdoor programs. It is conceived of as an alternative to the conventional sculpture garden that might otherwise be placed in such a transitional zone. This arena for cinema and outdoor performance accommodates a variety of uses from informal gatherings to large events with an audience of 3,000 in the amphitheater seating and adjacent grassy slopes. This re-naturalized landscape incorporates principles encouraged in the "Master Plan," such as reforestation to regenerate native forest species; grove plantings to provide shaded areas for viewing and picnicking; and plantings such as wildflowers and agricultural crops of cotton, corn, or tobacco to reflect the changing character and history of this part of the site.

Detail model of Amphitheater and Projection Booth with letters "T," "H."

Site model.

Museum site showing existing correctional facility.

Detail model of Amphitheater and Projection Booth with letters "T," "H."

Design Team

Henry Smith-Miller, Laurie Hawkinson / Smith-Miller + Hawkinson Architects
Barbara Kruger, artist
Nicholas Quennell / Quennell Rothschild Associates, landscape architect

Smith-Miller + Hawkinson Architects:
John Conaty, associate in charge / The Textualized Landscape
Annette Fierro, associate in charge / Imperfect Utopia
with Knut Hansen, Peter Morgan, Ruri Yampolsky, Kit Yan, and Elizabeth Ashford, Ben Dunkley, Eugene Harris, Michael Hirsch, Virginia Navid, Brian Ostner, Jennifer Stearns

Quennell Rothschild Associates, landscape architects
Andrew Moore, Mauricio Villarreal, Kate Cleary
Judy Harmon, landscape consultant

Ove Arup and Partners, structural engineer consultant
Guy Nordenson, Mel Garber

Frank Harmon, Associate Architect, Raleigh

Funded by

National Video Cave Art, New York, New York
The North Carolina Museum of Art, Raleigh

Models and construction of bleachers contributed by Richard Loring/Archetype

# ConceptualMasterPlan

***STUDIO WORKS in collaboration with Trivers Associates, Mary Miss, and James Turrell***

Model of Grand Center with an example of one portion of the proposed lighting design for the area.

# for Grand Center St. Louis

Historical photograph showing the theater district in its heyday.



A master plan for the Grand Center Arts and Entertainment District of St. Louis offers a number of unconventional strategies for revitalization of this formerly thriving eight-block theater district. The project approaches the site itself as theater, seeking to intensify aspects of its functional, physical, and conceptual identity. Working in collaboration with a design team including artist Mary Miss, dancer Vivian Watt, graphic designer Kiku Obata, Trivers Associates architects, and EDAW, Inc., landscape architects, Los Angeles architects Robert Mangurian and Mary-Ann Ray of STUDIO WORKS generated a conceptual master plan of seven different, yet overlapping strategies. Taking their cues from the site's identity as an arena for the performing arts and as an already dense and coherent urban fabric, each of the "Seven Layers—Seven Compositional Strategies" of the master plan—"Grand: On Stage Off Stage"; "Street and Green"; "Discrete Elements"; "Acropolis"; "Clusters"; "Overlaid Patterns"; and "Patchwork Quilt"—was intended to respond to and enhance its existing character rather than sweepingly to transform, reform, or reorder it. Each of the layers makes a strong proposal for at least one architectonic aspect; for example, the fourth layer, "Acropolis," configures the topography of the district, while the sixth layer, "Overlaid Patterns," designs small-scale elements and recognizes the importance of surface, material, and detail within the overall structure of the city.

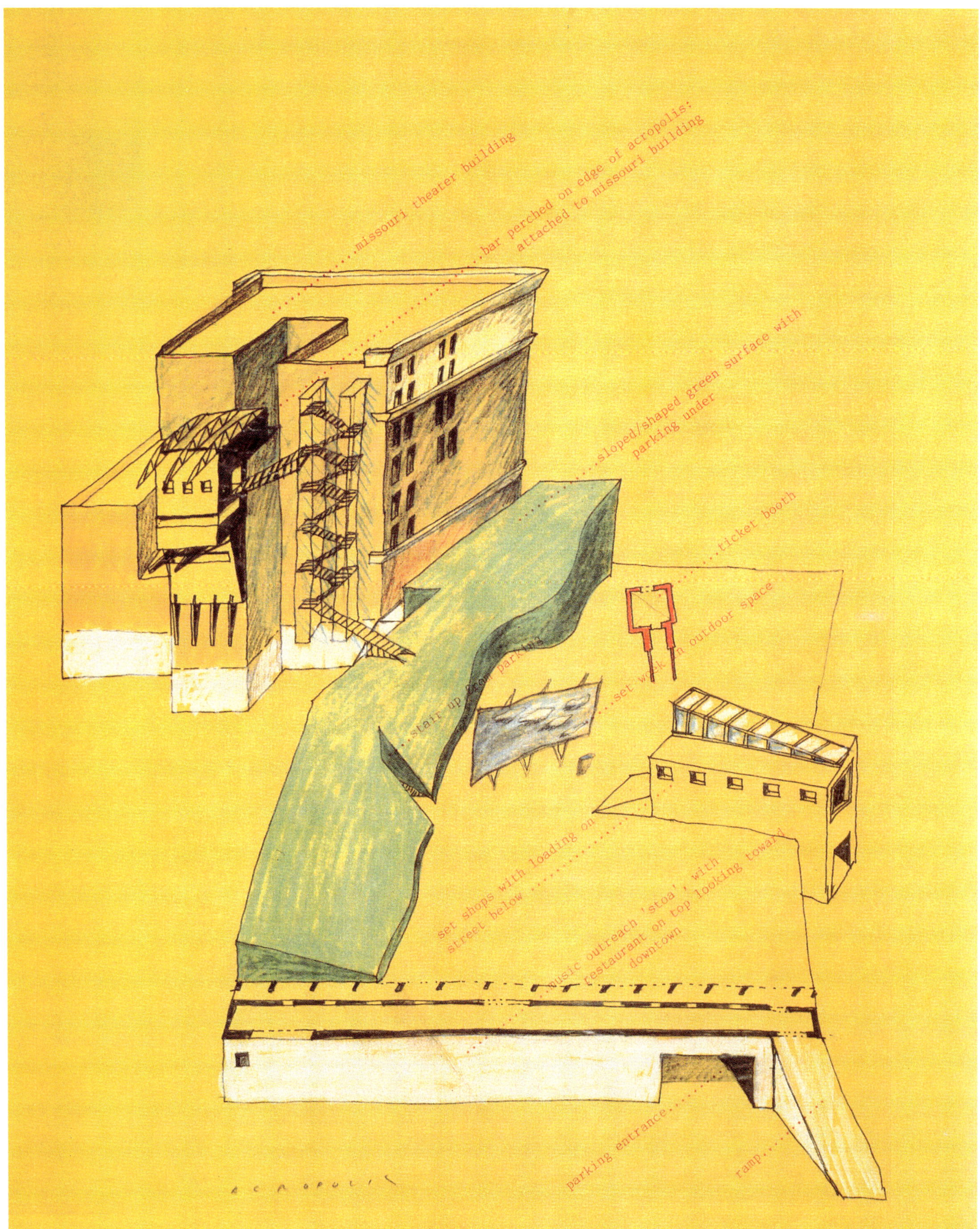


Acropolis behind Powell Hall.

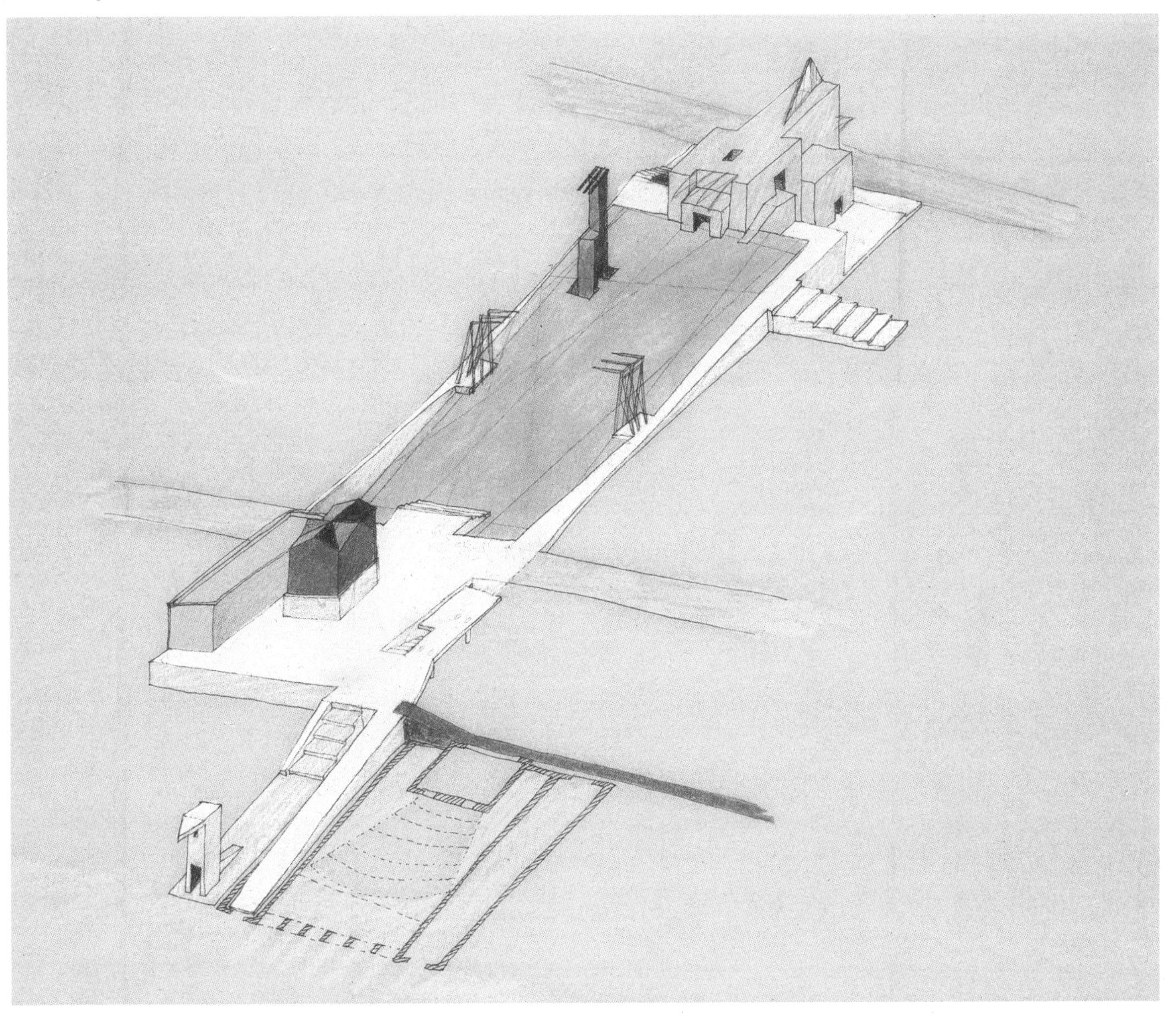

The Green.

Within the framework of the master plan is a series of lighting proposals by STUDIO WORKS with artist James Turrell. The lighting proposals transform this part of the city through minimal means, yet in spectacular ways. While some of the proposals deal with daytime conditions, most have their strongest expression at night. They take their cue from the interpretation of the street as theater and of the back lots as backstage elements. For instance, the project "Cross Light" consists of banks of theatrical cross lights mounted high on Grand Boulevard building walls, spotlighting other nearby buildings. "Laser Lid" proposes to draw networks of lines in the sky, forming a ceiling over an immense urban clearing. In "The Big Glass," empty billboards facing Grand Boulevard are surfaced with banded reflective surfaces on which are projected large fields of light. "Shadow Cast" and "Shadow Projection" are projects occurring in the offstage back lots, casting patterns and figures of shadow on the big blank walls—using fire escape stairs and moving pedestrians—from light sources that appear like strange props or theater machinery.

While the Grand Center master plan did not evolve into a full-blown plan for implementation, certain of its key features continue to inform the activity and overall approach to the evolving urban landscape being undertaken by Grand Center, Inc., in this transitional neighborhood. Remarkable for its departure from conventional modes of urban revitalization, the project is powerfully transformative not only on a poetic but also on an economic level, suggesting possibilities for regeneration of city form and function with a highly concentrated yet minimal approach.

Shadow cast with the Big Glass and the Moorage in the distance.

## Design Team

STUDIO WORKS
Robert Mangurian, Principal
Mary-Ann Ray, Principal

David Gregor
Michael Gruber
Irene Keil
Kathy Lindstrom
Nicholas Lowie

Trivers Associates
James Turrell
Mary Miss

## Consultants

Kent Hodgetts
Kiku Obata & Co.
EDAW, Inc.
Crawford, Bunte, Brammeier
Emily Pulitzer
Vivian Watt
Eugene Kupper

"Steel Cloud" model; detail of Plaza with Time Museum.

# "Steel Cloud" West Coast Gateway Los Angeles

The urban design approach of New York-based architects Hani Rashid and Lise Anne Couture is based on giving appropriate physical form to the "information city" and the technologically globalized nature of contemporary life. Their **"Steel Cloud" : West Coast Gateway** project for Los Angeles, the winning entry in a city-sponsored 1988 competition for a national immigration monument, expresses a variety of competing facts, identities, and usages of its proposed site in the airspace over a major downtown freeway. These include the linearity of the freeway and its space-time continuum of movement; the airplane as the mode of arrival of new immigrants; and the fact that technology (media, telecommunications, computers, etc.) represents the true shared cultural infrastructure linking business, government, the region's commuters, and the ethnically-diverse residential and business communities surrounding the site. Functioning as a monument to the largely intangible but highly pervasive forces at work in the modern information city, "Steel Cloud" : West Coast Gateway is a highly dynamic design seeking to embody the urban form of not only the contemporary immigrant experience, but also the very character of late twentieth-century life.

Site model. "Steel Cloud" elevation in urban context.

Rashid and Couture have described the "Steel Cloud" as "an architectural assemblage of situations and spectacle where scale is purposely disconcerting. Here aquariums and suspended landscapes hover above the city's skyline and oscillate to its arcane rhythms. The lifted horizon lines that configure and delineate this structure meld with the endless horizontality that is Los Angeles. This is a living monument, accommodating galleries, libraries, cinemas, parks, and plazas that are intersected by the fluid and transient space of the city. This is an architecture for the territories devoid of perspective, depth, frames, or enclosure."

"Steel Cloud" model; elevation.

Following a heated controversy surrounding the design after it was announced as winner of the competition, as well as shifts in funding priorities on the part of the sponsor, "Steel Cloud" will remain unbuilt. A highly visionary response to the complex program outlined in the competition brochure, its inclusive, technological character and unconventional architectural appearance struck many as chaotic and even threatening, and it was portrayed in the media as a monumental folly. Others passionately defended the "Steel Cloud" as a brilliant, deeply poetic concretization of the nature of its site and moment in time. What this polemic obscured was one aspect of the project's potential role as connective tissue within the urban fabric by its reclamation for pedestrian, cultural, and recreational usages of an otherwise "dead" zone of space over a sunken freeway in a city center.

"Steel Cloud" model; overall view with library and word screens in foreground.

Design Team

Hani Rashid, Principal
Lise Anne Couture, Principal

Project Team

Raoul Bustos
Richard Cress
William Deegan
Kevin Estrada
Begonia Fernandez-Shaw
Eytan Kaufman
Wissam Jabr
Marisabel Marratt
Nuno Mateus
Ignacio Salas
Mark Wamble
Chris Warnick
Beth Weinstein

Associate Architects

Gruen Associates / Los Angeles

Landscape Architects

Ursula Kurz / Paris

Structural Engineers

Ove Arup + Partners / New York

Model Makers

D.O.K. Labs / Brooklyn, N.Y.

Photography

Douglas Whyte Photography / New York
Eduard Hueber / New York

# UhuruGarden

Uhuru Garden site, 103rd and Grape Streets.

**Uhuru Garden** is a two-and-one-half-acre demonstration public garden project on a currently empty lot located in Watts adjacent to Jordan Downs, the largest public housing project in Los Angeles. The intent of the project is the creation of an environmental education center connected to successful existing programs and institutions in the city. Conceptual designs were developed by Los Angeles-based landscape architect Achva Benzinberg Stein, working with neighborhood residents and community organizations. Embodying Stein's ideas about the productive role of open space in the urban context, Uhuru Garden seeks to provide a variety of tangible services to its neighborhood, tied into the city's political, social, and economic systems, instead of standing merely as a green oasis or as undifferentiated recreational space.

Aerial view showing surrounding neighborhood.

# Watts Los Angeles

*Achva Benzinberg Stein, BLS Environmental Planning and Design, Los Angeles*



Axonometric view.

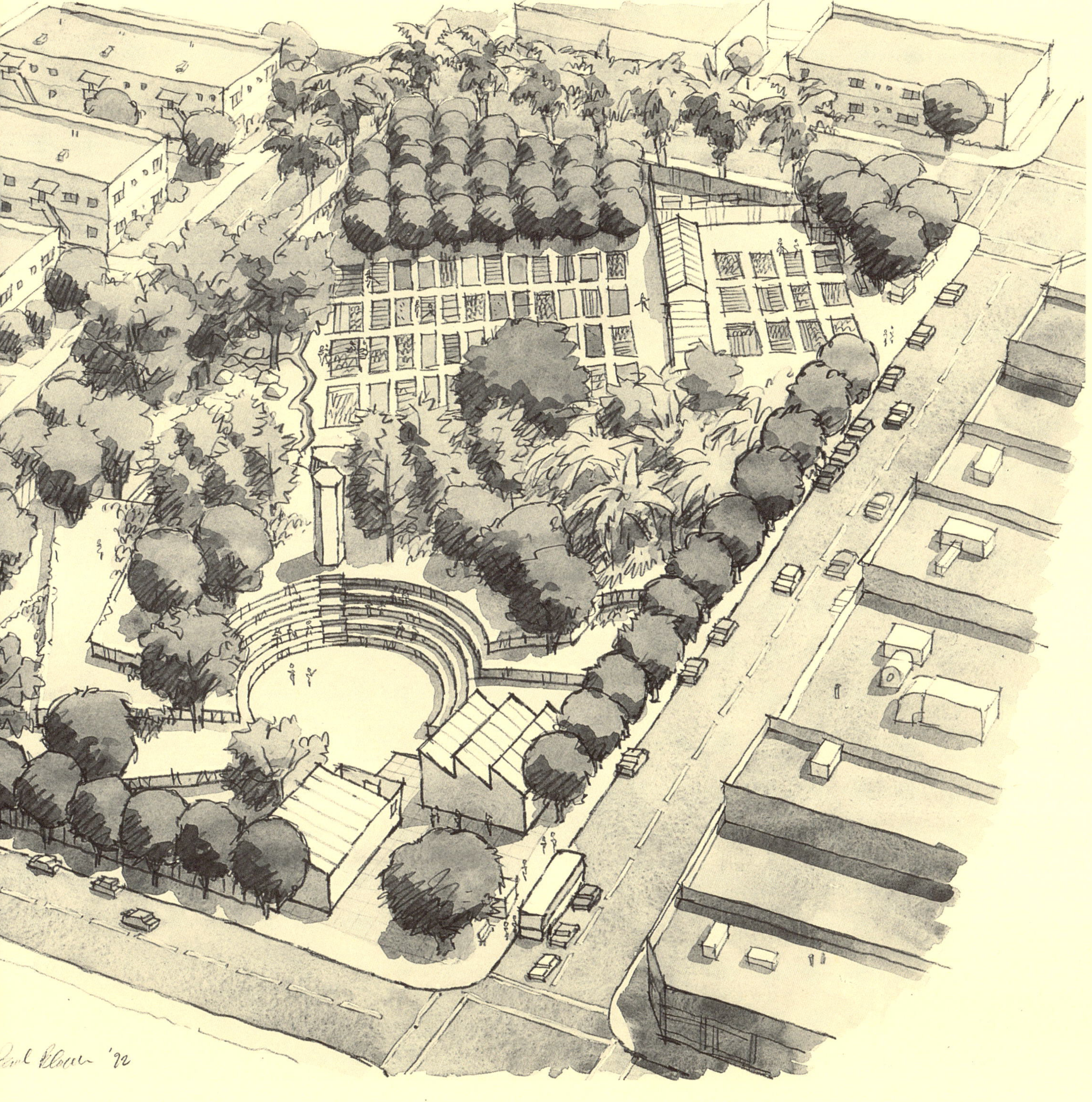

The Garden Environment as an Urban Refuge.



Included in the project are a community "victory" garden for sixty individual family plots, a market garden and horticultural teaching area for the Watts drug rehabilitation program, a recycling and composting area, an herb garden and orchard under the supervision of the Common Ground Program, a demonstration garden showing drought-tolerant plants native to Southern California, Latin America, and Africa, and an "energy-wise" community center. To reinforce the idea of puposeful service to its community, access to Uhuru Garden will be limited to those who work, volunteer, or study on the site.

The design solution is based on the idea that land is precious and that connections to it need to be fostered through work that sustains both the body and the soul. The project also explores the need to enlarge the opportunities for employment for inner-city youth. Much of the growth in the job market in the next century will be in both high-tech and intermediate biotechnology, with opportunities in recycling and the various "green" industries. In Uhuru Garden, youth counseling, teaching, and other educational activities will play a major role in creating a level of facility with and an understanding of the issues behind sustainable and environmental rehabilitation.

The Educational Garden : The Natural Forces of Wind, Water, and Solar Energy.

African Garden : Vernacular Dwellings Serve as a Setting for Crafts and Performing Arts.

Dwelling Precedent

African Garden
Place for Community Art Activities

Baobab Trees.

Arroyo Garden :
Physical Environment of Southern California's San Gabriel Mountains.

The Fire Pines

Arroyo Woodland

The Pasadena Oaks

Agricultural Garden : Traditional Crops and Cultivation Techniques of Spanish California.

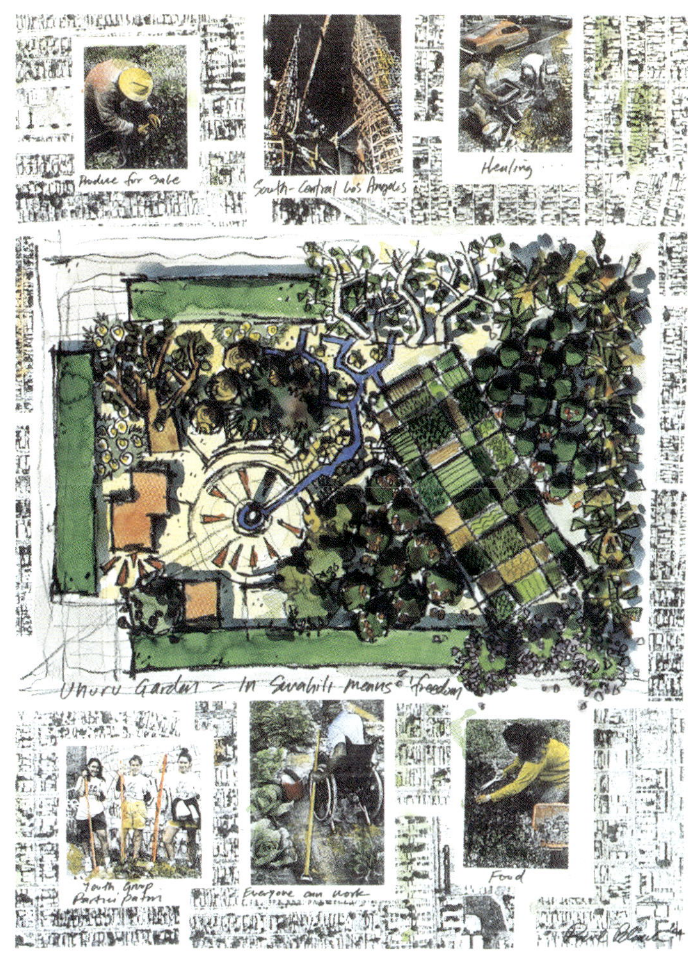


Concept Plan, Proposed Uhuru Garden, Watts.

San Gabriel Mountains

The Wash

California Sycamore

| Design Team | Community Organizations |
| --- | --- |
| Mark Motonaga | Brenda Funches, LA Harvest |
| Paul Blazek, Artist | Sheryl Hopkins, Common Ground |
| Leo T. O'Brian | Garden Program, |
| | University of California Cooperative |
| **With assistance from** | Extension |
| | The Trust for Public Land |
| Shaun Jennings | Green Industries Council, Rebuild LA |
| Farouk Tadros | Watts Health Foundation |
| Danny Koo | |
| Mark Lee | The working drawing was partly |
| Shlomit Stein | funded by the National Endowment |
| Mohammed al-Lahham | for the Arts |
| Jingbo Lou | |
| Steve Flusty | |
| and others | |

*Baratloo-Balch, Architects*

# Territorial Imperative: MasterPlan

# Bronx New York

Site.

# for Bathgate Avenue Community Park

Site model. Photo: Jack Pottle/Esto.



New York architects Mojdeh Baratloo and Clifton Balch have developed a **Master Plan for Bathgate Avenue Community Park** in the Bronx area of New York City. It seeks to establish a conceptual structure for the community's effort to create, within a barren urban neighborhood, a verdant, meaningful, and lasting public place. Recognizing the need to provide clearly for purposeful activity on this vacant two-and-one-half-acre site rather than leaving it as unstructured open space, the Master Plan for Bathgate Avenue Community Park defines a strategy for its reoccupation and control. The site shares a city block with a public school (P.S. 59) and two community gardens, one of which was established in conjunction with a Cornell University Extension Program and plays an important role as a center for the community and its links with the school.

Conceptual design documents : idealized plan to actual plan.

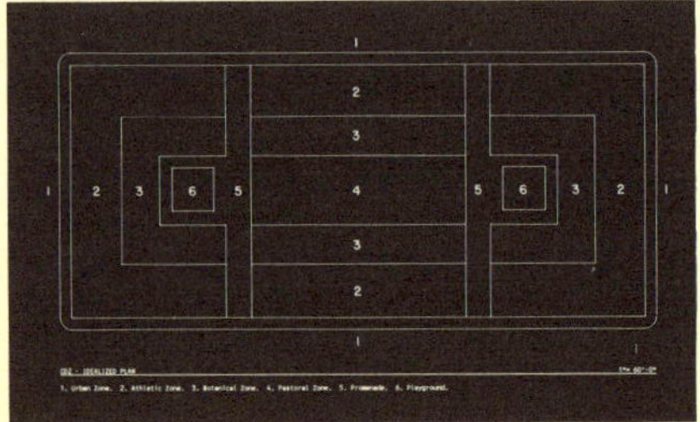

Idealized plan.

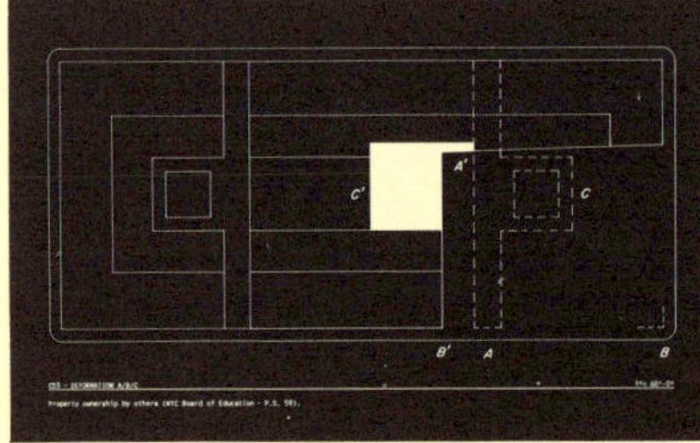

Property ownership by others.

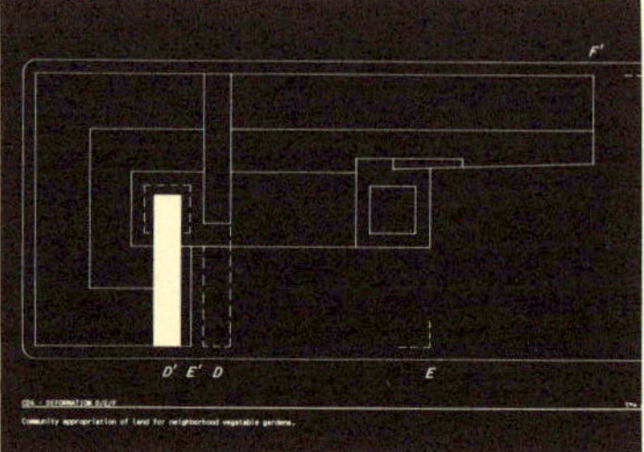

Community appropriation of land for neighborhood vegetable gardens.

The community's need for a public park is desperate, and therefore the activities to be accommodated are many. P.S. 59 and another school being built across the street will use the park for their school yard and outdoor sport activities. The park must also sustain, on a relatively small site, the disparate needs of all generations of a large surrounding area, from toddlers and their caregivers, to young adults and a growing population of elderly residents. The topography of the site is unusual in that it includes an elevated plateau. With the exception of some dying trees on the plateau and intermittent street trees at the sidewalk, the site vegetation consists of grass and weeds. Over the years sporadic attempts have been made to add amenities to the site—asphalt paths, a sandbox, and even a small amphitheater. None have been able to survive the rampant vandalism in the neighborhood.

The Master Plan envisions the site as a series of zones which respond to and structure these various conditions and activities. The zones wrap the site in continuous bands, each with its distinct character, in an attempt to perceptually enlarge the park. These zones are crossed by alleed walkways which correspond to the primary entrances into the park. An "Urban Zone," including new street trees and perimeter fencing, defines the world immediately outside of the park. Taking advantage of the lower flat areas of the site, an "Athletic Zone" supports all of the various sport activities. On the hillside, maximizing visibility of vegetation and controlling erosion, a "Botanical Zone" is established, to be developed over time with the assistance of an ongoing program of donations of plant materials from the nearby New York Botanical Garden. The upper plateau is treated as a simple but luxurious sodded lawn, a "Pastoral Zone" for children's play, family picnics, and a variety of community and school events. "Promenades," the only paved areas in the park, provide access to all of the zones and are sites for game tables and seating, allowing for supervision of the park by older members of the community. The promenades are lined with flowering trees. Within the promenade adjacent to, and with direct access from, the P.S. 59 school yard is the children's playground, also shaded by flowering trees and defined by the community as the "heart" of the park.

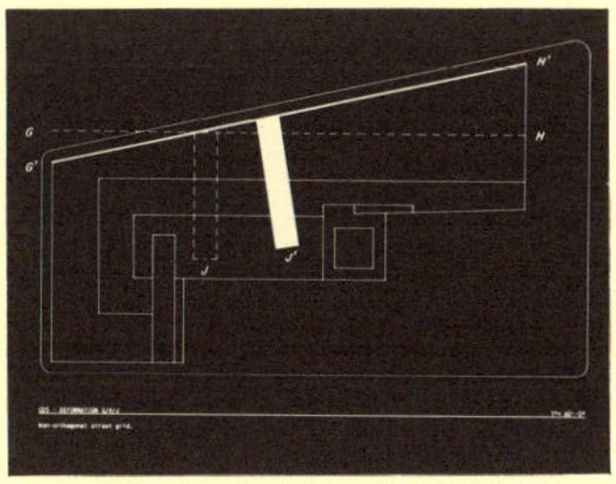
Non-orthogonal street grid.

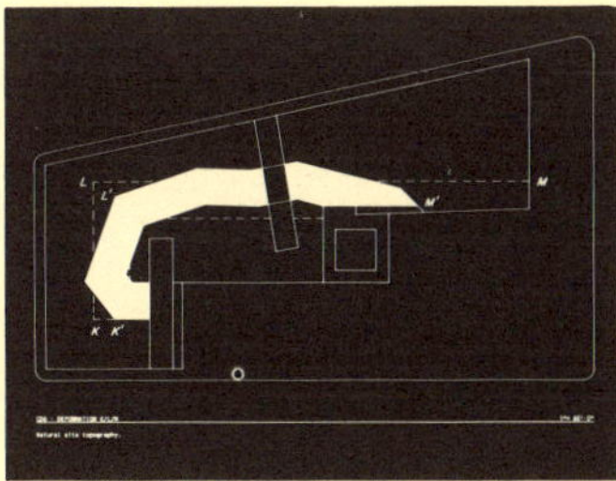
Natural site topography.

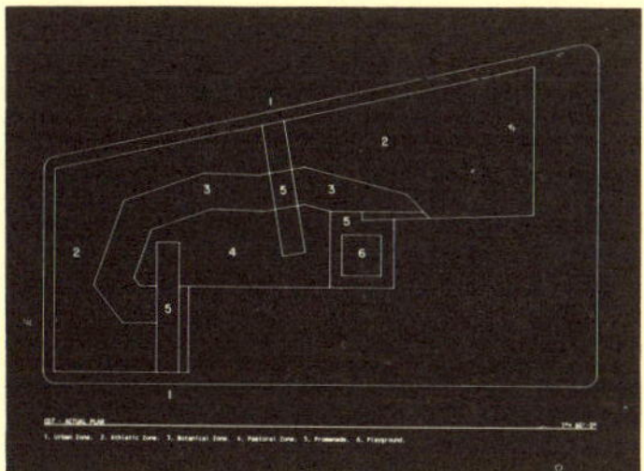
Actual plan.



**Design Team**

Mojdeh Baratloo
Clifton Balch

**Landscape Architects**

Teresa Chenney, Master Plan
Quennell Rothschild Associates, Design Development

**Project Administration**

Bronx Council on the Arts

**Participants from the following community groups**

Bathgate Avenue Tenants and Homeowners Association
Public School 59
Public School 159
Public School 23
Bronx Community Planning Board #6

**Sponsoring Organizations**

Community Involvement Program of the New York City Board of Education
New York State Council on the Arts
National Endowment for the Arts
The Parks Council

# Two Los Angeles

*Video compendium of neighborhood-based urban plans and projects, including, in Los Angeles, the Crenshaw Neighborhood Plan and Cultural Explainers ( South Central, Koreatown, and Pico-Union )*

Crenshaw area streetscape.

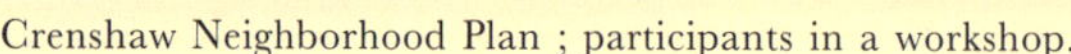

Crenshaw Neighborhood Plan ; participants in a workshop.

# Community-Based Projects

The phenomenon of design for and by communities, a potent form of empowerment and participation in the shaping of a truly public realm, is crucial not only to the future of the urban design field but also to the cultural, social, political, and economic health of our cities. A number of significant and innovative community-oriented planning and design initiatives are currently or have recently been underway in a variety of American urban contexts, including New York's South Bronx and Los Angeles's Crenshaw, South-Central, Koreatown, and Pico-Union districts. Together, these represent a rich spectrum of activism regarding the physical and social improvement of neighborhoods and public spaces.

Cultural Explainers, Koreatown workshop.

The processes characteristic of community-driven efforts—discourse and consensus-building—help to establish a greater stake within communities for the creation and implementation of ideas and solutions to a wide variety of problems. In efforts such as the neighborhood plans sponsored by Los Angeles's Coalition of Neighborhood Developers, initiated in the wake of the civil disturbances of spring 1992, these range from the provision of economic opportunities, affordable housing, and social service networks to the creation of recreational facilities and well-maintained open spaces. The Crenshaw Neighborhood Plan, one of ten plans developed under the CND's aegis, took the form of a series of participatory planning charrettes addressing specific concerns raised by and debated among the citizen-participants.

Contrasting with the breadth and intricacy of such large-scale efforts as the Bronx Center project and the Los Angeles neighborhood plans, other noteworthy projects are highly specialized in their nature and goals. Also in Los Angeles, the Cultural Explainers project of the Social and Public Arts Resource Center aims to promote dialogue among members of the ethnic groups that were most affected by the events of spring 1992. These discussions, taking place in the South-Central, Koreatown, and Pico-Union districts, are leading to the creation of temporary, movable public monuments that will be generated directly from the input of neighborhood participants in collaboration with artists and architects. These and related projects are providing a mechanism not only for self-definition and consensus-building but also for creativity in terms of ongoing experimentation with the portrayal of collective identity and the articulation of social space.

Section of Western Avenue, Los Angeles, following civil disturbances of Spring 1992.

Crenshaw Neighborhood Plan

Sponsoring Organizations :
Coalition of Neighborhood Developers
Local Initiatives Support Corporation
The Crenshaw Cluster
Corridor Economic Development Corporation
Crenshaw Chamber of Commerce
Crenshaw Neighborhood Development Corporation
Crenshaw Neighborhood Housing Services
Crenshaw Neighbors
Helpers for the Homeless and Hungry
Rebuild Crenshaw

Planning Team

Michaele Pride-Wells, Community Planning Consultant
Valerie Lynne Shaw, Administrator and Organizer
Fathia Macaulay, Planning Assistant

Crenshaw Cluster Steering Committee

Ted Lumpkin, Joe Gardner, Leslie Bellamy,
G. Landry Humphrey, Sharon Sumpter, Joi Oubre

Cultural Explainers

Sponsoring Organization :
Social and Public Art Resource Center (SPARC)

The success of this project, an ongoing effort, is predicated upon the contributions and participation of many individuals and groups, among them :
Judith F. Baca, Artistic Director, SPARC
ADOBE LA, Design Architects for all sites
Michael Cho, Video Documentation, ADOBE LA

South Central Los Angeles :
Pat Ward Williams, Artist
Franklin Westbrook, Community Coordinator, SPARC
Cecil Fergerson, South Central Cultural Activist/Historian

Koreatown :
David Chung, Artist
Jae Kim, Community Coordinator, SPARC
Kyong Shin Ko, Community Coordinator, ADOBE LA
Kiana Lee, Filmmaker, ADOBE LA

Pico-Union :
Judith F. Baca, Artist
Lindsey Haley, Community Coordinator, SPARC
Alessandra Moctezuma, Community Coordinator, ADOBE LA

“Zamora,” artist unknown.

# Saber es poder LosAngeles

ADOBE LA

"Gato," artist unknown.

Architects and Designers Opening the Border Edge of Los Angeles **(ADOBE LA)** is an organization of Latino architects, artists, and designers whose main objectives are, first, to observe and document the Latino physical presence in the Los Angeles urban landscape, and second, based on those observations, to create work (urban design, architecture, and public art) and resources for the community with its participation. An ongoing project of ADOBE LA is to document Latino manifestations of the cultural landscape of Los Angeles, which they have identified within the following categories:

### I. SPIRITUALITY AND THE LANDSCAPE.

Religious expressions in the urban landscape take the form of domestic altars, garden shrines, or images that adorn walls of private businesses, such as the images of the "Virgen de Guadalupe." Serving as "markers" of history and culture, they are traditions brought by the immigrants from their homelands that express a sense of identity.

### II. BARRIO ART.

This expression fills the Los Angeles urban landscape in the form of murals, as decoration on low-riders, or as tattoos. It is an outward artistic expression, meant to be seen and to become part of the landscape in the common scenario of the street. The murals on the sides of the local store serve as icons that communicate visually to the neighborhood.

### III. CODED MESSAGES: GRAFFITI AND TAGGING.

Graffiti and tagging reflect and respond to the particular socio-cultural conditions and aspirations of urban Latino youth. "Graffiti" is not merely a reflection of social dysfunction but, more importantly, a sign of creative resistance, spiritual tenacity, and a cohesive, coherent, and positive self-identity. In the context of ownership and appropriation of space, tagging is often used by gangs to delineate territory. Tagging is meaningless to mainstream culture because it is a code which is inaccessible.

### IV. ART OF SURVIVAL: STREET VENDORS AND TACO "TROCAS."

Street vendors are becoming ubiquitous in the city of Los Angeles. They are redefining the urban landscape by establishing their "store" within the street. They transform residential streets into commercial ones. They also bring life to the streets, as one can see in a Saturday evening on Cesar Chavez Avenue and Soto, something that is almost absent elsewhere in Los Angeles.

The presence of street vendors is an expression of Latino cultural identity and so is the way in which some of their cars and "trocas" are decorated. The images on these vehicles represent churches or villages in Mexico, or mythical characters taken from popular songs.

Most of these elements present in the cultural landscape are invisible to people who do not live in these communities because, as in many major cities, communities are divided. This isolation is further emphasized in Los Angeles because of its freeways; one can drive from the beach in Santa Monica to downtown Los Angeles every day without having to pass through Koreatown or Pico Union. Furthermore, many of these manifestations disappear behind all the visual information with which one is bombarded in the urban landscape.

In the Los Angeles presentation of "Urban Revisions: Current Projects for the Public Realm," ADOBE LA explores the concept of Latino appropriation and transformation of space in our city by appropriating certain spaces within the exhibition, the configuration and physical presence of which serves as a metaphor for the actual urban landscape. ADOBE LA defines these as "negative" spaces because, analogous to the spaces in the urban landscape that are appropriated and transformed by common people, they are often invisible. They are the back alleys filled with graffiti or tagging, or the almost imperceptible markets with their painted product images camouflaged behind the forest of billboards.

The exhibition will also provide a forum for discussion of the meanings of these vernacular interventions. By exploring the ways in which these elements are used as means of empowerment, the exhibition will allow viewers to read the spaces between the structures and to better read their city or, for that matter, any city.

"Jungle Temple."

| ADOBE LA | Additional Collaborators |
|---|---|
| Ulises Diaz | Amalia Mesa-Bains |
| Ignacio Fernández | Guillermo Gómez-Peña |
| Gustavo Leclerc | Wiro |
| Alessandra Moctezuma | Inner City Murals Project |
| Elpidio Rocha | Urbanos LA |
| Rosa I. Velasco | Judith F. Baca |
| | Carrol Flax |
| | Tania Martinez-Lemke |
| | Ruben Martinez |
| | Mandoe, Angst, Relic, Duke |
| | Lalo Lopez |

"Dos Rosas," artist unknown.

Abrams, Janet. "The Form of the (American) City." Lotus International 50. Milan: Industrie Graphiche Editoriali, 1986.

Alexander, Christopher, et. al. A Pattern Language: Towns, Buildings, Construction. New York: Oxford University Press, 1977.

Alexander, Christopher, Artemis Anninou, Ingrid King, and Hajo Neis. A New Theory of Urban Design. New York, 1987.

Anderson, Martin. The Federal Bulldozer: A Critical Analysis of Urban Renewal 1949-62. Cambridge, Mass.: MIT Press, 1964.

Anderson, Stanford, ed. On Streets. Cambridge, Mass.: MIT Press, 1978.

Attoe, Wayne, and Donn Logan. American Urban Architecture: Catalysts in the Design of Cities. Berkeley: University of California Press, 1989.

Bachelard, Gaston. The Poetics of Space. New York: Orion Press, 1964.

Banerjee, Tridib, and Michael Southworth, eds. City Sense and City Design: Writings and Projects of Kevin Lynch. Cambridge, Mass.: MIT Press, 1990.

Baratloo, Mojdeh, and Clifton J. Balch. ANGST: Cartography. New York: SITES/Lumen, 1989.

Bellush, Jewel. Urban Renewal: People, Politics and Planning. Garden City, N.J.: Anchor Books, 1967.

Bender, Thomas. Community and Social Change in America. New Brunswick, N.J.: Rutgers University Press, 1978.

Berman, Marshall. All That Is Solid Melts into Air: The Experience of Modernity. New York: Viking Penguin, 1988.

Boyer, M. Christine. Dreaming the Rational City: The Myth of American City Planning. Cambridge, Mass.: MIT Press, 1983.

Branch, Melville C. Comprehensive City Planning: Introduction and Explanation. Washington, D.C.: Planners Press, American Planning Association, 1985.

Broadbent, Geoffrey. Emerging Concepts in Urban Space Design. London and New York: Van Nostrand Reinhold, 1990.

Buder, Stanley. Visionaries and Planners: The Garden City Movement and the Modern Community. New York and Oxford: Oxford University Press, 1990.

Burns, Wilfred. New Towns for Old: The Technique of Urban Renewal. London: L. Hill, 1963.

Calthorpe, Peter. The Next American Metropolis: Ecology, Community, and the American Dream. New York: Princeton Architectural Press, 1993.

Calthorpe, Peter, and Sim Van der Ryn. Sustainable Communities: A New Design Synthesis for Cities, Suburbs and Towns. San Francisco: Sierra Club Books, 1986.

Carr, Stephen, et al. Public Space. New York: Cambridge University Press, 1992.

Castells, Manuel. The City and the Grassroots: A Cross Cultural Theory of Urban Social Movements. Berkeley: University of California Press, 1983.

Cherry, Gordon, ed. Shaping an Urban World. London: Mansell, 1980.

Cook, Peter, and Rosie Llewellyn-Jones. New Spirit in Architecture. New York: Rizzoli, 1991.

Cranz, Galen. The Politics of Park Design: A History of Urban Parks in America. Cambridge, Mass.: MIT Press, 1982.

Creese, Walter. The Search for Environment: The Garden City Before and After. New Haven: Yale University Press, 1966.

Crow, Dennis, ed. Philosophical Streets: New Approaches to Urbanism. Washington, D.C: Maisonneuve Press, 1990.

Davis, Mike. City of Quartz: Excavating the Future in Los Angeles. London: Verso, 1990.

———. "The Postmodern City." New Left Review. 151 (May/June 1985).

Dodson, Reynolds. Urban Renewal. Garden City, N.J: Doubleday, 1984.

Fishman, Robert. Urban Utopias in the Twentieth Century: Ebenezer Howard, Frank Lloyd Wright and Le Corbusier. New York: Basic Books, 1977.

Frieden, Bernard J., and Lynne B. Sagalyn. Downtown, Inc.: How America Rebuilds Cities. Cambridge, Mass.: MIT Press, 1989.

Gandelsonas, Mario. The Urban Text. Cambridge, Mass.: MIT Press, 1991.

Garreau, Joel. Edge City: Life on the New Frontier. New York: Doubleday, 1991.

Ghirardo, Diane, ed. Out of Site: A Social Criticism of Architecture. Seattle: Bay Press, 1991.

Girouard, Mark. Cities and People: A Social and Architectural History. New Haven: Yale University Press, 1985.

Glazer, Nathan, and Mark Lilla, eds. The Public Face of Architecture: Civic Culture & Public Spaces. New York: The Free Press, 1987.

Goodman, Robert. After the Planners. New York: Simon and Schuster, 1973.

Gottdiener, M., and C. G. Pickvance, eds. Urban Life in Transition. Newbury Park: Sage, 1991.

Gottschalk, Simon. Communities and Alternatives: An Exploration of the Limits of Planning. New York: Wiley, 1975.

Hall, Peter. Cities of Tomorrow: An Intellectual History of Urban Planning and Design in the Twentieth Centery. Oxford and New York: Blackwell, 1988.

Halpern, K. Downtown U.S.A.: Urban Design in Nine American Cities. New York: Whitney Library of Design, 1978.

Hayden, Dolores. The Grand Domestic Revolution: A History of Feminist Designs for American Homes, Neighborhoods, and Cities. Cambridge, Mass.: MIT Press, 1981.

Helman, Claire. The Milton-Park Affair. Montreal: Véhicule Press, 1987.

Jackson, Kenneth T. The Suburbanization of the United States. New York: Oxford University Press, 1985.

Jacobs, Jane. Cities and the Wealth of Nations: Principles of Economic Life. New York: Random House, 1984.

———. The Death and Life of Great American Cities. New York: Vintage Books, 1961.

Jellicoe, Geoffrey, and Susan Jellicoe. The Landscape of Man: Shaping the Environment from Prehistory to the Present Day. New York: Van Nostrand Reinhold Co., 1982.

Kaminsky, Jacob. How to Evaluate a Development Proposal in Your Community. Reston, Va.: Environmental Design Press, 1979.

Katz, Peter. The New Urbanism: Toward an Architecture of Community. New York: McGraw-Hill, 1994.

Koolhaas, Rem. Delirious New York: A Retroactive Manifesto for Manhattan. New York: Oxford University Press, 1978.

Kostof, Spiro. The City Assembled: The Elements of Urban Form Through History. Boston: Little, Brown & Co., 1992.

———. The City Shaped: Urban Patterns and Meaning through History. Boston: Little, Brown & Co., 1991.

Krieger, Alex. "The American City: Ideal and Mythic Aspects of Reinvented Urbanism." Assemblage 3 (1987).

———, ed. Andres Duany and Elizabeth Plater-Zyberk: Towns and Town-Making Principles. New York: Rizzoli, 1991.

Lampugnani, Vittorio Magnago, ed. Berlin Tomorrow: International Architectural Visions. Architectural Design Profile 92. London: AD Editions 1991.

Laska, S., and D. Spain, eds. Back to the City: Issues in Neighborhood Renovation. Elmsford, N.Y: Pergamon Press, 1980.

Lejeune, Jean-François, ed. The New City: Foundations. Coral Gables, Fla.: University of Miami School of Architecture, 1991.

Liebs, Chester H. Main Street to Miracle Mile. Boston: Little, Brown & Co., 1985.

Lozano, Eduardo. Community Design and the Culture of Cities: The Crossroad and the Wall. Cambridge and New York: Cambridge University Press, 1990.

Lynch, Kevin. Good City Form. Cambridge, Mass.: MIT Press, 1981.

———. The Image of the City. Cambridge, Mass.: MIT Press, 1960.

Mertins, Detlef, ed. Metropolitan Mutations: The Architecture of Emerging Public Spaces. Boston: Little, Brown & Co., 1989.

Mumford, Lewis. The City in History: Its Origins, Its Transformations & Its Prospects. New York: Harcourt, Brace, 1961.

Norberg-Schultz, Christian. Intentions in Architecture. Cambridge, Mass.: MIT Press, 1965.

Papadakis, Andreas, ed. Denise Scott Brown: Urban Concepts. London: Academy Editions, 1990.

Pickvance, Christopher, ed. Urban Sociology: Critical Essays. London: Tavistock Publications, 1976.

Pike, Burton. The Image of the City in Modern Literature. Princeton, N.J: Princeton University Press, 1981.

Relph, Edward. The Modern Urban Landscape. Baltimore: Johns Hopkins University Press, 1987.

Rowe, Colin. Collage City. Cambridge, Mass.: MIT Press, 1978.

Rowe, Peter G. Making a Middle Landscape. Cambridge, Mass.: MIT Press, 1991.

Scully, Vincent. American Architecture and Urbanism. Rev. ed. New York: Henry Holt., 1988.

Sennett, Richard, ed. Classic Essays on the Culture of Cities. New York: Appleton-Century-Crofts, 1969.

———. The Conscience of the Eye: The Design and Social Life of Cities. New York: Alfred A. Knopf, 1990.

———. The Fall of Public Man. New York: Vintage Books, 1977.

Sharpe, William, and Leonard Wollock, eds. Visions of the Modern City: Essays in History, Art, and Literature. Baltimore: Johns Hopkins University Press, 1987.

Smith, Neil. Uneven Development: Nature, Capital, and the Production of Space. Cambridge, Mass.: B. Blackwell, 1991.

Smith, Neil, and Peter Williams, eds. Gentrification of the City. Boston: Allen & Unwin, 1986.

Soja, Edward W. Postmodern Geographies: The Reassertion of Space in Critical Social Theory. London: Verso, 1989.

Solomon, Daniel. Rebuilding. New York: Princeton Architectural Press, 1992.

Sorkin, Michael. Local Code: Constitution of a City at 42° N Latitude. New York: Princeton Architectural Press, 1993.

———, ed. Variations on a Theme Park: The New American City and the End of Public Space. New York: Hill and Wang, 1992.

Spirn, Anne Whiston. The Granite Garden: Urban Nature and Human Design. New York: Basic Books, 1984.

Sudjic, Deyan. The 100 Mile City. London: A. Deutsch, 1992.

Tafuri, Manfredo. The Sphere and the Labyrinth: Avant-Gardes and Architecture from Piranesi to the 1970s. Cambridge, Mass.: MIT Press, 1987.

Teaford, Jon C. The Rough Road to Renaissance: Urban Revitalization in America 1940-1985. Baltimore: Johns Hopkins University Press, 1990.

Tod, Ian, and Michael Wheeler. Utopia. London: Orbis Publications, 1978.

Tuan, Yi-Fu. Topophilia: A Study of Environmental Perception, Attitudes, and Values. Englewood Cliffs, N.J.: Prentice-Hall, 1974.

Venturi, Robert, Denise Scott Brown, and Steven Izenour. Learning from Las Vegas. Cambridge, Mass.: MIT Press, 1972.

Vidler, Anthony. The Architectural Uncanny: Essays in the Modern Unhomely. Cambridge, Mass.: MIT Press, 1992.

Wallis, Brian, ed. If You Lived Here: The City in Art, Theory, and Social Activism, A Project by Martha Rosler. Seattle: Bay Press, 1991.

Webber, Melvin, ed. Explorations into Urban Structure. Philadelphia: University of Pennsylvania Press, 1964.

Whyte, William H. City: Rediscovering the Center. New York: Doubleday, 1988.

———. The Social Life of Small Urban Spaces. Washington, D.C.: The Conservation Foundation, 1980.

Wilson, Elizabeth. The Sphinx in the City: Urban Life, the Control of Disorder, and Women. Berkeley: University of California Press, 1992.

Wilson, James Q., ed. Urban Renewal: The Record and the Controversy. Cambridge, Mass.: MIT Press, 1966.

Wright, Gwendolyn. Building the Dream: A Social History of Housing in America. New York: Pantheon Books, 1981.

Photo Credits

Photographs reproduced in this book have been provided, in the majority of cases, by the architects, except where noted. The following list, keyed to page numbers, applies to photographs for which a separate acknowledgment is due.

6, 73, 100 (top and bottom right), 101, 102, 103: Brian Forrest; 10: Ville de Montréal; 14, 111, 112, 113, 152-157: Douglas Whyte; 28: courtesy of The Western Reserve Historical Society, Cleveland, Ohio; 74 (bottom), 108, 109: Bureau de projet Faubourg Québec; 75: Tom Bonner; 152 (top): Matilda Haywood, courtesy of Los Angeles Downtown News; 165: Jock Pottle/Esto; 171: Stanley Tom; 172-173: Alessandra Moctezuma; 174: Julie Easton; 176-177: Ulises Diaz; 177 (bottom): Julie Easton.

Colophon

The typefaces used in this edition are Monotype Baskerville and Bitstream Bell Gothic. Baskerville was originally designed by John Baskerville, of Birmingham, England, in 1770. It has its beginnings in the Romantic Movement. It is a letterform which began the transition from Old-Style typefaces such as Garamond to a form known as Modern. Bitstream Bell Gothic is based on a typeface designed for the Bell Telephone Company in 1938. A derivation, Bell Centennial, was designed by Matthew Carter in 1978 for AT&T to replace Bell Gothic.

The paper in this catalog is all recycled.